— VILLAGE ENGLAND —

Village England

A Social History of the Countryside

— TREVOR WILD —

I.B. TAURIS

LONDON · NEW YORK

Published in 2004 by I.B. Tauris & Co Ltd
6 Salem Road, London W2 4BU
175 Fifth Avenue, New York NY 10010
www.ibtauris.com

In the United States of America and Canada
distributed by Palgrave Macmillan a division of St Martin's Press
175 Fifth Avenue, New York NY 10010

International Library of Historical Studies 30
ISBN 1 86064 939 4
EAN 978 1 86064 939 4

A full CIP record for this book is available from the British Library
A full CIP record is available from the Library of Congress

Library of Congress Catalog Card Number: available

Typeset in Galliard by JCS Publishing Services
Printed and bound in Great Britain by MPG Books Ltd, Bodmin

Contents

List of Figures

List of Plates

———

For Joan, my wife,
who has accompanied me on my journeys through
village England, and has been a constant source of
encouragement in the writing of this book

———

Preface and Acknowledgements

The idea of writing this book began to emerge several years ago on a grey November day, deep in the Lincolnshire countryside. The author was in charge of what university and college geography and history departments still describe as a 'field trip' – a pleasurable and, weather permitting, very effective way of building upon lectures and infusing interest among students. This particular field trip, run for the first time and forming part of a course on 'the historical geography of rural Britain', was attended by some thirty final-year undergraduates, coming from a broad social spectrum. The morning had been spent looking at the Brocklesby estate of the Earls of Yarborough and examining a fine example of a Union workhouse (built in 1837 and converted into a county hospital in 1932) in the archetypal market town of Louth. The afternoon was devoted to studying two markedly different types of villages: the picturesque estate village of Tealby and the workaday village of Binbrook, both set in the rolling countryside of the Lincolnshire Wolds. The procedure was to brief the students first and then put them into small groups and let them wander around to observe things for themselves. It was interesting to watch them. At Tealby they worked rather mechanically, strolling past the pretty cottages and stopping only at the 'arts and crafts' village hall and the beautiful medieval church. Inside the church some of the groups made a few notes about the tablets and monuments of the Tennyson d'Eyncourt family. Outside, others contemplated the view over the village and the adjoining parkland. I pointed out the spot where the Gothic mansion of Bayons Manor – the seat of the d'Eyncourt family and the place where, as a child and later as a young man, the poet Alfred Tennyson used to come to visit his uncle – stood prior to its demolition in 1966. The students, however, asked few questions about Tealby, and I was left with the impression that they were already very familiar with all this – the cosy cottages, the ancient church and some literary association – having seen similar places many times before, on excursions with their parents and in the plethora of 'coffee-table' countryside literature and jigsaw and chocolate-box village scenes.

It was different at Binbrook, however. This was a village that had been built not for a pleasing visual effect, but principally in the nineteenth century to house a large accumulation of agricultural labour. The church (not as old nor as conspicuous as the one in Tealby) was closed, yet the students took their time, each group inspecting the several disused crafts-men's workshops, the mid-Victorian 'National' school, the commodious but rather austere-looking Wesleyan chapel, the still quite substantial numbers of untreated, brick-built, labourers' dwellings and an original inter-war garage built out of concrete and corrugated iron. They asked many questions here, and darkness was falling as we finally trooped back into the bus and the driver started the engine. On the journey back to Hull, I reflected on the day. The students had just demonstrated to me that there was a strong appetite for a fuller history of village England, and an enthusiasm for learning about ordinary buildings and the lifestyles of ordinary rural people.

Village England contains something in the order of 9,000 villages today, the large majority of which are easy enough to define. A commonly used rule of thumb is population size, with a lower limit of, say, 200 inhabit-ants and an upper limit of 2,500. But one should not be too rigid in applying these figures. For one thing, they are not always appropriate to 'pre-suburban' times when many villages were much smaller than they are now, and several countryside market towns had populations quite well below 2,500. For another, census population counts are for whole par-ishes, and thus include people living in outlying farms and hamlets. In individual cases, therefore, it is sometimes better for the purist to use his or her own eyes, perhaps with the assistance of a 'One Inch to the Mile' (1:63,360), or larger scale, Ordnance Survey map. The existence of a nat-ural focus, a church, and a variety of buildings – not just a cluster of farmsteads (or former farmsteads) – will help confirm village status; and the combination of a market place, more than just a couple of interacting streets, and a small concentration of shops and other commercial premises is the hallmark of a countryside town. One final problem that needs to be addressed here derives from the suburbanization process that, to a varying extent, has affected most villages over recent decades. Some have been overrun by new residential expansion, causing their population figures to rise well past the 2,500 mark. In these instances, deciding whether or not a village has been lost to modern development can be rather arbitrary. If it has, one indicator is its absorption into a general suburbia and its ceasing to be a free-standing settlement surrounded by open countryside. Another indicator is the commercialization of its his-toric core. The church will remain; but, if the farmhouses and cottages have been removed or converted into business premises, then there is no longer a village 'feel'. Such reductions to village England have some parallels in the industrialization of the nineteenth and the early twentieth centuries when in certain parts of the country numerous former agricultural villages were engulfed by heavy industrialization and ever-spreading urban growth. Over the last two centuries, therefore, village England, as a geographical expression, has been in a constant state of retreat.

The author's transition from geographer to historian has followed a fairly well-trodden path along which some of his early-acquired academic habits have been worth keeping. A predilection for using maps is one of these, though this has never been solely the preserve of the geographer. A fondness for describing landscapes is another, and is an issue that has undergone something of an intellectual revival in recent years. Then there is the so-called 'spatial dimension', which the author feels should not be left aside, since the history of village England and the English countryside has always contained major regional and local differences. When referring to these, use is made of a variety of area-orientated terms, some of which need to be clarified to the reader. First of all, there is a range of words for different scales of space. The largest of these is 'region', as applied for example in East Anglia, Wessex, and the Home Counties; the next is 'district', such as the Vale of Evesham and the Somerset Levels (but after the Local Government Act of 1894 used in connection with the usually much less extensive 'Rural District' local authority areas); and the smallest is 'locality' – a small grouping of parishes that have similarities of natural landscape, agricultural economy, historical traditions and perhaps vernacular building-style. Counties are also frequently mentioned. These are the old counties as had existed in England prior to the widespread reorganization of county administrative areas in the early 1970s.

Most of the regions referred to in the following chapters do have an identity, but there are some that can only be arbitrarily defined and there are some too that are not mutually exclusive. To assist the reader, the most contentious of regional terms are expressed as follows: 'Wessex', immortalized as the name of Alfred the Great's Anglo-Saxon kingdom and the location of Thomas Hardy's Wessex novels; is taken to be the old counties of Dorset, Wiltshire, Hampshire, Berkshire, Somerset and the southern part of Oxfordshire; the 'south midlands' consists of Gloucestershire, Oxfordshire, Northamptonshire and Bedfordshire; the 'west midlands' is made up of Warwickshire, Worcestershire and Staffordshire; and the 'Home Counties' are Kent, Surrey, Middlesex, Hertfordshire and Essex.

Several people have helped me in the production of this book. I am indebted to Keith Scurr of the University of Hull Department of Geography for drawing the Figures and advising me on their design. I am also grateful for the valuable administrative and technical assistance of John Garner, Nigel Ibbotson, Paul McSherry, Dick Middleton, John Spencer and Anita Watson of the same university. Thanks are also due to my son, Nathan, and my daughter, Christine, who have come to my rescue in the filing and copying of the manuscript and, more frequently, when something has gone wrong with the word-processor. Lastly, I am indebted to the editorial team at I. B. Tauris for all their work and encouragement.

Permission to reproduce photographic images for Plates 17 and 23 has been kindly given by Getmapping plc.

Trevor Wild,
Walkington,
East Yorkshire

Introduction

The idealization of village England and the English countryside is part and parcel of a general affection for all things rural. It embodies an idyllic vision of rurality that has historical roots going back to the blossoming of the English Romantic movement in the early nineteenth century when, turning their backs against the burgeoning Industrial Revolution, Keats was writing his rustic odes, Jane Austin was setting her novels in the country houses and parklands of southern England, and landscape paint-ers and the 'Lakeland' poets were nurturing an aesthetic taste for nature, Arcadian scenery and ancient Gothic ruins. However, it was not until later in the nineteenth century – in that prosperous and very settled period in English rural history known as the Age of High Farming – that villages and village communities were given a prominent role, most nota-bly perhaps in George Eliot's *Silas Marner* (1859) and *Adam Bede* (1861), and in Thomas Hardy's *Under the Greenwood Tree* (1872) and *Far from the Madding Crowd* (1874). By the time these novels were written, Britain had become a dominantly industrial nation – the very first urban industrial society in world economic history. But the unrestrained 'laissez faire' industrialism that underpinned this achievement was seen by many writers, including such influential thinkers and cultural critics as Charles Dickens, Mathew Arnold, John Ruskin and William Morris, to have destructive power. To them the Industrial Revolution was responsible for just about everything that was deemed to be wrong with mid- and late-Victorian urban life, especially its social alienation, its restlessness and the vast aggregation of inhuman, disease-infested and poverty-ridden slums. As the cultural historian Martin Wiener has forcibly argued,[1] it was from this critique of the 'new civilization' and growing doubts about the ide-ology of material 'progress', that anti-urbanism emerged as a powerful cultural and intellectual force, reinforcing the romantic conception of rurality and 'natural', slow moving, rustic existence.

Not even six decades of agricultural depression and rural decay, from 1875 to the late 1930s, could disturb the comforting images of verdant pastures, rolling cornfields, picturesque cottages and ancient church tow-ers. Indeed, the appeal of rural idyllism became stronger than ever as the nation, in the turbulent first half of the twentieth century, became embroiled in the huge emergencies of the First World War, the mass unemployment and social unrest of the 1920s and 1930s and the threat of invasion and the Blitz of 1940–1. It was in these grim times that the romanticized virtues of rural England and its timeless villages were elevated to beacons of moral character and a metaphor for national identity, even though more than three-quarters of the population were 'townsmen' living in towns and cities.[2] The rural idyll struck a chord with the whole nation, since it confirmed that England was an 'old' country with traditional values and a rich historical experience.[3] Not only did it continue to provide a perfect antidote for the ugliness and dehumanization of urban industrialism, but it now served as a psychological haven against the menaces of class conflict from within and of military conquest from without. It was with good reason, therefore, that Prime Minister Stanley Baldwin called upon the traditional 'Tory' vision of an older, socially cohesive and contented rural England as he sought to 'heal' the nation in the aftermath of the 1926 General Strike. And to help guide it through the turmoil of the Second World War, there was good reason too for the propagandist Ministry of Information to make repeated references to a 'real' England of independence, tolerance, patience and continuity, as opposed to Nazi Germany's assumed national characteristics of tyranny, persecution, aggression and modernity.[4] The former were derived from rural virtues: the latter, to use Wiener's words, were perceived as the maladies of an 'industrial society run amok'.[5]

The vast, predominantly middle-class, appetite for 'discovering' and learning about this real or 'Deep' England was fed by a plethora of rural literature, landscape painting and (making good use of the new forms of media) radio broadcasts and films on countryside life and rural heritage. In all of this, the economic and social realities – long-term agricultural depression, the continued poverty of farm labourers, the persistent decline of centuries-old village crafts and the seemingly unstoppable depopulation of countless villages – was given scant attention. And, apart from the angered criticism of countryside preservationists and members of the new profession of town and country planning, there was little mention of the advancing tide of suburbanization; a process that, even before the mass car-ownership of the post-war age, was threatening to damage much of the English rural landscape and was already engulfing many of its villages. Ironically, this intrusion of suburbia, with its haphazard ribbon development, unsightly plotland settlements and stark lines of modern infrastructure, was itself driven largely by this heightened idealization of the rural landscape and the rural way of life. Distaste of urban life, especially its smoke and noise, its lack of open space and its proneness to ill health, made people want to leave their towns and cities; but it was the image of a satisfying Arcadian existence that drew them into the countryside and village England. And the modern means of transport – the suburban railway, the motor bus, and the motor car – enabled them to do so, without having to change their employment and lose contact with friends and relatives.

Lured by the rural idyll, living in the country became a cultural goal for a widening spectrum of society; though whether or not this hope was achieved depended upon each person's financial resources or (until the regulatory 1947 Town and Country Planning Act) his or her personal ingenuity. The highest ambition, of course, was a Cotswold or Suffolk manor house as frequently advertised in the journal *Country Life*; but this could be attained only by a very small and very wealthy minority. The best that most ex-urbanites could aspire to was a vacant cottage, a bungalow or a semi-detached house in a ribbon development; or, for those with the least income, just a plotland shack.

Very prominent in the present-day imagination of rural England is the idealization of the village and the values that it is assumed to embody. Today the village is visualized as an anchorage and sanctuary from the current urban anxieties of increasing crime, inner-city riots, stressful lifestyles, the destructive impacts of globalization and the fracturing of society. Despite many years of social change, suburbanization and the debilitating impacts of the depletion of the agricultural occupation and the disappearance of most traditional rural crafts, village life is still perceived as peaceful, satisfying and always permeated with a strong feeling of community. We need only turn to the television and the radio for confirmation of this myth. It is not by coincidence that four of today's most popular serial programmes, namely 'Last of the Summer Wine', 'Emmerdale', 'Heartbeat' and the perennial 'The Archers', are each drawn around tightly-knit village communities in which everyone knows each other (for better or for worse) and nobody lives in isolation.

In reality, however, most villages can not fulfil these expectations. Invaded by consumerism, they are no longer peaceful places, as can be testified by anyone who has tried to relax out of doors at weekends amidst the incessant din of traffic, garden machinery and building and 'makeover' work. Moreover, few villages today possess a genuine community spirit or what the social historian Howard Newby has described as 'a sense of belonging, of sharing a social identity'.[6] Indeed, it is here that we see arguably the most salient contrast between the past and the present. Although there have been many attempts to relive it in village festivals and pageants, articles in parish magazines and passages in local histories, the traditional communal way of life, as immortalized in the Wessex novels of Thomas Hardy and the pastoral poetry of Oliver Goldsmith and John Clare, disappeared long ago. It was undermined by the dispossessions of the Georgian parliamentary enclosures, and was finally extinguished by the combined forces of agricultural mechanization and rural depopulation in the latter half of the nineteenth century. Today the organic village community exists only in the mists of nostalgic imagination.

Romantic perceptions of the English village and the English countryside tend to be the most compelling at times of rapid economic and social change when, as a reaction to these uncertainties, the desire for stability and traditional values is at its greatest. At these times too, affection for the past becomes a prevalent mood; and arising from this there is born a sense of regret and a yearning for 'the world we have lost',[7] especially that which is enshrined in literature and folk memory. In the words of the agricultural historian Alan Armstrong, 'it was always yesterday's countryside, ever receding, that embodied rural virtue to the full';[8] but 'yesterday's countryside' – the resting-places of this retrospective regret – always seems to be set in the good times and the so-called 'golden ages' of English rural history. Moving backwards through time we come first to the heroic years of the Second World War when rural England is seen to have been saving the nation from starvation and to have regained something of its ancient 'shoulder to shoulder' spirit. What the literary critic Raymond Williams has described as an 'escalator', taking his readers back from the present to various 'Old Englands',[9] then carries us to the prosperity of Victorian 'High Farming' and the highly functional and controlled rural society that underpinned it. From here – the closest history ever came to achieving the traditional 'Tory' vision of rural stability and perfect moral economy – we can move further back to the relaxed, squire-dominated, countryside of the Georgian agricultural revolution; to the 'merrie' rural England of the days of Shakespeare and Elizabeth I; and ultimately to the organic rural communities of the Feudal era. The myth of a happier past has always been more attractive than the realities of the present.

Each of these golden ages, however, lies between long periods of rural disquiet and economic difficulty – times, indeed, when rural history took a wrong course. But these dark ages of the rural past, including the plague-stricken and rebellion-torn late Middle Ages, the intolerant and politically divided seventeenth century, the poverty-ridden 'Bleak Age' of the 1810s, 1820s and 1830s, and the deep agricultural depression of the late nineteenth and the early twentieth century, are largely ignored.

Indeed, most conventional rural literature presents a selective and one-sided version of rural England's historical experience; a 'progressive' history of overlapping rather than well separated ages of material advancement and rustic bliss. Moreover, what this idealized view of rural history also evades is any critical assessment of the long process of agricultural capitalization and its transforming effects upon the rural landscape and rural society. In the rural idyll and its representation in art, literature and the media, the caprices and failures of commercial agriculture are not featured; and we are told nothing about the extent of rural poverty and the huge social disproportion that existed (and, in a different way, continues to exist) in most English villages. Uninformed about these issues, we are treated to a nostalgic and sentimental appreciation of the very things and the very values that capitalization and materialism have themselves swept away. This book, therefore, departs from the popular romanticized conception of the history of rural England, which stresses ancient origins, social harmony and stability. Instead, it explores a deeper and unromantic history that includes dispossession, impoverishment, social transformations, agricultural failure, destruction of tradition and widespread suburbanization. Taking the Tudor 'rural renaissance' as a starting point, the focus throughout is on the impacts of this deeper history on the ever-changing (and sometimes quickly changing) social values, landscape and way of life of the English village and the English countryside.

Plate 1: Cavendish, Suffolk. A quintessential English village scene. The ancient church, the green, the thatched cottages, and the backcloth of trees present an idyllic picture.

CHAPTER ONE

Origins, Organic Quality and Geographical Context

The old village homes of England are a precious heritage of the past. Of singular beauty, and fair to look upon, they create a wide and lasting interest. In all parts of the country are to be found many unpretentious examples of quiet and homely taste, erected by native craftsmen of a sturdy and vigorous peasantry. These buildings are fraught with an appeal to the mind and have a significance deeper than is conveyed by mere terms of stone, of brick, of timber. They stand for much that is peculiarly and characteristically English.
(Sidney Jones, *The Village Homes of England*, 1912)[1]

If the Englishman did not invent the village idea he has perfected it, and he has made his villages as unique as the countryside in which they are placed.
(Thomas Sharp, *Town and Countryside*, 1932)[2]

Historical Origins

It was once widely believed that the majority of English villages were first established by waves of German colonists – Saxons and Angles – in the fifth, sixth and seventh centuries and that these were supplemented in much of eastern England by a later phase of village foundation with the arrival of Danish settlers in the ninth and tenth centuries. This 'ethnic' and diffusionist interpretation of village creation was sustained by a whole generation of historians and historical geographers writing in the 1940s and 1950s. Prominent among them was the landscape historian W. G. Hoskins who, in his highly popular book *The Making of the English Landscape*, sweepingly declared: 'The Anglo-Saxons covered the whole of England with their villages, much more thickly in some parts than others.'[3] The first part of this assertion, however, has always been lacking in proof and does indeed contain a number of serious flaws. First and foremost, it is tenuously based upon the frequent appearance of Anglo-Saxon place-name suffixes such as 'ing', 'ington' and 'ingham' in the names of English villages. However, there is no real evidence to indicate that, at the time they are presumed to have been given, a substantial proportion of these suffixes had related to settlements any larger than a small grouping of farmsteads or a hamlet. Secondly, most historians and archaeologists today consider that settlements of true village proportions were mostly created through a process of gradual evolution, and did not become a common feature of the rural landscape until the widespread adoption of the open-field system of farming. Communal open-field farming, for which the nucleated village was far more logical than was scattered or dispersed settlement, is no longer thought to have been brought into England by the waves of 'Dark Age' German settlers. It is now believed to have taken root much later, emerging in the tenth century in some of the more populated parts of lowland England and then slowly spreading into other areas during the eleventh and twelfth centuries.[4] Thirdly, recent archaeological research has shown that the primitive habitations and the layouts of Dark Age settlements, like those of the preceding Iron Age and Romano-British cultures, were ephemeral rather than enduring features of the evolving rural landscape.[5] Their primitive wattle and daub huts, with roofs made from turf or some other vegetation material, often had to be rebuilt and were periodically reorientated and repositioned. All that Dark Age settlements did bequeath to the villages of later ages were their names, some relics of their small Anglo-Saxon churches, and, in places where there has been a long continuity of occupation, the selection and initial usage of their sites.

Throughout the Middle Ages, the pattern of rural settlement was constantly changing.[6] Countless hamlets and loose clusters of farmsteads did eventually grow into villages, many of them having done so by the time of the Domesday Survey in 1086; but many too, usually ones that were disadvantaged by a poor physical site and marginal natural conditions, disappeared entirely.[7] Some settlements were resited following a disastrous flood, the drying up of a spring, the engrossment of land for a monastic estate, or (as most famously in north and north-east England after William the Conqueror's onslaught there in 1069 and 1070) the devastation of a military campaign. Even towards the end of the Middle Ages the rural settlement pattern was still unstable. In the fourteenth century a series of famines and pestilences, culminating in the bubonic plague or 'Black Death' of 1348–50, brought about a catastrophic reduction of England's population. According to one frequently-quoted estimate this fell from around five million at the beginning of the fourteenth century to no more than three million at the end.[8] Rural England, with its crowded, often rat-infested, dwellings and its easily infected water supplies, suffered nearly as badly as urban England, perhaps even worse in some localities. Certainly many villages suffered heavy mortality, and some became completely depopulated as survivors fled in panic. Most of the plague-afflicted villages were partly or wholly repopulated a generation or so after the Black Death, but there were a few, for example Tusmore and Tigarsley in Oxfordshire and Elkington in Northampton-shire,[9] that were abandoned for ever.

Another wave of village depopulation and desertion came in the latter half of the fifteenth and the first quarter of the sixteenth century, this time to make way for large-scale enclosures for commercial sheep and cattle farming, or for the new fashion for emparkment and the building of secluded country mansions. Hoskins claimed that, over the country as a whole, more than a thousand villages and hamlets and their communal open fields 'were wiped off the scene' during this period.[10] More specifi-cally, in his comprehensive study of *The Lost Villages of England*, the historian and archaeologist Maurice Beresford identified as many as 427 deserted or 'lost' villages within the thirteen counties – all of them in the midlands and eastern England – that had been the most severely affected.[11] The process of evicting peasant cultivators and converting their open fields into large private sheep ranges or cattle-grazing pastures, some as extensive as an entire parish, resulted in the desertion of one out of every eight villages in Warwickshire, Northamptonshire and the East Riding of Yorkshire, and between 10 per cent and 12 per cent of villages in Leicestershire, Oxfordshire, Buckinghamshire and the Kesteven divi-sion of Lincolnshire. Many more villages in these and in other counties shrank to hamlets or were reduced to a mere handful of surviving cot-tages and farmsteads.

The removal of villages, such as Wharram Percy in the Yorkshire Wolds, Ingarsby in Leicestershire, Sulby in Northamptonshire, Chester-ton in Warwickshire, and Clopton in Cambridgeshire, was helped by the rudimentary nature of the medieval peasant dwellings. Most of these were nothing more than a single-room hut, typically built upon an earth or rubble foundation, with walls made out of dried mud and straw held together by roughly-hewn timber posts. The roofing consisted just of turf, brushwood or the crudest type of thatch, resting on rafters or the simplest of cruck-frames. In many of Beresford's lost villages every build-ing had been levelled, leaving their sites to become jumbles of grassy mounds, nettle-filled hollows and sunken trackways. Indeed, in places where there have been long periods of ploughing and cropping, some lost village sites have been entirely obliterated. They are identifiable today only after careful field investigation and scrutiny of air photographs.

At the most, just the manor house and one other building remained after a village was deserted. In some cases the latter would be a solitary cottage for the landowner's shepherd: in others it was the ancient church, left without a congregation and standing strangely alone within the new unpopulated landscape. Yet, around the middle of the sixteenth century, not long after the final phase of these devastations, there began an era of rural population growth and extensive rebuilding of those much larger numbers of villages that had not been casualties of sheep enclosure or emparkments. This 'rural renaissance' was accompanied by a great flourishing of rural domestic architecture – what Hoskins has described as 'the flowering of English peasant building'[12] – that was strongest within those parts of the country where soils and topographic conditions were conducive to prosperous yeoman and peasant farming, or (most notably in the thriving cloth-working districts of the Cotswolds, East Anglia, Wiltshire and Devon) where cottage industry had become firmly established and was providing many rural communities with a profitable additional source of income. The Tudor and Elizabethan craftsmen, with their rich variety of regional and local vernacular building styles, built their villages to last as, in all save the humblest of dwellings, wattle and clay gave way to more durable materials and building features such as dressed stone, tiles, angle-posts, dormer windows and brick chimneys. For the first time too, the entire physical structure of villages – no longer just the stone church and here and there a moated manor house and perhaps a medieval tithe barn – became permanent features of the rural landscape.

The renaissance or flowering of English villages and their domestic architecture continued well into the seventeenth century and did not come to an end until the military and political upheavals of the Civil War and its aftermath. Indeed, it is in this long golden age of vernacular craftsmanship, with its widespread rebuilding of cottages and yeomen's farmsteads, proliferation of squatter settlements and restyling of manor houses, that we find a definite starting point in the history of village England in terms of what can be seen in the landscape today. For, besides the well-publicized heritage of ancient churches, barns and manor houses, only in a small minority of villages have more than a handful of pre-Tudor domestic buildings survived in something like their original state. Even in the oldest and best-preserved villages just the occasional unaltered late-medieval cottage or farmhouse may be seen, either standing on its own or existing with two or three others in a small group or a row. Not only did the sixteenth- and early seventeenth-century renaissance of rural building witness the growth and crystallization of many formerly insubstantial settlements into solidly built, fully-fledged villages, but, in their carefully crafted thatching, stonework, half-timbering and plentiful variety of early brickwork, it also saw the blossoming of villages that have become emblematic in today's idealized and historically-orientated imagery of English rural life. And, whenever we take pleasure in viewing such charming exemplars of the English village tradition as, say, Castle Combe and Bibury in the Cotswolds, Weobley and Pembridge in Herefordshire, Emley Castle in Worcestershire, Corfe and Sydling St Nicholas in Dorset, Chilham in Kent, Polperro in Cornwall, and Kersey and Stoke-by-Nayland in Suffolk, what always heightens their appeal is their inherent organic quality and their consonance with the countryside in which they are framed.

The Organic Village of 'Olde England'

The Old England was the England of the organic community, and in what sense it was more primitive than the England that has replaced it needs pondering.
(F. R. Leavis and D. Thompson, *Culture and Environment*, 1964)[13]

Long before the construction of turnpike roads, improvement of navigable rivers and digging of canals made it practical for builders to bring in materials from further afield, villages had to be built out of the very rock-beds upon which they stood, or from whatever other local materials were near at hand. Every cottage, house, farmstead and barn was derived from the countryside to which the village belonged:[14] stone and flint were hacked out from some nearby quarry, timber was taken from the parish woodland, thatch was gathered from rush-beds or from fields of straw just outside the village, wrought iron was forged out of the nearest beds of ironstone and, until the railway age and the advent of mass production, bricks were fired from local bands of clay. England contains a very wide range of geological formations, soil qualities and natural vegetation, and this has provided a remarkable geographical diversity of organic materials for builders and craftsmen to call upon. Over the centuries, they have applied their skills to these materials to produce a rich variety in the architecture and texture of pre-modern villages, and to create such distinctive statements of regional vernacular style as the honey-coloured villages of the Cotswold oolitic-limestone country, the timber-framed villages of Herefordshire and Worcestershire, the thatched villages of Berkshire, Hampshire and Dorset, the cob-wall villages of Devon and the flint villages of north Norfolk and the Chiltern hills. Strong enough to withstand the elements and mellowed by long exposure to the sun and

rain, it was this rich wealth of local natural building-materials and craftsmanship that prompted the early twentieth-century antiquarian writer
the Reverend P. H. Ditchfield to comment in 1910: 'There is a sense of
stability and wondrous variety caused by the different nature of the materials used, the peculiar stone indigenous in various districts and the
individuality stamped upon them by traditional modes of building.'[15]
Although Ditchfield warned that this could all disappear as an outcome
of twentieth-century rural decay in some areas and the march of suburbanization in others, there was, a generation later, still enough of this
vernacular village England left for the countryside writer H. J. Massingham to declare: 'The reason for the diversity of the English villages are
the varieties of our native rock, and the English village is a better hand-
book of geology than any printed text. It is not only a guide to the strata
underlying it but an exposition of their qualities, capacities and natural
vegetation.'[16] Travelling through the scarp and vale countryside of south
Warwickshire and its strings of what were still unmodernized agricultural
villages, he then asserted:

> I can test the geographical and vegetational changes taking place between
> the oolite and the lias drawn from the north-western Edge of the Cotswolds
> to the Valley of the Warwickshire Avon just as well by going from village to
> village as by studying the landscape and tapping about with a geological
> hammer. The transitional architecture from village to village exquisitely reg-
> isters and translates into vernacular terms the hidden history of the earth on
> which the homesteads rest.'[17]

The villages that were fashioned in the 'Olde' or 'Merrie' England of
the sixteenth and early seventeenth centuries were organic not only in the
physical sense of being built out of materials derived from the immediate
vicinity, but also in their economic self-sufficiency and the degree to
which their inhabitants depended upon each other. With the notable
exception of cloth-making for which the raw materials were quite easily
transportable, everyone's livelihood and everything that the villagers grew
or made ultimately came from the soil and the rock-beds beneath. The
type of farming, in terms of the crops that were cultivated and the proportions of arable and pasture, varied from region to region, from locality
to locality and, indeed, in many parts of rural England, from one parish
to the next. Likewise the range of village trades and craft industries varied
across the country, depending very much upon which particular natural
resources were readily available. As Massingham stressed, most, if not all,
of the materials used by traditional village craftsmen came from within
just two or three miles from where they lived and worked.[18] In the Chiltern Hills and the Sussex and Kent Weald, for example, the abundance of

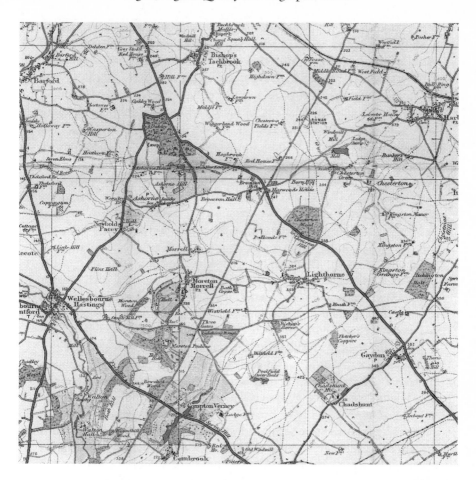

Plate 2: 'Old' village settlement in south Warwickshire. South Warwickshire, with its fertile loamy soils, is an area of early emergence of open-field farming and associated village settlement. A variety of villages is shown here, including the 'clustered' villages of Bishop's Tachbrook and Harbury, the 'linear' villages of Lighthorne and Wellesbourne Hastings, the estate villages of Moreton Morrell and Cornbrook and, two miles northeast of Lighthorne, the lost village of Chesterton (with just the medieval church and the manor house remaining).

Reproduced from Ordnance Survey, One Inch to the Mile, *Popular* edition, sheet 82, published in 1919.

beech, hazel and oak woodlands were encouraging people to turn to wood-working and charcoal-burning in many villages and hamlets. In areas such as east Shropshire, the Stour valley in north-east Worcestershire, and the Gloucestershire Forest of Dean, where both heating coal and locally worked iron were readily available,[19] craft metal-working industries, especially nail making and the forging and finishing of agricultural implements, were displacing farming as the main source of livelihood in several places. And, to take one more set of examples, in the Somerset Levels, the Cambridgeshire fens and the flood plain of the river Ouse in Bedfordshire and Huntingdonshire, the existence of good quality reed-beds and osiers had given rise to a thriving rural basket-making and matting industry. Even the most ubiquitous of rural crafts were attached to nature in one way or another: corn milling required a suitable streamside site for a water-wheel or, if this was not available, an exposed position for a windmill; thatching needed local supplies of reed or straw; and the village mason had to obtain his stone from a local quarry.

Although the feudal social system was slowly disintegrating, more so in some parts of rural England than in others, little had been lost of what had always been a highly cohesive, communal way of life – a folk society in which the lives of all village inhabitants were mutually connected as if each person existed as a part of a natural organism. There was no apparent conflict of interest and no one, other than the most disinterested and detached of landowners, lived in isolation without any positive social role or sense of responsibility. Governed by their annual or half-yearly manorial court-leets (until these began to be replaced by parish vestries towards the end of the sixteenth century), the villages of this old England housed heterogeneous but very tightly knit communities. Whilst few of these had exactly the same social composition, nearly all had a backbone of small independent yeomen farmers. These people, mostly descendants of medieval freemen, had come to possess land as freeholders or to hold it through time-honoured, if vaguely defined, copyhold agreement: they were indeed countrymen who had control over the land that they tilled.[20] Villages in this formative age also housed husbandmen and peasant cultivators who held small acreages of plough-land through customary tenure, and also enjoyed ancient rights to use communal pastures and, where it existed, common heathland and woodland waste. At the bottom of the social spectrum were the sub-communities of squatters and other smallholder-cottagers, some of whom became part-time craftsmen or seasonal labourers.

In most Tudor and Elizabethan villages the lord of the manor still presided as ruler and paternal guardian of the whole community. Moreover, where he had retained the authority to impose manorial dues, he continued to profit from the labour service that his villagers were still obliged to provide and the various taxes and petty fines they had to pay. However, by the time of the Civil War, the more materialistic-minded of the manorial lords had reduced, or in some cases entirely discarded, their once strong sense of social responsibility. Many of them were now giving much greater attention to the accumulation of personal wealth, in which the acquisition of land beyond their original manorial demesnes was an obvious and often easy approach.[21] In the rural landscape this particular aspect of the long transition from feudal to capitalist organization of land and labour was reflected in the pulling down of medieval timber-framed manorial halls, and the replacement of these by elegant stately homes built in the new, classical Renaissance architectural style. The feudal title of lord of the manor was becoming an anachronism and that of 'country gentleman' – the private owner of a landed estate – was becoming more appropriate, especially among the increasing numbers of new entrants into landownership who were emerging from the ranks of military and political leaders, civil servants and wealthy city merchants. One manifestation of this increasing detachment was the tendency for the new mansions and stately homes to be built outside the village, unlike the medieval halls, which in most cases had been positioned intimately within it or in close proximity.

At harvest time and during the ploughing season, the communality of the pre-capitalist village was nowhere more clearly in evidence than within its surrounding open fields. These hedgeless expanses (some of the original versions were over a thousand acres in extent) were the places in which the villagers were allocated their individual strips and furlongs of arable land, used principally for the cultivation of wheat, oats and barley. In its simplest form the open-field system consisted of just two such fields, often called the 'north field' and the 'south field', or the 'west field' and the 'east field', depending upon their position and orientation. Over the centuries, however, the system in many parts of the country became more complex as farming communities, seeking to grow a wider range of crops and to reduce the proportion of fallow, increased the numbers of open fields to three or four, and in some cases even to as many as five or six. This was achieved partly by rearranging the original fields and partly by converting wasteland and perhaps common pasture into new plough-land.

The strips of each farmer varied in length and breadth according to the local terrain, and were scattered within each open field rather than being grouped together as a single compact block of land. This, of course, meant much extra expenditure of time and effort for the peasant and yeomen cultivators, but it did ensure that all farmers had a fair share of the different qualities and locations of arable land. Moreover, to the advantage of everyone, the open-field system facilitated the communal use of horse-teams or ox-teams for ploughing; and, crucially, it enabled farmers to operate a collectively organized cycle of rotation in which each year one of the open fields could be rested as fallow and the fertility of its soil could be naturally replenished.

Close to the villages too, and almost invariably on the lower and damper land by the side of a stream or river, were the common meadows or 'ings' that were traditionally used for the gathering of hay in late spring and early summer and the grazing of cows and draught-oxen from the end of haymaking until the approach of winter. Beyond the open fields, in the remoter and often the higher parts of the parish, were tracts of general common pasture that usually included sheep walks, rabbit warrens and areas of rough-grazing land. In certain parts of the country there were also some residual stretches of uncleared 'forest' and waste, consisting variously of woodland, barren heath or, as in the fenlands and wetlands of Lincolnshire, Cambridgeshire and the Somerset Levels, waterlogged marshes and reed-beds. The common pastures were used principally for sheep-grazing whilst the forest land and wastes, though they came to be disparaged as 'sterile wildernesses' and 'useless moors' by the Georgian enclosers and agricultural improvers, provided several important needs for village communities. Rich in natural vegetation and wildlife, they served both as natural playgrounds and as sources of supplementary food – places where people were free to wander about to gather berries, nuts and mushrooms in the autumn, and to cut furze for fuel in the winter. They were also places where villagers were allowed to keep their pigs, geese and beehives, catch the odd rabbit or hare and collect timber, bark, rushes and stone for craft industries and building materials. However, unlike the open fields and the common pastures, the wastes were not communal spaces in the fullest sense. Most were owned by the lord of the manor or his legal descendant, whilst rights of access and usage were often hazily described and were handed down through custom rather than as legally defined entitlement.[22]

At times of heavy population pressure on the land, as was the situation in various parts of rural England in the Tudor age, many of these wastes and primaeval woodlands were encroached upon by squatter settlers, creating a type of landscape – a disorderly unofficial countryside[23] – that is still recognizable today in areas like the New Forest, the Weald, the Forest of Arden, the Forest of Dean and some parts of the southern Pennines.

Here the process of piecemeal eating away of the edges of wastelands and commons has produced a haphazard pattern of old cottages and small-holder farmsteads, many of which have coalesced into hamlets or loosely arranged villages (see Plate 3). The names of such settlements tell us something of their origins. In the Forest of Arden, for example, one comes across places like Tilehouse Green, Hockley Heath and Tanner's Green that, protected by the Birmingham green belt, have not become engulfed by twentieth-century suburbanization and still contain small clusters of sixteenth- and early seventeenth-century cottages and small farmsteads. Since their migrations went unrecorded, knowledge of the origins of these squatter settlers will always be scant. However, there are enough clues in the landscape and evidence in local manorial records to indicate that the heaviest incidence of wasteland colonization here took place during and shortly after the most intensive phase of Tudor enclosures. It can be reasoned, therefore, that many of the squatters moving into areas like the Forest of Arden had been uprooted from villages that had recently been deserted or reduced as a consequence of a major land engrossment or emparkment. In the case of rural Warwickshire this would have meant movements of people over quite long distances, principally from the numerous depopulated villages in the fertile Avon valley and Jurassic limestone country in the south of the county[24] to the sparsely settled woodlands and commons of Arden in the north. If this was what did happen in this area, then it may well be indicative of a broader, perhaps nationwide, partial redistribution of rural population away from areas of long-established village settlement and into marginal lands.

England's historic villages have a diversity of form and physical structure. The most widespread type of layout is the linear village, some of which, such as Clare and Long Melford in Suffolk, Combe Martin in Devon, Piddletrenthide in Dorset, and Kilham in the Yorkshire Wolds, are over a mile in length. In such villages the church is normally situated at the higher end, whilst the various cottages and farmsteads are strung out along both sides of the long main street, often with no more than a narrow grass verge or a strip of earth separating them from the roadway. In a number of linear villages the street divides to embrace a small green, a duckpond or perhaps a stream and former source of water supply. Used variously as gardens, orchards, paddocks for sheep, or spaces to accommodate barns and other outbuildings, narrow crofts run back at right angles from the main street to a back lane or other property-line marking the physical limits of the village. Until a strong surge in rural population growth and infilling of settlements in the late eighteenth and early nineteenth century, most linear villages were straggling in appearance with

Plate 3: Clearance settlement in the Forest of Arden, north Warwickshire.
The Forest of Arden, with its Triassic rock-beds and difficult soils, offered little scope for communal open-field farming and development of village settlement. In medieval times it was a landscape of woodland wastes and heathy commons, punctuated by hamlets and small isolated farms. The settlement pattern filled out extensively in the Tudor 'rural renaissance', mainly through squatter encroachments and expansion of some of the hamlets into small villages. The beginnings of suburbanization can be seen near the railway station at Dorridge on the main Oxford to Birmingham line.

Reproduced from Ordnance Survey, One Inch to the Mile, *Revised Popular* edition, sheet 72, published in 1933.

their two, often sinuous, lines of buildings frequently being broken up by small pieces of undeveloped land. Some, however, were much more compact. More often than not these were failed market towns – settlements that at one time had been granted the right to hold a market but had been unable to grow into anything more substantial than a larger than average village.

Rather less common than the linear village is what has often been described as the 'clustered' or 'agglomerated' village,[5] typical examples of which are Finchingfield in Essex, East Hendred in Berkshire, Aldbourne in the Wiltshire Downs, and Blockley and Ilmington in the Cotswolds. These and other villages of this type consist of an irregular assemblage of farmsteads, cottages and other buildings, mostly grouped around a unifying feature such as the church or a variously shaped green with its chestnut tree and communal well. Even more amorphous, and also less compact, are the village-size clusters of homesteads that have evolved in association with piecemeal – acre by acre – squatters' encroachments into commons and wastes. These settlements are not as old as the linear and the agglomerated villages, most of them emerging during the long span of time from the late Middle Ages to the onset of the Georgian parliamentary enclosures.[26]

Very much different are the quite considerable numbers of villages that were built in an orderly fashion, with each building, each street and a central green conforming to a preconceived plan. They include several villages in various parts of the country that (mostly in the twelfth and thirteenth centuries) were repositioned on more suitable sites with better supplies of water and better accessibility to their land. Some of them, usually those that were associated with a castle or an abbey, were laid out as a regular linear village with straight building-lines and a fairly even spacing of dwellings and crofts. Others, however, were designed as compact villages, focusing on a rectangular or a square-shaped green. Interestingly the latter, the so-called 'green villages' of northern England,[27] occur most frequently in County Durham, lowland Cumberland and Northumberland, and the Vale of York and Vale of Pickering in north Yorkshire, where they are thought to date back to the reconstruction of the settlement landscape in the aftermath of the Norman Conquest and that systematic campaign of genocide and devastation known as the 'harrying of the north'.[28] The builders of these villages no doubt would have been well aware of the vulnerability of this portion of the country to marauding Scottish raiders. Very likely, therefore, the distinctive central greens were initially intended to carry something of a protective function.

Whenever an attack was threatened, cattle could be herded inside the village, whilst defenders could keep watch from the rear of their dwellings.

The Geographical Context of Village England

Measured simply as the areas where villages are common features of the rural landscape, the geographic extent of village England covers nearly three-quarters of the country, with every county having some share. As shown in Figure 1, which is based upon the comprehensive empirical work of the historical geographer Harry Thorpe,[29] village England exists in the non-urbanized and mostly lower-lying parts of northern England, the midlands plains, East Anglia and the scarp and vale country of Wessex and southern England. It stretches continuously north to south from Northumberland to Devon, and west to east from the Shropshire and Herefordshire vales to Norfolk, Suffolk, Essex and Kent. Within this great sweep of English countryside, Thorpe made a distinction between what he described as 'the belt of strong village development', where villages abound and are rarely any more than three miles apart, and 'other areas' that have a mixed pattern of settlement with villages occurring less frequently and a large proportion of their populations living in hamlets or isolated cottages and farmsteads. The former, which can be regarded as the geographic heartland of village England, stands out in Figure 1 as a broad but irregularly shaped arc of territory, encompassing the Cretaceous chalklands and the great Jurassic stone-belt of 'Deep England', and stretching right across the country from the Yorkshire–Durham border to the south midlands and Wessex. The areas of mixed settlement, or what may be described as 'peripheral' village England, are rather less extensive, but they do include much of Cheshire, Staffordshire and the marchland counties of Shropshire and Herefordshire in the west, the 'High' or 'inner' Weald in the south-east, and large parts of East Anglia and Lincolnshire in the east.

Elsewhere, there are several outliers of village England. These are areas where natural conditions, cultural history and a long tradition of arable farming have led to a nucleated pattern of rural settlement, though in most cases this is not as strong as in the heartlands. In northern England such outliers are to be seen in lowland Northumberland (outside the Tyneside conurbation), in the Vale of Eden and Solway Plain in Cumberland, and in the Ribble valley and Furness lowlands in north Lancashire. Moving southwards, there is a small outlier in the White Peak of Derbyshire, a part of the southern Pennines that was quite favourable for early

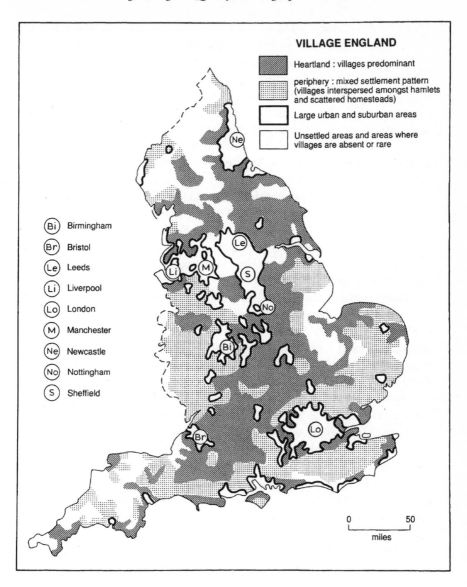

Figure 1: Village England: its geographical context.
The map is based on the work of Thorpe (1964),with the
'large urban and suburban areas' being updated.

agricultural settlement and contains some of the highest farming villages in the country; and there are others in the West Country, mostly in north-west and south Devon and along the south coast of Cornwall.

The parts of the country that are left unshaded in Figure 1 include the major urban areas and conurbations. By the time Thorpe published his survey in 1964, the suburbanization process had been long established and large acreages of countryside had already been lost. Since then, the process has continued (despite the operation of green belt planning policy), and further inroads have been made into village England, especially around London, Birmingham, and the towns and cities of south Lancashire and west Yorkshire. The unshaded spaces also include the uninhabited hills and moorlands of Pennine England, the Lake District, the North York Moors, Dartmoor, Exmoor, Bodmin Moor and a number of lowland heaths and forests such as the Breckland in central East Anglia and the New Forest in Hampshire. Unshaded too is some countryside that is in fact farmed and populated, but where natural conditions and settlement history have meant that hamlets and scattered homesteads prevail and rural communities large enough to be described as villages are few and far between. Such countryside exists over much of Devon and inland Cornwall, the hillier and most westerly parts of the Welsh Marches, and the Lincolnshire and Cambridgeshire fenlands, though in the latter it is still difficult to distinguish between what some may regard as very straggling villages and what others might look upon as loose linear clusters of farmsteads and smallholders' cottages.

Thorpe also took into account the localities, mostly on the coalfields and in the west Yorkshire and east Lancashire Pennines, where mining or other kinds of industrial villages prevailed. These too are left blank in Figure 1, so that what the shaded portion of the map is really identifying is the extent of a village England that, apart from some stretches of coastline where fishing has for long been important, is historically rooted in the soil and the farming occupation. This, however, is more extensive than the popular imagination of a cultural 'Deep England' in which the village, in idealized form, is everywhere very prominent. Deep England, with is strong southerly or 'south country' emphasis and its blissful vista of charming, timeless villages, each grouped around its ancient church, its peaceful green and its vernacular manor house, has been depicted by the cultural historian Angus Calder as stretching 'from Hardy's Wessex to Tennyson's Lincolnshire, from Kipling's Sussex to Elgar's Worcestershire.'[30] Excluded from this image and also absent from any geographical representation of village England are, of course, London and its sprawling suburbs, and the urban-industrial areas of the midlands and the north. Deep England is very much a rural construct: it includes only the more human-scaled and least industrialized of urban landscapes.

Few people would argue against enlarging this mental map of Deep England to embrace Mary Webb's Shropshire and the rolling, orchard and hop-growing countryside of Herefordshire, with its 'olde world', black and white, 'magpie' villages. And few people too would wish to leave out 'cob-wall and cream tea' Devon and Somerset (Thomas Hardy's Wessex is really just Dorset with the occasional excursion into another county) nor omit, on the other side of the country, Constable's Suffolk, the Norfolk of the Norwich School of painters and Rowland Hilder's rural Kent and garden of England. Even so, this wider interpretation of the geography of Deep England still ignores the northern counties and the various localities within them that do contain attractive rural landscapes and homely villages of agricultural origin. However, Yorkshire, Lancashire, Durham and Northumberland are counties that nearly always conjure up visions of nineteenth- and early twentieth-century industrialism and its ugly urban development. Moreover, even the Lake District counties of Cumberland and Westmorland do not have a proper place in Deep England, despite possessing some of the nation's most spectacular natural scenery and finest pastoral countryside. Cumberland and Westmorland, and the High Pennines too, are normally associated with rugged peaks and barren, windswept moorlands. They exist in the mind as a mountainous backcloth to Deep England rather than as parts of the actual stage.

Within both the heartland and the peripheries of village England, villages are not scattered randomly across the rural landscape. In most regions and localities there is a distinct pattern in their siting and their distribution, which is closely related to topographic features, drainage and soil conditions. It needs to be emphasized here that the sites of the large majority of present day English villages were first chosen and occupied long ago when techniques of farming were very undeveloped and when rural people were highly dependent upon the natural environment and what it could provide. Only certain types of soil were suitable for cultivation: the primitive dwellings were always highly vulnerable to bad weather, and supplies of water had to come either from springs and streams or from shallow communal wells. Thus the small groups of cultivators who established their embryo villages sought out places where the soil was both easy to work and contained good natural fertility; and, where the local terrain gave them the opportunity to do so, they chose sites that were sheltered from cold northerly and easterly winds. These considerations explain why so many of England's villages are situated

Plate 4: Stourpaine, Dorset. Like so many English villages, Stourpaine nestles in a hollow at the foot of a steep escarpment where natural shelter, a spring-line and favourable soils could all be found. The view is from the Iron Age and Romano-British hill fort of Hod Hill, the earthworks of which can be seen in the foreground.

along the edges – in geological terms the scarp foot and the bottom of the dip-slope – of a chalk, a sandstone, or a Jurassic limestone outcrop, where springs, natural shelter and the most productive and most easily worked soils could all be found in close proximity. Other typical village sites are the gravel terraces on either side of a river flood-plain; the drier margins of wetlands and fenlands (and any 'island' knolls within them); and, in upland areas underlain by porous limestone, chalk or coarse sandstone, the broader and better-watered valleys.

An illustration of the strong relationship between natural environmental conditions and the siting of villages is presented in Figure 2, which shows the distribution of nucleated settlements in the Somerset Levels and adjoining uplands – a part of south-west England that is noted for its geological and topographic diversity. In its humanized landscape, the most impressive feature is the line or chain of villages following the foot of the limestone Mendip hills and stretching some fifteen miles from Bleadon in the west to Wells in the east. Occupying sites where springs issue out from the base of the limestone and where also the steep south-facing escarpment gives way to gently sloping and well-drained ground on the edge of the Levels, villages here have always been sheltered from the coldest winds. Furthermore, for centuries their inhabitants have benefited from the existence of three markedly different types of terrain: the rich and easily cultivated farming land at the foot of the escarpment; the marshlands and wetlands of the Levels that, before they were reclaimed (principally in the seventeenth, eighteenth and early nineteenth centuries), provided an additional source of food in their abundance of wildfowl, fish and eels; and, lastly, the Mendips themselves, where sheep and cattle could be grazed and, as alternatives to farming, lead ores and building-stone could be mined and quarried.

In the south-east corner of the area shown in Figure 2 a somewhat less distinct grouping of villages can be seen in the undulating clay and marl-stone country formed out of the Liassic (Lower Jurassic) rock-beds that outcrop to the east of the Levels and run southwards from the vicinity of Shepton Mallet. Here, as along the foot of the Mendips, natural conditions have been very favourable for the development of village settlements. The numerous small streams, flowing down from the Liassic hills, provide reliable supplies of surface water; the many small entrant valleys and hill spurs afford plenty of shelter; and the fertile and generally well-drained loam soils have always been beneficial for farming communities. Other concentrations of villages can be seen on the various upland islands within the Levels, the two largest of which are the elongated ridge of the Polden hills and the broader, but mostly lower-lying, Isle of

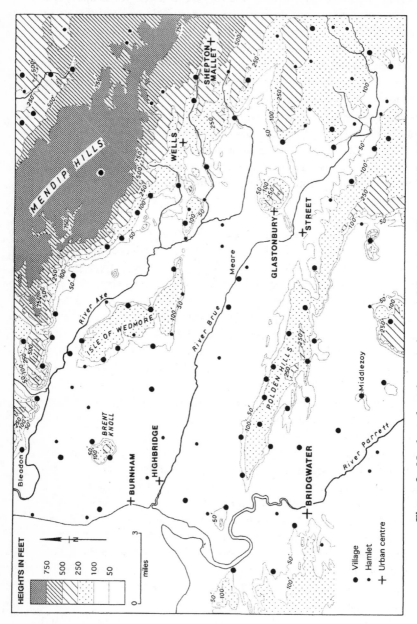

Figure 2: Nucleated settlements in central Somerset. The map is based on the Ordnance Survey, One Inch to the Mile, fifth edition, sheets 120 and 121, published in 1937.

Wedmore. In both of these localities small strings of villages follow the contouring just above the places where the better-drained land meets the flat and, in early times, seasonally inundated Levels. Streams and springs are very infrequent on the Polden hills and on Wedmore. However, the underground water-level here is nowhere much below the surface, which, together with the friable nature of the underlying rocks, meant that wells could be easily dug and rarely ran dry. Moreover, the marshland nearby not only served as an extra food resource but, at times of unrest, it could also afford some security from attack. Elsewhere in the Somerset Levels, a similar combination of advantages for early farming communities had existed on the smaller island of Brent Knoll, the miniature Liassic outlier at Meare, and the deposits of shelly material – the quaintly named 'Burtle Beds' – upon which the long-established 'Zoy' villages of Ched-zoy, Westernzoyland and Middlezoy are situated.

— CHAPTER TWO —

The First Transformation: Village England and the Parliamentary Enclosures

There once were lanes in nature's freedom dropt,
There once were paths that every valley wound –
Inclosure came, and every path was stopt;
Each Tyrant fix'd his sign, where paths were found
To hint a Trespass now who cross'd the ground:
Justice is made to speak as they command;
The high road now must be each stinted bound;
– Inclosure, thou'rt a curse upon the land.

And every village owns its tyrants now,
And parish-slaves must live as parish kings allow.
　　　　(excerpts from John Clare, *The Village Minstrel*, 1821)

Despite the Tudor enclosures and some further privatization of land in the seventeenth century, the ancient culture of communal open fields, independent peasant farmers, sturdy yeomen and busy cottagers, still prevailed over large areas of rural England when George I came to the throne in 1714 and the Georgian age began. However, important changes in the economic geography of the country had certainly been taking place. In several parts, including Cornwall, Staffordshire, Shropshire, Lancashire, south and west Yorkshire and much of Pennine England, mining and industrial outworking had taken root. Indeed, in many villages this proto-industrialization was already vying with farming as the chief occupation and economic mainstay. Elsewhere, peasant farming, which for centuries had been mainly for subsistence, was quietly becoming more commercial in purpose and in some areas more specialized. Marshlands and fenlands were being drained and reclaimed, whilst new methods of farming, including the first scientific techniques of cattle and sheep breeding, the growing of root crops and the highly productive 'Norfolk four-course' rotation, were being adopted by the more enterprising and more progressive of landowners. Those with the wealth and the power to use it had continued to engross land whenever they had the opportunity, though generally speaking this was much smaller in scale and far less damaging to village life than had been experienced with the Tudor enclosures. Around many villages there was also a gradual and mostly unrecorded nibbling away – the joining together and piecemeal enclosure of arable strips through mutual agreement – of the nearmost parts of the open fields; a process that reflected an increasing desire among the more ambitious of peasant farmers and yeomen to have exclusive access to the land that they worked. However, where these changes did occur, they were usually slow to materialize and their impacts on the rural landscape and village culture were undramatic. At the beginning of the eighteenth century nearly five million acres of agricultural land, representing around one-half of the cultivated area of England, was still being worked under the traditional open-field system. Moreover, there was an even vaster acreage of communal pasturage, commons and waste.[1]

The pace of change quickened appreciably after the first quarter of the eighteenth century, when the long-established processes of engrossment of land and the breaking down of peasant subsistence entered the most decisive of their historical surges – the Georgian agricultural revolution that brought the first great transformation of village England. The driving force behind this transformation was parliamentary enclosure; that is, enclosure sanctioned by a private Act of Parliament. Prior to the eighteenth century, there had been just seven instances of this mode of enclosure, the earliest being that of Radipole parish in south Dorset in 1604.[2] Parliamentary enclosure was still uncommon in the reign of George I (1714–27), when just eighteen more private Acts were authorized; and it did not begin in earnest until around the year 1750. By then, the number of parliamentary enclosure schemes in England had reached the hundred mark, with most of them having taken place in the midland counties of Leicestershire, Warwickshire, Rutland and Northamptonshire, principally for landowner emparkments and the planting of private woodlands. Thereafter, the trend was nothing short of spectacular and was dominated almost entirely by enclosures for agricultural purposes. Some 2,000 local Acts were passed in the second half of the eighteenth century, and nearly the same number again during the period from 1800 to 1845.[3]

'A Curse Upon the Land':
the Georgian Parliamentary Enclosures

A villager who had played in the open fields as a boy, or watched the sheep in the common pastures, would have lived to see the modern landscape of his parish completed and matured, the roads all made, the hedgerow trees full grown and new farmsteads built out in the fields where none had ever been before.

(W. G. Hoskins, *The Making of the English Landscape*, 1955)[4]

Parliamentary enclosure was the means by which a huge acreage of rural England was converted from its ancient state of common occupation into the modern condition of individual ownership. It gave licence for the displacing of peasant cultivators, removing their arable open fields and their mosaics of strips and furlongs, and taking away their customary rights to usage of commons and wastes. It was also the vital legal instrument for the remodelling of the English rural landscape for the implementation of capitalist methods of agricultural production and the fostering of efficient and profitable exploitation of the land resource. Through enclosure, land immediately became a private commodity: hitherto, most of it had been used for communally organized cultivation of crops and grazing of animals. The placing of fixed field boundaries in the form of fences, quickset hedges or, in some upland areas, drystone walls signified this new role and proclaimed to any observer that enclosed land was indeed private property. Such boundaries also meant that only the owners, the tenant farmers and their workers had access to the new fields, and that all other people were excluded.

It was the husband and wife co-authors John and Barbara Hammond who, in their classic book *The Village Labourer 1760–1832*[5] (published nearly a century ago but still widely read), presented a social interpretation of the parliamentary enclosure movement and established it as a prime focus of interest and debate for future generations of social and economic historians. The Hammonds believed that the Georgian parliamentary enclosures were of unparalleled importance in the history of rural and village England. In their view not only had the enclosures completely reshaped the landscape in many areas but, by enabling landowners to widen their control over land and to strengthen their power over the rural population, they had also revolutionized rural life and its class relationships. H. J. Massingham, invoking the spirit of Oliver Goldsmith, John Clare and William Cobbett, wrote in a similar vein. Denouncing the parliamentary enclosure movement as 'a "hundred years" war between the landowner and the peasantry',[6] he saw only its destructive effects,

blaming it for 'shattering' the self-contained village community and elim-
inating its ancient peasant 'folk-life'. Rather different, however, was the
view expressed in the 1960s and 1970s by historians with Marxist lean-
ings, in particular E. P. Thompson (1963)[7] and Eric Hobsbawm and
George Rude (1969),[8] who saw the movement less in isolation and much
more as part of a continuous general historical process of agricultural capitalization and social transformation of rural England; a process that,
hastened by the enclosures but by no means wholly attributable to them,
had involved widespread appropriation of land, dispossession of peasant
farmers, marginalization of the rural poor and ultimately the creation of a
mass agricultural working class or 'rural proletariat'. More recently, the
pendulum of opinion has swung back some way from this stance. Today
there is broad agreement among historians that the Georgian enclosures,
by fundamentally altering the organization of land, by removing traditional customary rights, and by dispossessing large numbers of the
farming population, undoubtedly did have a profound impact upon the
English rural landscape and contributed greatly to the social transformation of countless English villages and parishes. And it is widely accepted
that, whilst enclosure was not the only force in this transformation, it was
certainly the cutting edge.

In the late fifteenth and sixteenth centuries the state, responding to a
rising tide of anti-enclosure unrest and believing that it was in the public
interest to stem the decline of crop cultivation and the desertion of villages, had attempted to check the Tudor enclosures by promoting a long
succession of government enquiries and restrictive statutes of varying
effectiveness. This had begun with the Husbandry Act of 1489 and, over
the following six decades, had continued with an assortment of Acts and
Commissions, all aimed at checking large-scale conversion of tillage into
pasture and stopping the distress and depopulation that this was seen to
be bringing about.[9] Then, in the much different context of the eighteenth
century – when the emphasis of policy shifted towards stimulating agricultural 'improvement' and encouraging the application of 'rational'
methods of farming – the state intervened again. But this time it acted for
the private domain by becoming a vehicle for extinguishing the ancient
communal farming culture and, in many areas, replacing this with an
entirely new agricultural landscape.

Those who stood to profit most from the 'new husbandry' and 'scientific farming' of the Georgian agricultural revolution needed the sort of
efficient and legally defined means of enclosure – and one that strongly
favoured the larger landowners at the expense of peasant farmers – that
only a private Act of Parliament could provide. The procedure that had

been introduced with the Radipole enclosure was for interested parties to meet together to draw up an initial, usually parish-wide, proposal and present it to parliament for acceptance as a private Bill. For a petition to be approved and a local Enclosure Act and Award to be passed and made legally binding, it was necessary for the promoters to gain the consent of the owners and occupiers of at least four-fifths, or in some instances three-quarters, of the land that was to be affected. It was not obligatory, however, for the promoters to have the backing of a majority of the actual holders (occupiers, tenants and customary users) of land, nor indeed a majority of the parish population. The level of consent, therefore, was expressed purely and simply in terms of land ownership, not democratically in accordance with the numbers of people who would be directly affected. In many instances a few larger landowners, or not uncommonly just one, could override the interests of everyone else. In a large number of parliamentary enclosures, therefore, the small yeoman farmer, the cottager and the squatter were excluded, becoming, in the words of the Hammonds, 'merely dim shadows in the very background of the enclosure scheme'.[10]

In each Enclosure Bill commissioners and surveyors were appointed, first to define the provisions of the Award and its allocations, and then to supervise the actual enclosure work and carry out what E. P. Thompson has pointedly described as 'a plain enough case of class-robbery played according to fair rules of property and law laid down by a Parliament of property-owners and lawyers'.[11] More often than not the commissioners, normally three in number, had already been nominated by the promoters in their initial enclosure petition. With few exceptions they were chosen from members of the rural and country-town establishment; people such as magistrates, solicitors, surveyors, land-agents and clergymen, who could be trusted to side with the landowning interest. Indeed, it was not until 1801 that a House of Commons Standing Order ended the anachronistic and blatantly unfair practice of the lord of the manor or his representative acting as one of the commissioners.

Earlier Standing Orders in 1774 and 1775 did attempt to establish some element of democracy at the parish level. Previously a petition for enclosure, provided that it met with the approval of the lord of the manor (in parishes where this title still existed) and the clerical or lay tithe owner, could be carried through without a public notice and with the peasant community knowing little or nothing about what was happening until the legal process was well underway. Indeed, in some villages it was not until the commissioners and surveyors had arrived to draw up a new map of the parish that villagers first became aware that enclosure was due to take place.[12] These Orders provided some scope for counter-petitions, and they stipulated that notices of any proposed enclosure had to be posted for all to see on the church door on at least three consecutive Sundays in August and September. However, there was no departure from the long-established principle that only landowners, the larger freeholders, and ratepayers with a property qualification could vote at a parish meeting. All too often the peasant class still had no real say and, at this crucial stage in its history, its interests remained undefended.

Wartime conditions (the Napoleonic Wars) and their inflationary impact on food prices pressed the government into passing the first General Enclosure Act in 1801. This important legislation was designed to make enclosure simpler and less expensive by establishing a number of general terms and conditions all aimed at speeding up the authorization of individual Bills. In particular it made it easier for landowners and other promoters to enclose commons and heathland and moorland waste. Thus the period after 1801 saw the enclosure of a large acreage of marginal, formerly uncultivated, land; and with this there came widespread extinction of commoners' rights and the last vestiges of traditional peasant subsistence and independence. Significantly it was this late phase in the history of the parliamentary enclosure movement that provoked the strongest opposition from the dispossessed, leading in some cases – most notably in the villages around the Otmoor marshes in central Oxfordshire in 1814 and 1830 – to open rioting and other acts of violence.

Further General Enclosure Acts were passed in 1836, 1840 and 1845. The Act of 1836 lowered the consent threshold to two-thirds of land ownership and removed the need for a private Act if seven-eighths of the interested parties were in agreement that the scheme could be undertaken without the need for commissioners to be appointed.[13] The General Enclosure Act of 1845, which perhaps was as much a response to the anxieties of a growing body of commons preservationists and outdoors enthusiasts as it was a belated attempt to place enclosure on a more equitable footing, authorized parliament to appoint central commissioners and entrusted them with giving greater consideration to the needs and objections of local cottagers and small farmers.[14] However, this effort to avert any further injustices was far too late. By then, there was little potentially productive land left to be treated, and the enclosure movement had become nothing more than a mopping up of the odd remaining pocket of non-privatized land. Eventually it ceased altogether in the face of mounting opposition from the influential Commons, Open Spaces and Footpaths Preservation Society formed in 1865. The very last parliamentary enclosures were made in 1901 for Skipwith in the Vale of York (but interestingly preserving much of the common here) and in 1914 for part of the Gloucestershire parish of Elmstone Hardwicke. If we include the thousand or so awards made after the General Enclosure Act of 1836, the total numbers of parliamentary enclosure schemes in England come to a final figure of 5,226.[15] In aggregate they covered nearly seven million acres of land, or around one-quarter of the country's total farming area; and they had taken place in nearly 3,000 parishes.[16] Approximately two-thirds of the enclosed acreage had previously been arable open fields, whilst one-third had been common pastures, commons or waste.

To a large extent the parliamentary enclosure movement was driven by the eighteenth- and early nineteenth-century zeal for national economic progress, in which agricultural improvement and efficient cultivation of the land was seen to have a vital role. Whereas the traditional, self-sufficient, peasant farming culture, with its archaic open fields, fragmented holdings, wasteful bare fallow, scrubby commons and half-starved cattle, was regarded as a public encumbrance standing in the way of modernization and encouraging idleness and immorality among the rural poor, the new scientific and highly profitable agriculture, as praised by such influential advocates as Arthur Young (1741–1818), William Marshall (1745–1818) and Thomas Coke (1752–1842), was deemed to be rational and virtuous. Enlightened farmers knew that the latter mode of farming, with its new crop rotations, improved techniques of drainage, superior methods of cattle breeding and planned layouts of farm buildings, could prosper only within a remodelled landscape of large consolidated holdings and an orderly arrangement of permanently hedged or fenced fields.

Whilst in the minds of the agricultural modernizers the ethos of progress and improvement provided all that was needed as moral justification for the enclosure movement, the principal economic influence was the growing domestic market for food commodities and the increased profits that this promised to the new breed of capitalist farmers and landowners. Almost three-quarters of all parliamentary enclosure was concentrated within two waves of intense activity, both coinciding quite closely with a period of high prices for agricultural products, especially cereals.[17] The first of these waves, involving the conversion of around two million acres of land, began in 1760 and lasted until the early 1780s. The second, which affected an even larger acreage, commenced around 1790 and continued until the end of the Napoleonic Wars in 1815. In the earlier wave most of the enclosures were predominantly of arable open fields: in the later wave, however, the emphasis in many areas turned to the enclosure and reclamation of commons, heaths and other marginal land.[18] General inflation and food scarcities during the Seven Years War

(1756–63), the American War of Independence (1775–83) and the French Revolutionary and Napoleonic Wars (1792–1815), aggravated in the latter case by a run of poor harvests, fuelled the price increases; but the reason why food prices never fell back to previous levels was the quickening of urban population growth, stemming from Britain's burgeoning industrialization and flourishing trading economy. At the census of 1821, just a few years after the second great wave of parliamentary enclosures, there were nearly three times more urban mouths to feed in England and Wales than there had been in the middle of the eighteenth century.

There were appreciable regional and local variations in the timing, the intensity and the long-term impacts of parliamentary enclosure; and, as can be seen through comparison of the two maps in Figure 3, there were major differences between the geography of enclosures of arable open fields and that of enclosures of commons and wastes. The map of the former (Map A) shows that conversion of open fields was absent or, at the most, only thinly represented in those regions and districts that had either never been open-field country in the first place or had already been extensively enclosed prior to the Georgian agricultural revolution. Thus there was little or no parliamentary enclosure of open fields in Cornwall, west Devon, Lancashire, Westmorland, Cumberland, Durham or the Welsh borderland counties of Shropshire and Cheshire, where in many localities communal crop farming had never been a part of the rural landscape and the rural way of life. And there was little of it too in the southeastern counties of Essex and Kent and in east Sussex, where most of the open fields that are known to have once existed had already been enclosed before the eighteenth century or had survived only as small remnants. This, however, still leaves us with a vast belt of countryside, stretching from the Vale of York and east Yorkshire, through Lincolnshire and central England, to northern East Anglia, the western Home Counties and Wessex, where in every district the amount of former open-field land enclosed through the parliamentary process ranged from a minimum of one-tenth to more than half of the total area. Prominent within this belt is a broad grouping of heavily shaded districts covering much of the east and south midlands, and extending northwards into Lincolnshire and east Yorkshire. Here the proportion exceeds 30 per cent and in several localities, mostly in Northamptonshire, Buckinghamshire, Huntingdonshire and Cambridgeshire, it rises above the very high figure of 50 per cent.

The map of parliamentary enclosure of commons and wastes, (Map B in Figure 3) shows a far less distinct pattern. Over wide areas of the midlands and southern England this type of enclosure features only

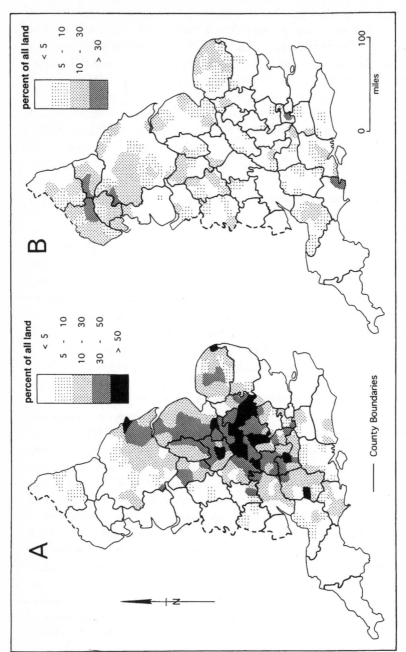

Figure 3: The geography of parliamentary enclosure. Map A is of enclosure of open-field land; Map B is of enclosure of commons and wastes. Both maps are based on the work of E. C. K. Gonner (1912).

sporadically – here and there in a few localities where there had been a sizeable tract of old heathland, unreclaimed marshland or common grazing land. It does, however, exceed the acreage of open-field enclosure in much of northern England, especially the Pennines and most of Cumberland and Westmorland, where there were large expanses of moorland and other uncultivated uplands. It also features quite extensively in the sandy heathlands of Staffordshire, Norfolk, the New Forest and south-east Dorset; and likewise in the fenlands and marshlands of south Lincolnshire, north Cambridgeshire, coastal East Anglia and the Somerset Levels.

The visual impact of parliamentary enclosure varied from parish to parish depending upon the amounts of former communal land and how much or how little of it had been subjected to earlier forms of enclosure. In some parishes parliamentary enclosure was merely a clearing up of what were just small remnants of the original open fields and commons. In these instances the commissioners and surveyors could create just fragments of the new agricultural landscape, juxtaposed amongst pieces of old enclosure with their disorderly patchworks of irregularly shaped intakes and closes. In many other parishes, however, mostly within the former strongholds of open-field farming in the south and east midlands, Lincolnshire and east Yorkshire, almost all the land was transformed. Here the landscape of parliamentary enclosure still prevails today, though some of the original field boundaries have been pulled down or uprooted to create even larger units of agricultural production. Markedly different from the very informal and often quite picturesque landscape of old enclosure, its dominating characteristic is the rigid 'chequer-board' pattern of fields. There are, however, significant differences between the landscape of the eighteenth-century parliamentary enclosures, especially of arable open fields, and the landscape of the later versions carried out during and after the Napoleonic Wars. The former produced a rather softer landscape that in many places did incorporate some long-standing features, such as a winding lane, the curving line of an old open-field 'headland', and patches of ridge and furrow. The later parliamentary enclosures, many of which involved the conversion of large acreages of commons and wastes, obliterated everything that had existed before and imposed a geometric gridiron of characterless square and rectangular divisions of agricultural space.

After the new field pattern had been laid out, the landscape of parliamentary enclosure also came to include new roads, small plantations of trees, and new farmsteads built away from the village. Typically running in dead-straight lines and bounded by wide verges of greensward (to facilitate the movement of teams of horses, herds of cattle and flocks of

Plate 5: Landscape of parliamentary enclosure, Yorkshire Wolds. The landscape shown here was created in the early years of the nineteenth century, in the second great wave of parliamentary enclosures. The 'chequer-board' pattern of geometric square and rectangular hedged fields dominates the countryside as far as the eye can see, and is relieved only by post-enclosure farmsteads and windbreak plantations.

sheep), the enclosure roads, or 'occupation' roads as they were sometimes called, were designed to give access to the new farmholdings and in some cases to by-pass a village or to avoid some troublesome marshy ground. With agricultural output increasing all the time and greater quantities of materials, animals and crops needing to be moved, the new roads also eased the congestion of farm traffic along what was left of the old networks of meandering pre-enclosure lanes and trackways. After a few years, the tree planting, usually of sycamores, beeches or larches, brought some relief to the monotony of the new landscape. It also provided spinneys and coverts for fox-hunting and places where landowners and farmers could enjoy the increasingly popular leisure-pursuit of shooting pheasants, partridges and other game. However, the main intention of post-enclosure tree planting was to create natural shelter belts, giving the more exposed of the new fields and farmsteads some protection against strong winds and drifting snow.

In the days of the traditional open-field system, with its scattered and highly fragmented distribution of arable strips, the most logical place for the location of farmsteads had been the village. After parliamentary enclosure, however, it often made economic sense for landowners to relocate the homes and farm buildings of their tenant farmers within or adjoining the new holdings, especially those that were situated some distance away from the village. In some parishes several of the new farmsteads were built almost immediately after enclosure, but it was more usual for the dispersal process to take place at least a decade later.[19] Indeed, in some localities, especially in chalk or limestone country where the underground water-level was often deep below the surface, it was not completed until the sustained agricultural prosperity of the High Farming age in the third quarter of the nineteenth century. Whatever the actual timing, the benefits of relocation as far as the farmer was concerned were a comfortable and substantial new farmhouse to live in and spacious, well-built, farm buildings to make use of. However, these could only be at the price of becoming geographically and socially isolated from their workers and the rest of the village community.[20]

Social Effects

The divorce of the peasantry from the soil, and the extinction of commoners, open-field farmers, and eventually small freeholders, were the heavy price which the nation ultimately paid for the supply of bread and meat to its manufacturing population.

(Lord Ernle, *English Farming Past and Present*, 1912)[21]

The parliamentary enclosures, as well as creating a new agricultural land-scape, played a decisive role in the reordering of rural society and the transformation of English village culture. In conjunction with the under-lying process of agricultural capitalization, they were instrumental in destroying the traditional peasant mode of existence and fostering a hard-ening of social divisions – indeed, the forging of a rigid, tripartite class system and creation of what Hoskins has declared to have been 'one of the most unequal societies the world has ever seen'.[22] The new social order came to dominate the entire structure and tenor of English village life throughout the nineteenth century, and it did not begin to break down until the retreat of landowner power and 'landlordism' in the after-math of the First World War. Large landowners, who had gained the lion's share from the Georgian enclosures and indeed had been the sole beneficiaries in some parishes, stood firmly at the head of the rural class-hierarchy and formed an instantly identifiable ruling elite.[23] Parliamentary enclosures had enabled them to consolidate and enlarge their estates, usu-ally only at the costs of paying for the hedging or fencing of the new fields and meeting their share of the commissioners' and surveyors' fees. Tenant farmers and the remaining freeholders, whose forefathers in pre-enclosure times quite likely would have been yeomen, copyholders or just better-off peasant farmers, occupied the middle position. They repre-sented the most heterogeneous of the three classes, since their incomes and social status varied very much in accordance with the acreage and the quality of the land that they worked. Some, like Farmer Boldwood in Hardy's *Far from the Madding Crowd*, were wealthy enough to merit the description of 'gentleman farmer' and had pretensions to gentility. Oth-ers, however, were little or nothing more than struggling smallholders; for the parliamentary enclosures did not eliminate every small farmer (perhaps only a minority in some areas) and many of the lesser yeomen and the larger of the peasant farmers did manage to stay on the land, especially in diversified farming areas like Worcestershire, Herefordshire, the Weald and the fenlands. But, although they did manage to survive, they could not avoid becoming incorporated into the market economy, with some eventually joining the lower end of the tenant-farming class and others eking out their livelihoods as the smallest and most marginal of owner-occupiers.

Firmly at the bottom of the tripartite social system were the wage-dependent agricultural labourers and hirelings. Constituting by far the most numerous of the three rural classes, they had no land to call their own: indeed many did not even have a cottage garden or a parish allot-ment. People described as 'labourers' had been living in village England long before the parliamentary enclosures, but they had existed in much smaller numbers, with most of them having a fair chance of eventually being able to find their way into peasant proprietorship or some crafts-man's enterprise. By pushing many peasant farmers and cottagers off the land, the enclosures swelled the landless rural population and placed it at the mercy of market forces and all their rigours. The social repercussions soon became all too clear as more and more inhabitants of village Eng-land were put onto the road to pauperism, and were placed in a precarious state of total dependency upon farmer employers and a money wage. The loss of their strips of open-field land had taken away the ability of many villagers to produce crops both for their own consumption and for providing a small income and means of exchange. For many villagers too, the enclosures of commons and wastes had removed all other sources of food and the places where fuel, timber and thatching materials had previously been gathered. It was the loss of these important means of subsistence that convinced the Hammonds that enclosure had indeed made 'all the difference between independence and pauperism' and had proved 'fatal' to the peasant farmer, the cottager and the squatter[24] – the very groups of people who, from time immemorial, had represented the corner-stones of traditional rural society.

The reduction of peasant families into this condition of dispossession and exposure to impersonal hire – the 'parish-slaves' of John Clare's remonstration – owed much to the undemocratic nature of an enclosure process that excluded them from any of the decision making and more often than not treated their claims very unfairly or ignored them entirely. In the old, communally organized, farming regime peasant cultivators and yeomen had held strips of land within the open fields and had enjoyed rights to use commons and wastes. For many, however, these rights had been no more than ancient customary practices or just unde-fined permissions passed down through the ages. If put to the test, not many peasant families could demonstrate a clear, written-down, legal entitlement; and few had the knowledge and the nerve to put their case forward or to organize a counter-petition. Moreover, those who were allocated one or two pieces of land soon found themselves being pre-sented with a share of the enclosure costs. All too often this was disproportionately high and had to be met before any economic benefits could be gained. Whilst the expense of enclosure could be easily borne by the landowners, it was a severe obstacle for common village people. For many of the latter, the commissioners' and surveyors' fees, together with the costs of planting quickset hedges or installing lengths of fencing, were prohibitive. Rather than attempt to pay for all this, they either sold their allocations or accepted an offer of compensation, very often for just a paltry sum of money.

Impacts on the Village Landscape

William Cobbett, one of the strongest and most persistent critics of the new economic and social order, was mistaken in his belief that the parliamentary enclosures, and the dispossessions that they brought about, caused a mass migration of people out of rural England and widespread depopulation of its villages. From the middle of the eighteenth century onwards, few enclosures of open fields were accompanied by a change from arable landuse to mainly animal husbandry and a pastoral landscape. In a large majority of cases these, and also many of the enclosures of commons and wastes, paved the way for labour-intensive cereal growing or mixed, cereal-cum-livestock, farming. The new, increasingly capitalized, mode of crop cultivation applied advanced rotations and did away with much of the land wastage of the old communal system; but often it required considerably more agricultural labour, not less. Furthermore, the actual process of enclosure, which usually took several years to complete, itself created a substantial amount of additional rural employment. Fences and gates had to be erected, hedges laid, ditches dug, roads constructed and new farmsteads built. Accordingly, rather than precipitating an immediate exodus of the dispossessed in the way that Cobbett and, later, the Hammonds have supposed, parliamentary enclosure was in fact commonly followed by an appreciable population increase. Whilst certain other factors, most notably the continued operation of outdoors Poor Law relief which encouraged the rural poor to have large families and to remain in their native villages, played an important part in this, much – certainly over the short and medium term – has to be attributed to enclosure.

That strong population growth did often occur following the implementation of an Award has been demonstrated in Gleave's work on the impacts of parliamentary enclosure upon the landscape and settlement pattern of the Yorkshire Wolds,[25] a predominantly mixed cereal-growing and sheep-pasturing area, and a part of rural England where several enclosure acts conveniently came shortly after the first national census of 1801. In each of a dozen parishes, including those of East Heslerton, Middleton-on-the-Wolds, Thwing, Weaverthorpe and Wold Newton that Gleave selected for closer investigation, the completion of an enclosure scheme came during a time of fast population growth and the building of several new cottages and tradesmen's workshops. In Middleton, where parliamentary enclosure commenced in 1805, the population rose sharply from 286 at the 1801 census to 441 in 1821, whilst during the same period the numbers of dwellings increased from forty-six to eighty-eight. In Weaverthorpe parish, to take another illustration, the enclosure process was initiated a few years earlier and was followed by even stronger demographic growth and building activity. In 1801, the year before the Weaverthorpe Enclosure Award was passed through parliament, there were 182 inhabitants living in just thirty-one cottages and farmhouses. Two decades later, the population here had risen to 334, and the numbers of dwellings had more than doubled to seventy. Here, as in Middleton, and indeed in countless other villages elsewhere in agricultural England, what in pre-enclosure times had been small village communities developed into much more substantial settlements, and they did so within the time-span of just a single generation.

The amount of post-enclosure population growth and the numbers of new cottages and other dwellings that were built to accommodate it varied considerably from village to village, with the largest differences occurring between those villages that were situated within 'close' parishes and those, such as Middleton-on-the-Wolds and Weaverthorpe, which lay within 'open' parishes. The distinction between close and open parishes is older than the Georgian agricultural revolution. It was first given official recognition in the Elizabethan Poor Law legislation of 1598–1601 that made the parish vestries and parish overseers responsible for the granting of relief to the poor, with resident landowners and other ratepayers having to bear the financial burden. Indeed, in many instances the status of close parish had its roots in the Tudor enclosures when entire open fields were engrossed for the creation of private grazing land or for an emparkment, in some cases involving the removal of the village but more commonly leaving it to survive in a diminished state. Broadly speaking, the parts of the country that had experienced the strongest incidence of Tudor enclosure, namely the east and south midlands, western East Anglia, south-west Lincolnshire and east Yorkshire, were the same as those that came to have the greatest numbers of close parishes and close villages. Eventually, in each of these areas more than one-quarter of rural parishes were of this type, and in some localities, such as west Norfolk and the Lincolnshire and Yorkshire Wolds, the proportion was higher than one-third.[26]

Historically, close parishes were parishes in which by far the largest share of the land was the property of one principal landowner or, at the most, just two or three smaller landowners who quite likely would have had some family connection. Because of their concentrated ownership, close parishes and the villages within them were always dominated by landowner authority and the far-reaching social control that this conferred. To exclude unwanted incomers, particularly the sort of people who might well become paupers and burdens on the parish Poor Rate, the construction of cottages was strictly regulated. Parish-based Settlement Laws, brought in during the seventeenth century primarily to control the movement of the rural poor, were rigidly applied, and any new tenants were carefully selected. There could be no squatting within close parishes, and the building of cottages by the villagers themselves was rarely permitted. Landowners preferred to have a deficiency of agricultural labour in their own villages, leaving their tenant farmers to recruit casual and seasonal workers from the population accumulations of neighbouring open villages and the nearest market town. Always mindful of their self-interest in restricting population growth and keeping parish rates in check, landowners built new cottages only when and where these were really necessary. Moreover, in many instances they took the precaution of demolishing old dwellings if they became untenanted for long and were falling into a poor state of repair. Enid Gauldie, in her book *Cruel Habitations*, an in-depth history of urban and rural working-class housing, provides us with some further insight into their actions: 'They preferred to keep down the numbers on the land so that they might remain benevolent to a few rather than resentfully burdened with many.'[27]

This control over people and housing supply is the reason why the population trend in most close parishes and close villages was one of slow growth or stagnation. For example, in fifty-eight close parishes and townships (divisions of large parishes) in west Norfolk the average population growth from 1801 to 1841 was just 22 per cent, compared with an average 47 per cent increase in all rural parishes in this area. During the same period the population of thirty-two close parishes and townships in west Leicestershire and east Warwickshire rose by a modest 10 per cent, compared with an overall rural population increase there of approximately four times this rate; and in Dorset, Somerset and west Wiltshire a sample of thirty-eight close parishes experienced an average population growth of 11 per cent, which was less than one-third of the overall rural trend for these parts of Wessex.[28]

The extreme version of the close village is the model 'estate' village in which single ownership extends to every house and every cottage. Several Georgian estate villages, such as New Houghton in Norfolk, Nuneham Courteney in Oxfordshire, Harewood and Coneysthorpe respectively in west and north Yorkshire and, most famously of all, Milton Abbas in

Plate 6: A model estate village, New Houghton, Norfolk. Houghton Hall was built for Sir Robert Walpole, Prime Minister of George I and George II. The park was laid out in the 1730s, involving the destruction of the old village of Houghton. It was replaced by a model village, placed directly in front of the parkland entrance. The photograph shows some of the original early-Georgian cottages, built in blocks of four and very formally arranged. Note also the elegant iron gateway. A screen of trees hides the hall from public view.

Dorset were built as completely new settlements on fresh sites. Most, however, were formed through the rebuilding and formalization of long-established villages. Whichever the case, they were all heavily influenced by the improvement visions of wealthy landowners and the Georgian fashion for landscape design. The eighteenth-century estate village, whilst being physically set apart from the great house, was integral to it both as part of the wider landscaping idea and as a place to provide superior cottages and an easily supervised residential environment for the landowner's key workers, servants and bailiffs. Designed by some of the finest architects of the day, estate villages were the most appropriate places for their owners to display their paternalism and social accomplishments. Very often this took the form of building almshouses and erecting monuments in prominent positions, whilst the church became the obvious place to exhibit mural tablets, boards and inscriptions proclaiming generous acts of benevolence to the aged and the deserving poor.

Open parishes, on the other hand, had a diffuse pattern of ownership, with land and other property being held by several minor landowners and small proprietors. The village communities living within such parishes were not blessed by the benevolence and charity of the landed class, nor were they subjected to their presence and direct authority. Moreover, because the Poor Rate in open parishes was divided among a plurality of property owners, and also because farmers, tradesmen and craftsmen here saw that it was in their interests to have an assured supply of labour near at hand, incomers were encouraged, rather than discouraged, to settle. Thus, very different from the situation in close parishes and their land-owner-dominated villages, strong population build-up and an expanding pool of agricultural labour became the norm here. Taking the large and well-documented county of Lincolnshire as an illustration, we find that nearly three-quarters of its 214 rural open parishes and townships saw more than a 75 per cent increase in numbers of inhabitants between 1801 and 1851, with around one-third of them recording a doubling or trebling.[29] Even more emphatic are Pamela Horn's figures on house and cottage building in rural Oxfordshire. Here, in the 1840s, a total of 1,342 new dwellings were built within eighty-six open parishes, compared with a mere seven new dwellings in thirty-four close parishes.[30]

Whereas in close villages small numbers of good quality, attractive and well-positioned cottages were constructed under the direction of a wealthy landowner, in open villages much larger numbers of dwellings – mostly labourers' hovels – were run up by speculative tradesmen who had nothing but profit in their minds. These labourers' cottages were almost invariably built on the cheap and were scattered about the village in a typ-

Plate 7: An open village, Langtoft, Yorkshire Wolds. Langtoft is a typical example of an open village in which, over the centuries, there has been a plurality of ownership of land and property. Note the disorderly crowding of village farmsteads, labourers' cottages and what remains of craftsmen's workshops. The medieval church stands on higher ground and overlooks the whole community. Recently, some of the village farmsteads have gone out of agriculture, and two (in the right-hand foreground) have been partially replaced by new residential development.

Plate 8: Early-nineteenth-century labourers' cottages in Langtoft. Labourers' cottages like these, built in terrace rows and facing directly onto the street, tell us something about the living conditions of the lowest tier of rural England's rigid nineteenth-century rural class structure. Agricultural labourers once formed a majority among the population of most villages, and their humble homes were the most numerous type of dwelling. The row shown here comprises of ten cottages which, according to the census enumeration schedules for Langtoft, housed as many as sixty-two people in 1851. The dwellings look very small today but, with their two bedrooms and separate parlour and kitchen, they were of above-average size and standard. This is why, unlike most labourers' cottages, they have survived the rural slum clearances of the twentieth century. The nearmost cottage has been extended at the rear, almost doubling the amount of living space.

ically haphazard way. Many were constructed in short terrace rows, often backing onto each other as back-to-back housing. Some were erected as infilling on vacant plots, facing the main street, whilst others occupied sites along the back lanes or within the crofts and closes that stretched between these lanes and the village core. All too often new cottages were placed upon patches of damp and badly-drained land; sites that were useless for anything else and could only worsen the insanitary and unsound condition of these humble dwellings. Badly built and poorly maintained (it was normally quicker and cheaper to employ unskilled builders and carpenters from a nearby market town than to use village craftsmen), the worst of these late eighteenth-century and early nineteenth-century labourers' hovels were as wretched to live in as were the much more widely publicized urban slums. Their walls, flimsily made and usually lacking a proper dampcourse, became dilapidated and full of cracks; their roofs, particularly those made of thatch, often leaked; and shoddy workmanship meant that the windows and doors let in the wind and the cold. Moreover, the families of the rural poor tended to be larger than average and in many cases included an aged and perhaps infirm grandparent. Yet the cottages were very small, typically comprised of no more than a kitchen and parlour downstairs and just a single bedroom and perhaps a few square yards of attic above. Usually one part of the family – the husband and wife and the youngest child – slept in the bedroom. The rest slept elsewhere in the cottage, commonly having to share a bed or, if there was no bed, a straw pallet on the floor.[31] Adding to the untidy congestion of buildings within open villages were the workshops and sheds of the growing sub-communities of tradesmen and craftsmen. These premises could sprout up in just about any vacant spot, but more often than not they were built in a central position alongside the main street where it was easier to bring in the raw materials and to have the finished work collected. Here too were to be found the Methodist chapels that provided the religion for the rural working class, and the alehouses, which catered for a much different sort of comfort.

At the opposite end of rural England's widening social spectrum, much of the wealth accrued from the new husbandry and the land engrossment of the parliamentary enclosures was expended on a new and highly impressive era of country-mansion building and the creation of landscaped parks. In few instances, however, were these monuments of personal wealth incorporated inside the physical structure of a village. The large majority were built well outside, and in most cases this separation was reinforced by the construction of a walled surround, the placing of forbidding gateways and lodges, and the planting of dense screens of trees. Not unusually, in creating these barriers, obstructing cottages and farmsteads were removed, whilst roads and trackways were diverted.[32] Inside the parks nothing of the pre-existing human landscape was allowed to remain. Indeed, in some instances, as for example at New Houghton, Milton Abbas, Nuneham Courtenay and Shugborough (in Staffordshire), entire villages were pulled down and repositioned.

Despite their seclusion, the new mansions certainly had a profound effect upon the way of life of many landowner villages, both symbolically as declarations of class power and in material terms as places of regular employment for small armies of servants, estate workers, bailiffs and gamekeepers. Until the advent of Gothic revivalism in country-house architecture towards the end of the eighteenth century, most Georgian stately homes were constructed, or remodelled, in the fashionable Palladian style. Dominated by their imposing fronts and cold portal columns, and including some (such as Lord Arundel's Wardour Castle in Wiltshire, Richard Temple's Stowe House in Buckinghamshire and Thomas Coke's Holkham Hall in Norfolk) that were built on a monumental scale, they were designed to convey what Raymond Williams has forcibly expressed as a 'visible stamping of power, of displayed wealth and command'.[33] Usually positioned on rising ground, the grander of these mansions looked out over a carefully arranged prospect of flower gardens and shaven lawns in the foreground; verdant parkland, clumps of trees and a serpentine lake in the middle distance; and natural undulations, flocks of sheep, a roaming herd of deer and encircling woods in the background. Many of these vistas also contained such ornamental features as fountains, obelisks, statues and classical temples; later, perhaps an ivy-clad ruin or some other Gothic folly was added to add a sense of antiquity and surprise. Laid out in this way by professional landscape architects, the foremost of whom were William Kent (1685–1748), Lancelot 'Capability' Brown (1715–83) and Humphry Repton (1752–1818), the landscaped parks were shaped to provide the rural rich with private secluded worlds and leisured environments. Here their proud owners and their admiring visitors could indulge themselves in exclusive enjoyment of tamed nature, blissfully oblivious to the toil and poverty of that other rural world that existed in the productive agricultural countryside, out of sight and out of sound beyond the parkland walls, the iron gates and the woodland screens.

— CHAPTER THREE —

Villages of Poverty and Rioting:
Rural England in the Bleak Age

But go down into the villages; invited by the spires, rising up amongst the trees in the dells, at scarcely ever more than a mile apart; invited by these spires go down into these villages, view the large, and once the most beautiful, churches; see the parson's house, large, and in the midst of pleasure-gardens; and then look at the miserable sheds in which the labourers reside! Look at these hovels, made of mud and straw; bits of glass, or off-cast windows, without frames or hinges frequently, but merely stuck in the mud wall. Enter them and look at the bits of chairs or stools; the wretched boards tacked together to serve for a table; the floor of pebble, broken brick, or of the bare ground; look at the thing called a bed; and survey the rags on the backs of the wretched inhabitants; and then wonder if you can that the gaols and the dungeons and treadmills increase, and that a standing army and barracks are become the favourite establishments of England!
(William Cobbett, *Rural Rides*, 1830, Eastern Tour)[1]

Whilst Britain's involvement in the French Revolutionary and Napoleonic Wars, with its inflationary effect on food prices and the stimulus this gave for a new surge of enclosure activity, brought prosperity to landowners and their tenant farmers, it produced little or no material benefit to the rural working class. Shortages of labour – at the height of hostilities around 300,000 soldiers and seamen were enlisted – did lead to a quite appreciable rise in agricultural wages, but this was easily eclipsed by a near doubling of four-yearly average wheat prices during the period from 1791/5 to 1811/15.[2] Then, although food prices did fall back quite sharply, the end of the French wars saw the onset of a period of widespread impoverishment among the common people of village England, which continued right through the 1820s and into the following decade. This dismal period, or Bleak Age, to use the title coined by the Hammonds,[3] saw extensive pauperization of what, by the time Cobbett completed his *Rural Rides*, had become a much enlarged and very wage-dependent class of agricultural labourers. It also proved to be the final straw for all that remained of traditional peasant culture.

Not all the blame for rural England's Bleak Age should be placed upon the enclosure movement and its undermining of the old communal way of life. As we have seen in the previous chapter, enclosure did take away people's land, remove the commons and wastes that had enabled the poor to subsist, and put peasant families at the disposal of exploitive hire; but such outcomes, distressful as they were, do not fully explain why so many inhabitants of village England became reduced to destitution and pauperism. What the enclosures did to the rural poor was certainly to bring them to a condition of dependency and vulnerability, but it was the combined forces of sustained rural population growth, unrestrained market forces, and repressive government that finally settled their fate. Each of these pressures played an important part in what most writers agree was the grimmest period in the history of village England ever since the famines and pestilences of the fourteenth century.

Villages of Poverty

Contrary to the Hammonds' view that the parliamentary enclosures had precipitated an immediate exodus of the dispossessed and widespread depopulation of the countryside, the middle and later decades of the Georgian age are now known to have been a time of appreciable rural, as well as quickening urban, demographic growth. Whereas the population of rural England and Wales had changed very little during the first half of the eighteenth century, it rose from around 4 million to a figure of 5.8 million during the second. An even stronger build-up of rural population was recorded in the early nineteenth century when the numbers of rural inhabitants increased by 38 per cent during the period 1801–31, to reach 8 million at the latter date.[4] Indeed, in many parishes and villages, mostly within areas that had experienced a high incidence of parliamentary enclosure, the trend was considerably faster. This can be demonstrated by turning to a sample of localities and examining their parish-level population figures. In the highly rural Ploughley Hundred in east Oxfordshire, to take one example, population growth between 1801 and 1831 exceeded 40 per cent in 16 out of the area's 37 parishes, whilst in 5 others the increases were higher than 50 per cent. In the cereal-growing and sheep-grazing countryside of the Yorkshire Wolds, to take another example, 7 out of a total of 44 parishes saw a doubling of population during this period, and in 11 others increases ranged between 50 per cent and

100 per cent. Lastly, in the Berkshire Vale of the White Horse as many as 19 – nearly one-half – out of 42 parishes recorded increases above 50 per cent. In each of these three areas, as in most other parts of rural England, population growth tended to be rather faster in the market towns than it was in the open villages; and, in turn, it was very much faster in the latter than it was in the close and estate villages. Thus, inside each rural area there were wide differences in the rate of population build-up, with a clear trend towards a concentration of this growth within the larger and less-controlled settlements.

During the first three decades of the nineteenth century agricultural output in Britain, though much increased as a consequence of the war-time wave of parliamentary enclosures and further improvements in farming methods, was unable to outpace what proved to be the fastest rate of population growth in the nation's recorded demographic history. This and, after 1815, the protection of the Corn Laws (which prohibited the purchase of imported wheat at prices below eighty shillings a quarter) explain why cereal prices, despite dipping sharply towards the end of the Napoleonic Wars and again in the economic depression of the early 1820s, only once, in 1822, dropped back to a pre-war level. However, causing even more hardship for the rural working class was the prolonged decline in agricultural wages, a trend that began soon after the declaration of peace in 1815. By the mid-1820s, the average wage for regularly employed married male labourers had fallen to a mere eight to nine shillings a week, having been around thirteen shillings just a decade or so before.[5] Indeed, in the Wessex counties of Berkshire, Wiltshire and Dorset, where outside the towns there was very little alternative rural employment, it had been driven down even further to a pitiful seven shillings a week. In Berkshire, a county in which the condition of the rural poor was typical of the cereal-growing regions of southern England, Cobbett claimed that the purchasing value of a farmworker's average weekly pay in 1826 was less than two-thirds of what it had been at the end of the eighteenth century.[6]

Rural England's Bleak Age was also a time of widening geographical differences in labourers' wages and levels of rural poverty. By the 1820s, farm wages in the agricultural counties of the south and south-east were between just one-half and two-thirds of those in the north and the midlands where nearness to industrializing areas and quickly expanding urban centres was exerting competition upon the labour market. Cobbett, with his extensive knowledge of the English countryside and the people who worked within it, more than once commented upon the close correspondence between the locales of greatest rural distress and the locales of strongest emphasis upon capitalized cereal cultivation. 'The more purely a corn county the more miserable the labourers'[7] was how he saw it on his travels across the southern counties in the mid-1820s. To his sharp eyes, poverty was in fact at its worst in the places where agricultural productivity was greatest and the fertility of the ground was highest; and it seemed to be at its least in places where there was still an abundance of woodland waste, unenclosed commons, and a flourishing cottage industry. The paradoxical relationship between rural poverty and agricultural 'progress' was also noticed by some later writers, including the Hammonds who saw the impoverishment and marginalization of thousands upon thousands of rural people principally as an outcome of agricultural modernization and in particular the enclosures and dispossessions upon which this was based.[8]

For many inhabitants of village England the effects of the widening disparity between food prices and agricultural wages were compounded by the wartime wave of enclosures of commons and wastelands. This 'fencing off' of the rural poor from the places where, from time immemorial, they had been able to enjoy customary rights of squatting, collecting fuel, picking berries, gathering nuts and mushrooms, snaring the odd rabbit and keeping a pig and perhaps one or two cows, removed the last vestiges of former peasant self-sufficiency. In John Clare's poem 'To a Fallen Elm', which he wrote in his native Northamptonshire village of Helpston sometime in the 1820s, this type of enclosure meant:

> The common heath became the spoiler's prey;
> The rabbit had not where to make his den
> And labour's only cow was drove away

Following the enclosure of commons and wastes, all items of food, save the produce of a small vegetable plot and perhaps, every now and then, the rewards of a successful night of poaching, had to be paid for out of cash wages or from Poor Law handouts. Then in 1816 came the notorious Gaming Act, the most punitive piece of legislation in a succession of repressive Game Laws, each aimed at protecting the recreational pleasures of the landed class and making wild animals and edible birds private possessions. The Game Laws, with their strict code against trespass and their licence for landowners to install spring-guns and man-traps on any part of their land, made even the 'rabbit in the pocket' type of poaching a hazardous activity. Very often a landowner had created or had enlarged his private game-preserve out of a newly enclosed common or piece of wasteland. To the rural poor, many of whom had lost much of their livelihood through this very process, poaching in such places was regarded not as a criminal activity but as a morally justified part of the working-class sub-culture. It was, indeed, both a symbol of rural independence and a time-honoured means of providing tasty additions to the family's normally very plain and modest diet. Thus, in the minds of the dispossessed, poaching represented a nocturnal act of defiance and a reassertion of the lost right of bringing in food from the wild. However, because of the new code, poaching had become a pursuit that carried a high risk of severe punishment, including flogging, a gaol sentence, and transportation. For those who were caught in possession of a gun and had threatened to use it, there was the ultimate penalty of death by hanging. According to government figures, at the height of the 'poaching wars', from 1827 to 1830, as many as 8,502 people – equivalent to the population of a quite substantial town and representing one-seventh of all criminal convictions in England and Wales – were convicted for offences under the Game Laws.[9]

That the appropriation of wild nature, the criminalization of poaching, and an increasing enthusiasm among the landed class for fox-hunting and shooting were all taking place at a time of widespread poverty and hunger says much about the extent of private power in the rural and village England of the Bleak Age; and it underlines how vast the gulf had become between the rich and the powerful and the poor and the powerless. Fox-hunting, more so than any other rural pastime, was emblematic of this social division, as it was also of the authority and opulence of landownership. The landowners and country gentlemen, riding their fine horses and dressed in their vivid scarlet coats and white breeches, always led the chase, followed by the tenant farmers. The common people were either permitted to trudge along on foot and well behind, closing the gates and mending the fences, or were excluded altogether.

Village England under Speenhamland

A Marxist interpretation of the deteriorating plight of the rural poor would stress the necessary condition of an assured and growing 'reserve army' of labour for agricultural capital to exploit. The build-up of rural population, the dispossessions that came with the parliamentary enclosures and in some localities the terminal decline of cottage spinning and weaving, each played a part in creating this situation. However, much significance has also to be attached to the operation of what became known as the 'Speenhamland system' of calculating parish outdoor relief – regular doles of money handed out at the recipients' own home – to the rural poor.

The Speenhamland system had been devised and first applied in the county of Berkshire in 1795 following a meeting of magistrates and other 'discreet persons' at the Pelican Inn on the outskirts of Newbury. Without departing from the humane principles of the Old, Elizabethan, Poor Law in which the parish and the local community had the responsibility for looking after their own poor, it established a sliding scale of allowances to paupers, with the individual allocations of relief being measured according to the current price of bread, the number of children in the family and, if the husband and father had employment, the wages that he earned. Introduced at a time of wartime emergency and rising food prices, Speenhamland was born partly out of a genuine humanitarian desire among the rural establishment to keep the poor from hunger and starvation, but (with the lesson of the French Revolution still fresh in their minds) partly also as a safeguard against large-scale social unrest. Its general acceptability among farmers, however, perhaps owed rather more to its capacity to sustain a constant surfeit of cheap, subsidized labour.[10] Certainly there was much to encourage a widespread adoption of the new system in southern England, especially Wessex, the south midlands, East Anglia, Kent and Sussex,[11] where in many areas capitalized cereal and mixed cereal and livestock farming prevailed, where poverty and the threat of social unrest were the highest, and where a regular reserve of farm labour was the most needed.

Following the adoption of the Speenhamland system, farmers came to realize that there was no longer any economic need for them to pay a fair wage, since they could now rely upon the parish to keep the labourers and their families above starvation level. Such reasoning, however, was not widely put into practice until after the end of the Napoleonic Wars. Then, as cereal prices plunged, farmers sought to stay in profit by cutting their costs of labour; and, because of the Combinations Acts of 1799 and 1800 with their prohibition of all 'combinations' or unions of workers, there was nothing to stop them from doing so. These Acts were eventually repealed in 1824, but the famous episode of the Tolpuddle Martyrs ten years later demonstrated to everybody that it was still easy enough in rural England to find a pretext for bringing members of a collective labour organization to trial and having them convicted with a heavy sentence. The six Dorset labourers were each sentenced to seven years' transportation for doing nothing more than administering 'unlawful' oaths to a few men joining the obscure and unthreatening Tolpuddle Friendly Society of Agricultural Labourers.[12]

Whilst one unforeseen effect of Speenhamland was to facilitate the reduction of agricultural wages to levels that could provide only the barest of livelihoods, another (as was later claimed by the Poor Law Commissioners in 1834 and such influential critics of the day as Thomas Malthus and Jeremy Bentham) was to fuel rural population growth. It did this, so the argument goes, by encouraging the poor to marry or cohabit earlier and to bring up larger families, in the sure knowledge that the more children they had the larger would be the assessment of their parish relief. Thus, despite its humane intention, Speenhamland stimulated demographic reproduction of rural poverty, and it did so to such an extent that, by the 1820s, it was not unusual to come across parishes and villages in which more than one-third of the inhabitants were either paupers, permanently dependent upon poor relief, or were unemployed labourers and their families receiving a temporary allowance. Indeed, in southern England there were some villages where the numbers of families relying upon Poor Law handouts were actually in the majority. In situations like these, rural communities had degenerated into a condition that was approaching universal pauperization.[13]

Under the Old Poor Law and the Speenhamland system, each parish was required to maintain its own poor from a local rate chargeable to landowners and other property owners. Only those who had been born and bred in the parish had a 'natural' entitlement to relief there. Incomers, who were unable to find regular work and were deemed likely to become a pauper and a burden on the rates, could be turned away and sent back to their parish of origin. In principle only people who had been assured gainful employment at their destination were free to migrate, though in practice, in most market towns and open villages, restrictions were applied either not at all or only to a small extent. As a general rule the better-off and more needed members of the rural working class, namely craftsmen, servants and skilled farmworkers, were able to follow their migratory instincts, in some cases even to a landowner-controlled close village. But they left behind them large numbers of paupers and unskilled casual labourers living out their entire lives in the same place and in the same state of unremitting poverty.

The Speenhamland system and the mass pauperization that it was often blamed for fostering had a calamitous impact upon Poor Law expenditure and parish rates. Over England and Wales as a whole annual payments of relief doubled from £2 million in 1795 to £4 million in 1802, and then almost doubled again to just under £8 million in 1817 – the highest outlay ever reached under the Old Poor Law.[14] Only a small fraction, approximately one-seventh, of this huge increase can be attributed to nationwide population growth: much the larger part came from the increasing proportion of paupers among the rural population and, in the last two years (due to the lowering of labourers' wages after 1815), the rising amounts of relief per family. In absolute terms the most pronounced escalation of Poor Law expenditure belonged to the aftermath of the Napoleonic Wars, a time not only of falling agricultural wages but also one when large numbers of demobilized soldiers and sailors returned to their towns and villages, swelling the pauper population and adding to the imbalance in the rural labour market. Faced with the mounting pressure on Poor Law rates, authorities, especially in the hard-pressed southern and eastern counties, responded by making economies wherever these could be achieved. One way of doing so was to save on other parish expenditure through the deployment of pauper labour. Thus, many parishes used their able-bodied paupers for such public undertakings as mending highways and bridges, constructing new enclosure roads and digging drainage ditches: previously they would have employed properly paid workmen to do these tasks. Some parishes also adopted what was known as the 'roundsman system' in which paupers, at the busiest times of the year, were sent round the parish from farm to farm where they were given tasks to do, often just on a day-to-day basis. By sending them to work, the parish was able to make some deduction in their Poor Law handouts; and by taking roundsmen on, farmers benefited from having the cheapest of all sources of labour at their disposal, with sixpence a day being a standard payment in the 1820s. Indeed, in the localities where it was widely practised, the roundsman system, by encroaching upon work that had formerly been performed by regularly employed labourers, made its own, not inconsiderable, contribution towards the worsening plight of the rural working class.

A more effective approach, however, was for the Poor Law authorities to economize on individual handouts by applying stricter definitions of the poverty line and introducing tighter scales of relief. This whittling away of Speenhamland assistance was pursued with such parsimony after 1817 that annual Poor Law expenditure in England and Wales, having increased so steeply since the 1790s, fell back to £7 million in 1820 and £5.7 million three years later; and it did so despite the continued growth of the pauper population.[15] During the 1820s and up to the introduction of the New Poor Law in 1834, it fluctuated between these two figures. Only in 1831, when the sum briefly touched £7 million again, did it threaten to climb back to the high point of 1817.

Reductions of Poor Law relief, made during a time when the purchasing value of agricultural wages was diminishing year by year, could only worsen what were already severe levels of deprivation and destitution in the English countryside. This deepening of rural poverty could not continue much longer without provoking something more serious than just the occasional isolated riotous protest; and eventually, in the autumn of 1830, it came to a head with the sudden and widespread eruption of rural arson and machine wrecking that came to be known as the 'Swing riots'. Whilst the increasing use of threshing machines, with the threat that this placed on agricultural employment, served as the catalyst for these disturbances, it was the desperate state of the rural poor that formed the underlying impulse. Cobbett, writing just before the outbreak of Swing, was in no doubt that the condition of the agricultural labourers and their families, including many who were not quite poor enough to qualify for the revised scales of relief, had been reduced to the verge of starvation. Tragically in some cases it had fallen below even this miserable level. In the corn lands of Wiltshire, where agricultural wages were amongst the lowest in the country, there were reports of men being found dead in ditches and hedges, with, in Cobbett's grim words 'nothing but sour sorrel in their bellies'.[16]

Village England in Conflict: the Swing Rioting of 1830–1

What do my readers think of such a state of things in the quiet, idyllic country districts of England? Is this social war or is it not?
(Frederick Engels, *Condition of the Working Class in England in 1844*,
English translation, 1892)

'Swing', or to give him his full title 'Captain Swing', was an invention; a mythical leader and folk hero in the minds of the rioters and their supporters, but a demonized apparition in the eyes of the rulers of the countryside and the forces of law and order. From either viewpoint the invention of Swing conveyed the impression of a semblance of control; as if one person – some unidentified commanding figure – was orchestrating the rioting and pursuing a deliberate strategy. The reality, however, was very different. Swing was not a person but a symbol for what was a spontaneous and unprepared conflagration of violence that swept across southern and eastern England in the autumn of 1830 and the early part of the following winter. It was a collective name for what were in fact hundreds of acts of desperation that were organized only at the very local, village to village, level. Yet, at its fullest intensity and geographical extent, the rioting was considered by many members of the establishment and the government at Westminster as something that threatened to develop into a nationwide rural uprising.

Although the geography of Swing (Figure 4), with its apparent encirclement of London and the existence of two principal centres of 'dispersal' in Kent and Norfolk, might suggest otherwise, there was no evidence of any set plan. Instead, there were large numbers of local cores of activity, made up of individual or small groups of parishes and villages. Whilst a regional pattern did emerge during the course of the rioting, and a remarkably clear one at that, this was only a reflection of the salient fact that rural poverty was very much worse in some parts of the country than it was in others. These worst-off areas were the regions and localities that had the interconnected economic and social conditions of an emphasis upon capitalized cereal cultivation, widespread adoption of the threshing machine, below-average agricultural wages, extensive pauperization and high dependence upon diminishing Speenhamland handouts. Such conditions were all strongly represented within the southern and south-eastern counties where an additional circumstance, the significance of which has neither been proved nor disproved, was their greater vulnerability to radical influences spreading across the English Channel from France and Belgium. In both of these countries a political revolution had taken place in the summer of 1830, and the news and excitement of this would have reached Kent and Sussex shortly before Swing rioting broke out in earnest. As Hobsbawm and Rude point out in their comprehensive and highly readable book, *Captain Swing*, an atmosphere of expectation, and perhaps some insurrectionary fervour too, were conveyed to market town audiences here by radical speakers including the persuasive figures of Henry ('Orator') Hunt and William Cobbett.[17] Indeed, after the suppression of Swing, Cobbett himself was prosecuted by the government and taken to trial for incitement. The jury, however, could not agree on a verdict and, fearing a huge public reaction, the authorities quickly backed down and discharged him.

Swing rioting did indeed commence in Kent, with the first rick-burning incident taking place at Orpington in June 1830 and the first threshing machine being destroyed at Lower Hadres, near Canterbury, two months later. By October that year, Kent was the scene of widespread rioting, and disturbances were spreading westwards across the county boundary into East Sussex. The violence reached its most intensive phase in November, when the numbers of incidents each day averaged nearly fifty.[18] These mostly consisted of deliveries of threatening 'Swing letters', breaking up threshing machines, and setting fire to corn ricks and barns; but they also included extortion, larceny, assaults on unpopular Poor Law overseers and, in some market towns, mobs fighting on the streets. By the final week of November, Swing rioting in all its various forms had reached a crisis point in the Wessex counties of Hampshire, Berkshire, Wiltshire and Dorset, whilst sporadic disturbances were now taking place in parts of Buckinghamshire and Bedfordshire to the north-west of London. Moreover, as if to complete the spectre of a strategic encirclement of the capital, a new centre of diffusion had emerged in central and north Norfolk where, it is worth noting, there had been a previous outbreak of rural violence in 1816. From here, Swing activity quickly moved south-

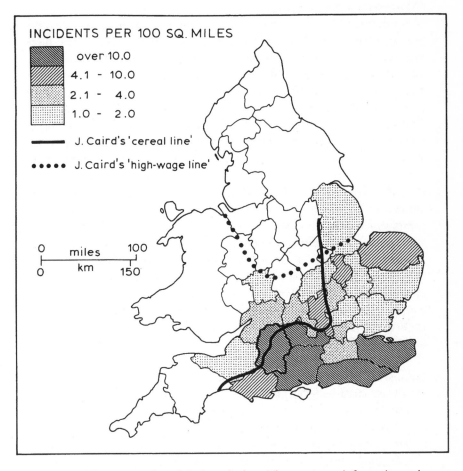

Figure 4: The geography of Swing rioting. The map uses information published by E. J. Hobsbawm and G. Rude in their book *Captain Swing* (1985), Appendix I. James Caird's 'cereal' and 'high wage' lines are from J. H. Clapham, *Economic History of Modern Britain* (1932), vol. 1, p 147.

wards into the corn country of Suffolk and north Essex, and also westwards and north-westwards into Cambridgeshire, Huntingdonshire and Lincolnshire. Then, in January 1831, Swing, now confronted with properly organized forces of law and order, subsided just as swiftly as it had begun. At its fullest extent it had reached as far as Somerset and east Devon in the West Country, the Cotswolds and the Avon valley in the west midlands, and Lincolnshire between the Wash and the Humber. For a few critical weeks it had seemed as if it was about to sweep through the whole of rural and village England.

As shown in Figure 4, the intensity of the rioting varied considerably amongst the Swing counties.[19] It was greatest in Berkshire where there were as many as twenty-three recorded incidents per 100 square miles (259 square kilometres). Berkshire was followed by Wiltshire with six-teen per 100 square miles, Hampshire with fifteen, Sussex with eleven and Kent with ten. Elsewhere the violence was much weaker and more sporadic. In Somerset, Worcestershire and Lincolnshire, representing respectively the western, north-western and northern extremities of the rioting, the frequency was no more than two incidents per 100 square miles. An interesting feature, which is indicated by the relative quietness of four of the five Home Counties (Kent is the exception), was the virtual absence of Swing activity within a radius of up to twenty miles from the centre of London. One plausible reason for this was the concentration of constabulary and militia resources in and around the capital, which meant a much greater risk of being caught and arrested. Another reason, an explanation that is favoured by Hobsbawm and Rude, was the influence of this huge city on the type of farming and the labour market in the sur-rounding countryside. In this part of south-east England the pull of the metropolis in terms of its large demand for meat, dairy produce, veget-ables and fruit had given rise to a diverse agricultural structure in which there were relatively few specialized cereal farms. Nearness to the metro-polis, with its vast concentration of employment, also meant that farmers here were faced with far greater competition for labour. This could only be met by paying their workers an adequate wage. In the villages around London, therefore, people had much less cause to join Swing.

Most of the Swing activity occurred within that part of the country which lies to the east of James Caird's well-known 'cereal line' (drawn in 1850 to distinguish between corn-growing and pastoral England) and to the south of his 'wage line' separating high-wage from low-wage rural England.[20] It was within this critical 'south-eastern quadrant', excluding London and its adjoining countryside, that all the economic and social ingredients of the Swing condition existed together and were the most strongly entrenched. However, the geography of Swing did transgress Caird's divisions in some locations, especially where the cereal line had to be rather arbitrarily drawn and where it could distinguish only between areas where cereal farms just about predominated and areas where there was in fact a balance between corn-growing and pastoral parishes. Most noteworthy was the situation in Buckinghamshire and in the south-west midlands counties of Gloucestershire, Worcestershire and Oxfordshire, which were all situated wholly or largely beyond Caird's definition of cereal-growing England, yet did play a part in the Swing rioting. Significantly each of these counties stretches across the grain of geological outcrops, and their topographies are largely composed of scarp and vale landscapes consisting of limestone uplands, broad clayland plains and tracts of river terraces. The uplands, with their generally drier and lighter soils, were dominated by corn and sheep husbandry, and several parishes here bore witness to Swing activity. Natural conditions and local agricultural economies, however, were very much different in the lowlands. These – the Severn Plain in Gloucestershire, the Vale of Evesham in Worcestershire, the Valley of the Middle and Upper Thames in Oxfordshire and the Vale of Aylesbury in Buckinghamshire – contain a wide range of soil types; their claylands being best suited to pastoral farming, whilst the silt and gravel-covered terraces, with their well-drained and easily cultivated soils, encouraged mixed farming and in some places the growing of fruit and vegetables. Villages here, like those within the ring around London, remained quiet, even at the height of Swing when rioting was breaking out just a few miles away.

It is worth looking at the local geography of Swing. For this we can turn to Figure 5 which maps out the distribution of Swing incidents in the county of Wiltshire where, as in other parts of Wessex, the rural settlement pattern is dominated by strings of villages along the larger river valleys and around the edges of the chalk uplands. Wiltshire experienced some of the very worst rioting in the country, the heaviest of it taking place in November 1830. Indeed, there were over 200 Swing incidents here, most of which involved the destruction of threshing machines.[21] As Figure 5 shows, the rioting villages (or strictly speaking rioting parishes, since some of the attacks were directed at outlying farmsteads) were very unevenly distributed. The large majority of them were situated within the Wiltshire 'corn belt' in the eastern and southern parts of the county. Here, following the parliamentary enclosures of the late eighteenth century and the Napoleonic Wars, the agricultural landscape had become one of capitalized wheat and barley cultivation on the lower chalklands, sheep grazing on the higher parts and steeper slopes and mixed, arable and

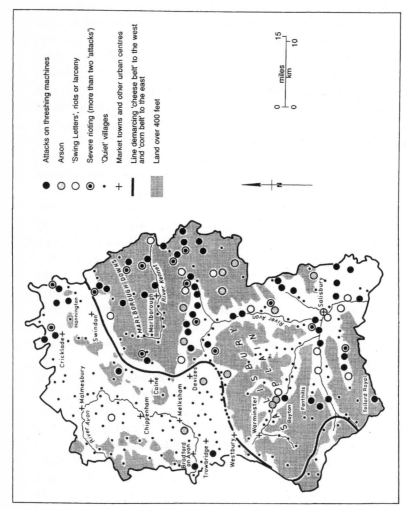

Figure 5: Swing rioting in Wiltshire. The information for this map is from E. J. Hobsbawm and G. Rude, *Captain Swing* (1985), Appendix III.

Legend:

● Attacks on threshing machines
○ Arson
○ 'Swing Letters', riots or larceny
◉ Severe rioting (more than two 'attacks')
· 'Quiet' villages
+ Market towns and other urban centres
▎ Line demarcing 'cheese belt' to the west and 'corn belt' to the east
▨ Land over 400 feet

0   miles   15
0   km   10

pastoral, farming in the broader valleys. East and south Wiltshire, where commercial cereal growing predominated and where agricultural wages were the lowest,[22] was typical Swing country: nearly half the villages and parishes here were involved in rioting in one form or another, and several of them were 'revisited' on more than one other occasion. Very much different, however, was the situation in the 'cheese belt' in the pastoral north-west of the county, where a prevalence of heavy clay soils and a grouping of urban centres (including the clothing towns of Bradford-on-Avon, Trowbridge and Warminster) had encouraged most farmers to concentrate on dairying, especially cheese making. Apart from the Cricklade area close to the Oxfordshire border, Swing disturbances here were few and far between.

A noticeable feature in the Wiltshire corn country, and one that was characteristic of other principal locales of Swing, was the tendency for the rioting to take place as distinct local clusters or 'contagions' of action, normally consisting of two or three nights of intensive violence. A striking illustration of this is to be seen in the line of rioting villages in the Vale of Pewsey, at the foot of the chalk slopes to the east of the market town of Devizes. Other examples, though less emphatic, can be observed in the clusters of Swing villages west and east of Salisbury and in the chalklands to the east of Marlborough. In each case nearly every parish and village was involved, suggesting that, in certain localities, the rioting was systematic and had as its objective the destruction of every single threshing machine. This supports the view expressed by Hobsbawm and Rude that the rioting was commonly performed by large bands of men, sometimes more than 200 strong, proceeding from village to village and from parish to parish.[23] Usually they moved at night along the minor lanes and trackways, collecting new members before each attack and releasing earlier recruits soon after. As they did so they could pass on the idea of Swing to the next group of rioters and inform them of what, by November 1830, had become well-tested and successful methods of violence. Thus, in many localities the disturbances assumed a wave-like pattern of movement, capable of spreading over quite considerable distances.

In nineteenth-century rural England rioting on this scale required the sort of informed local knowledge and trustful leadership that only village craftsmen and tradesmen could provide. Due to the nature of their work, which usually involved frequent visits to neighbouring villages and the nearmost market town, these people had connections and contacts with a wider world. Moreover, most of them were more literate than the rest of the rural working class and were regular attenders of Nonconformist chapels where they could learn of any new senses of injustice. Craftsmen and tradesmen, therefore, had some standing in the community, and in most villages it was from their ranks that there emerged the spokesmen and organizers of the rioters. The men who followed them were drawn very largely, perhaps exclusively in some areas, from open villages and countryside towns where rural poverty had sunk to its greatest depths. However, when writers refer to 'rioting villages' they really mean the places where the incidents actually took place, which in some cases were estate farms and in certain instances the home of an oppressive bailiff or foreman. This explains why it was not unusual for a close parish to feature in the rioting, though it is unlikely that its inhabitants would have provided much, if anything, in the form of active support. Interesting examples in Wiltshire were Boyton in the Wylye Valley, which included within its boundaries the estate and country residence of Boyton Hall – the seat of the Gifford family whose ancestors had fought in the Crusades – Fonthill Gifford and Fonthill Bishop, which contained Fonthill Park and the ruins of William Beckford's Gothic fantasy of Fonthill Abbey, and, a short distance to the south of the Fonthills, West Tisbury where in the woodlands around Pyt House (the residence of a landowner member of parliament) a pitched battle was waged between a gang of labourers and the Wiltshire Yeomanry, resulting in the death of one of the rioters and injuries to six others.[24] Rarely, even in places like these, did the targets of the Swing rioters extend beyond the wrecking of threshing machines and the threatening of unpopular individuals. Even more rarely – Pyt House was the most notable exception – were any of the landed class confronted in person. The Swing rioting was essentially a conflict between the labourers and the more exploitive of their farmer employers. It was not a conflict between the bottom and the top of the rural social hierarchy.

For some time, the government was confused and hesitant to intervene, preferring to leave everything in the hands of the local and county forces of law and order. Where the first contagions of rioting had occurred this included the swearing in of special constables and the deployment of watchmen and informers – often recruited from the ranks of trustworthy estate workers and reliable tenant farmers – to keep an eye on suspect villages. However, by November 1830 when Swing was spreading swiftly through the Wessex counties and, to many of the rural establishment, was beginning to look like an organized revolt, the government decided to take firm action. Troops of dragoon guards were dispatched to the most riot-stricken counties, and the Home Secretary, Lord Melbourne, offered rewards to anyone who helped to bring rioters to justice. In Wiltshire, where the rioting was particularly widespread, the Yeomanry cavalry was mobilized with orders to range over the countryside.

The government also appointed a Special Commission of Assize to deal with prisoners in the emergency counties of Berkshire, Buckingham-shire, Dorset, Hampshire and Wiltshire. Kent and Sussex, where, by late November, Swing had run most of its course and many trials were already in progress or had been completed, were not included in this list. Over England as a whole nearly 2,000 cases were heard, with the num-bers of trials being fairly evenly divided amongst the Assizes of the Special Commissioners and the normal sessions of the county courts. The punishments that they meted out easily surpassed the retribution for any other working-class conflict in nineteenth-century Britain. According to Hobsbawm and Rude, only two out of every five Swing prisoners were acquitted. Of those who were convicted, 252 were sentenced to death (though mercifully only nineteen hangings were actually carried out); 644 were sent to prison and 505, including most of those whose death sentences had been commuted, were transported to Australia.[25] In its harshness and intensity, and also in the long-lasting atmosphere of defeat, demoralization and resentment that followed, the suppression of Swing had something in common with the aftermaths of Sedgemoor and Cul-loden. Certainly the severity of the sentencing is ample enough testimony to the immense self-interest and power of the rural establishment and how seriously it viewed the whole Swing episode. Far from interpreting Swing as a desperate 'cry of outrage'[26] from people demanding nothing more than some modest betterment of their dismal quality of life, the rural establishment of landowners, gentlemen farmers and custodians of law and order were at one in seeing the rioting as little short of a major insurrection. To them, Swing was a near-nationwide upsurge in rural ter-rorism that, at its height, had carried the potential to undermine the entire structure of the rural social system and the huge disparities that underpinned it. The ruthless retribution that followed the rioting ensured that any protest and confrontation on this kind of scale, and with this degree of violence, would never break out again. Yet, for some considera-ble time afterwards, the conditions which had been at the root of the Swing rioting remained hardly changed, and working-class resentment, though pushed under the surface, continued to be a feature of English vil-lage life. Becoming ever more secretive, it was, in the words of E. P. Thompson: 'thrust back into the underground of the poaching war, the anonymous letter, the flaming corn rick'.[27]

In 1834, with memories of Swing rioting still fresh, the Poor Law Amendment Act was passed and with it the New Poor Law was established. Indeed, the events of 1830–1 and the introduction of the New Poor Law were strongly connected, since three of the underlying ambitions of this legislation were to reverse the decline of social discipline among the labouring class of rural England, to enforce its moral regeneration and to replace the iniquities of idleness, improvidence and immorality with a new ethos of gainful work and respect for authority. Another intention was to make rural poverty less visible. The worst of it was now to be kept out of sight, inside newly constructed Union workhouses; and, using the threat of these institutions, the rest of it was to be encouraged to drift away either to the towns and cities or across the oceans to far-off lands.

The New Poor Law of 1834: a New Rural Discipline

> Hodge ... comes in his old age under the dominance of his last masters at the workhouse. There, indeed, he finds almost the whole array of his rulers assembled. Tenant farmers sit as the guardians of the poor for their respective parishes; the clergyman and the squire by virtue of their office as magistrates; and the tradesman as guardian of the market town. Here are representatives of almost all his masters, and it may seem to him a little strange that it should require so many to govern such feeble folk.
>
> (Richard Jefferies, *Hodge and his Masters*, 1880)

The Poor Law Amendment Act was much more far-reaching than its title suggests. It did away with the outdated and wasteful Speenhamland system and, over most of the country, quickly extinguished or substantially reduced the ancient practice of the parish providing outdoor relief – 'the last inheritance of the rural poor' according to E. P. Thompson[28] – to its own paupers. It was replaced by an entirely different approach based upon 'indoor' relief within the new workhouses and organized under a centralized structure of administration. The New Poor Law revolutionized government social policy, instituting a new mode of social control that, in the minds of Hodge and others of the rural working class, was a great deal more foreboding and far more impersonal than anything that had existed before. The cornerstone of this new approach in dealing with the poor was the principle of less eligibility, in which the material condition of any person receiving assistance should not be better than that of the poorest-paid active labourer. The eligibility test, in conjunction with the building of the Union workhouses and the placing of severe restrictions on outdoor relief (particularly for the able-bodied) was devised to

Plate 9: Union workhouse, Louth, Lincolnshire. The Union workhouse at Louth was built in 1837, with accommodation for 240 inmates. Placed on high ground overlooking the market town, it became a familiar sight to all those who travelled into and out of Louth on its northern side. The wall, railings and traffic roundabout in the foreground were added after the workhouse was converted into a county hospital in 1932. The forbidding archway (now without its massive door) in the middle distance is the workhouse entrance. Behind it looms the original main block, with the master's quarters in the centre.

discourage the 'idle and dissolute' from seeking indoor relief and force them to seek some form of employment outside. It also ensured, in the localities where the test was fully applied, that only the 'deserving poor' – the temporarily unemployed, the destitute, the chronically sick and the infirm – would now burden the ratepayer. Effectively, after 1834, the lowest-paid labourers were faced with two choices: they could either struggle on, toiling away for very low remuneration and having lost their Speenhamland allowance; or they could leave their village in the hope of finding some better-paid work elsewhere. For the aged and the infirm, unless they were being looked after by one of their offspring or lived in a village where elderly paupers were still provided with some outdoor relief, the choice could hardly have been starker: they could either step inside the new workhouse or they could starve.

To dissuade all save the deserving poor from entering, the post-1834 workhouses and the conditions inside were designed deliberately to deter – to make these institutions a very definite last resort in which basic human rights and any lingering sense of freedom had to be left behind. There had been earlier versions of workhouses. Houses of Correction or Bridewells, some dating back as far as the sixteenth century, had been scattered sparingly and unevenly across the English counties. More numerous than these had been the village 'poor houses' and market town 'houses of industry' that had proliferated throughout the country in the eighteenth century. But these were typically small in size, often no larger than an average farmhouse or a couple of cottages: few were capable of accommodating more than thirty or so inmates at any one time. The workhouses of the New Poor Law differed in all respects. These were built on a much larger scale, most of them being designed to cater for upwards of 200 paupers and some having a capacity of over 400. Even more striking was their external architecture which, with its high surrounding walls, imposing archway entrance, prison-like main building and the commanding central position of the master's quarters (see Plate 9), was made to appear as forbidding as possible and to convey to any casual observer something of the sternness and regimentation of the life inside. One example in Victorian fiction was the Casterbridge (Dorchester) workhouse in Thomas Hardy's *Far from the Madding Crowd*. In this novel, Casterbridge workhouse was the building into which the country girl Fanny Robin staggered to spend the last few hours of her tragic life. It was in Hardy's words:

> ... a mere case to hold people. The shell had been so thin, so devoid of excrescence and so closely drawn over the accommodation granted, that the grim character of what was beneath showed through it, as the shape of a

body is visible under a winding sheet. ... The stone edifice consisted of a central mass and two wings, whereon stood as sentinels a few slim chimneys, now gurgling sorrowfully to the slow wind. In the wall was a gate, and by the gate a bell-pull formed of hanging wire. The woman raised herself as high as possible upon her knees, and could just reach the handle. She moved it, and fell forwards in a bowed attitude, her face upon her bosom.

Conditions inside the workhouse were organized systematically to fulfil the two imperatives of deterrence and rigid discipline.[29] For the former, families were not allowed to live together. Parents and children, brothers and sisters and (to prevent child-bearing) husbands and wives were kept apart and housed in separate blocks or segregated sections of the main building. They were allowed to see each other only at mealtimes and at Sunday service. The new workhouses, therefore, were made particularly repellent to people who, however desperate their circumstances, had enjoyed something of the positive side of family life. Yet, by the early 1840s, the numbers of workhouse inmates in England and Wales had passed 200,000, and in 1848 an all-time record of 306,000 was established.[30] 'The most eloquent testimony to the depths of poverty is the fact that they were tenanted at all' is E. P. Thompson's comment on these institutions.[31] That they became 'tenanted' in such large numbers adds further weight to this remark.

Workhouse inmates were not only segregated according to gender and age, they were also divided into different classes of pauper. A government order in 1847 required all 'indoor' paupers to be divided into seven categories: aged or permanently infirm men; able-bodied males over 13 years; boys between 7 and 13; aged or infirm women; able-bodied women and girls over 16; girls between 7 and 13; and, lastly, children of either sex under 7 years.[32] Each category had its own upstairs dormitory, wash-room, and stairway access. In the larger workhouses categorization of inmates went even further to include people who were declared to be 'lunatics', 'imbeciles' and 'incorrigibles'. To meet this increased complexity and, later in the century, also to provide better medical facilities, many workhouses were enlarged, with new wards and exercise yards being added and infirmaries being improved and extended.

All inmates were subjected to a stern regime of discipline. Strict rules, which included the wearing of pauper uniforms, maintaining silence at mealtimes, keeping to strict timetables, performing onerous work routines, and having to apply for formal permission before they could be visited by a friend or a relation, made life in some workhouses not very different from that of imprisonment. Disobedience, absconding and other, often trivial, breaches of regulations were summarily dealt with; the usual punishments being solitary confinement, withdrawal of any privileges, and reductions in what was at the best just a very basic diet. 'Life on relief should be more unpleasant than the most unpleasant way of living outside' wrote the historians G. D. H. Cole and Raymond Postgate,[33] describing the thinking behind the New Poor Law. To reinforce this purposefully contrived unpleasantness and inhumanity, workhouse life was made to be as unvarying and mechanical as possible. The Wiltshire author Richard Jefferies has depicted the scene:

> In the workhouse there is of necessity a dead level of monotony – there are many persons but no individuals. The dining-hall is crossed with forms and narrow tables. ... On these at dinner time are placed a tin mug and a tin soup-plate for each person: every mug and every plate exactly alike. When the unfortunates have taken their places, the master pronounces grace from an elevated desk at the end of the hall.
>
> (*Hodge and his Masters*, 1880)

The New Poor Law and its workhouses required a completely new administrative structure. For more than two centuries, ever since the introduction of the Old Poor Law at the beginning of the seventeenth century, responsibility for looking after the poor had resided with the parish vestry and the parish overseer. After 1834, however, this role was handed over to a combination, or Union, of parishes, functioning at first under the direction of the Poor Law Commissioners in London and then, after this body was disbanded in 1847, under a central Poor Law Board. Within each Union the administration of relief was supervised by a board of guardians under the chairmanship of a justice of the peace. The guardians, who were chosen by ratepayers to stand and act for each constituent parish, had to have a property qualification. Thus, in village England they were drawn very largely from the gentry, gentlemen farmers and the clergy, whilst in market-town England they were more likely to have come from the professional class and the more prosperous traders and manufacturers.

The short period from 1834 to 1840 saw the creation of 630 Poor Law Unions in England and Wales, more than half of which were in full operation by the latter date.[34] Outside the cities and other large urban centres, most of them stretched over quite extensive districts, ranging from around twenty to as many as seventy or even eighty ecclesiastic parishes. A few, such as Spilsby Union in Lincolnshire, Cerne Abbas Union in Dorset and Bradfield Union in Berkshire, were entirely rural. The large majority, however, were designed to incorporate a market town at the centre, which provided a logical location for the new workhouse. By 1839, after the most intensive phase of workhouse construction, some 340 of these institutions had been built in England and Wales, approximately two-thirds of them lying south and east of a line drawn from the

Exe estuary in south Devon to the Wash in south Lincolnshire.[35] By 1870, their numbers had been increased to 511, and few of the larger market towns were without one.

Most Union workhouses were positioned on the edge of a market town rather than within it, as if to signify that they were not really one of an urban community's 'normal' functions. In many instances, however, the new institutions were built on a prominent, clearly visible, site. Some were placed alongside a principal highway leading into and out of the town: others, where the local topography provided the opportunity (as, for example, at Totnes in Devon, Stroud in Gloucestershire and Louth in Lincolnshire), were located on higher ground and became familiar local landmarks. In either case, the conspicuous presence of the 'new Bastilles' could hardly fail to prey upon the minds of the rural poor as, in their fairly regular Saturday quests for cheap items of food and other necessities, they trudged into the nearest market town and, a few hours later, began their journey home carrying their small purchases.

In the words of the Hammonds, the Union workhouses 'hung like a cloud over the working-class world'.[36] Introduced just a few years after some parts of rural England had been in a state of widespread conflict and disorder, these grim institutions, with their uncompromising ethos of discipline, work and moral behaviour, remained in operation and stayed fixed in people's imagination throughout the rest of the nineteenth century. Indeed, most of them continued to function as places for the poor until the establishment of national unemployment insurance and the introduction of state pensions in the 1920s and 1930s; and some were still open for the sick and the elderly until the foundation of the National Health Service in 1948. Most workhouses too became equipped with infirmaries and special wards, which is why a large proportion of them were eventually converted into hospitals and other public-health institutions. Even so, in many urban centres, ranging from countryside market towns to large industrial cities, the original building structures (though much modified inside) can still be seen today as monuments to a repressive past and a harsh history of utilitarian social policy.

Whilst they had a stronger psychological impact upon the people of rural England than they had upon the industrial and urban population, the New Poor Law and its Union workhouses did fulfil two important conditions for nineteenth-century industrialization. Disciplining the poor and the working class in general was the first of these and one that was quickly resolved. Stimulating migration and making it easier for the rural population surplus to move out of the countryside and settle in the labour-hungry industrial towns and cities was the other. Perhaps it was not just by coincidence that the New Poor Law was introduced just as the main phase of nineteenth-century agricultural mechanization was about to commence and when large quantities of immobile rural labour were soon to become a requirement of the past.

Hitherto, large reserves of rural labour had been essential for the profitability of English agriculture, and, under Speenhamland and the long-established practice of granting outdoor parish relief, the poor had been dissuaded from leaving home. At the same time, enforcement of the antiquated Laws of Settlement in many places had severely restricted village-to-village migration, rendering it difficult, if not impossible, for the rural poor to move from their parish of birth and place of settlement entitlement to another parish where a right to relief could not be obtained. The New Poor Law, coming at a time when the pace of industrialization was calling for a greater circulation of labour and when the recent Swing rioting had demonstrated the dangers of having a large, underemployed excess of rural population, changed this situation for ever. From the outset it encouraged people, especially the young and the more ambitious, to leave the most poverty-stricken villages and hamlets simply by removing the strongest reason for staying – the assurance of being able to receive in one's native parish a known sum of outdoor relief assessed by a familiar overseer. Moreover, the New Poor Law was accompanied by some loosening of the Settlement Laws, giving greater scope for a migrant to secure settlement status at his or her destination. After 1834, therefore, the rural working class could move more freely, although it was still very difficult for anyone other than the most skilled and most needed type of worker to move into a landowner-controlled close village where, more often than not, restrictions continued to be rigorously applied. The Settlement Laws in fact did not become universally redundant until the Union Chargeability Act of 1865. This, in the interests of further centralization and greater administrative efficiency, removed the one last piece of the centuries-old tradition of community responsibility for the poor. Prior to this Act, the cost of relief had always been charged to each parish in accordance with its own numbers of paupers. After 1865, the old parish Poor Rate was replaced by a system in which the impersonal Poor Law Union became the sole unit of relief administration.[37]

The workhouses themselves made an important direct contribution to the drift of people from rural to urban England, since nearly all of them were located at market towns and larger urban centres but many of their occupants came from the surrounding countryside. Moreover, the Union workhouses were places where industrialists could make arrangements to recruit new labour, including orphan children at or approaching working age. The conditions inside these institutions ensured that inmates were only too willing to accept such a chance of escape, even if this meant the poorest of working conditions and migration to some unknown northern town or city. In this light the New Poor Law of 1834 can be seen as a medium for incorporating some of the most marginal of the country's surplus rural population into the ever-expanding industrial economy, and doing so to the benefit both of the rural ratepayer and the urban manufacturer.

CHAPTER FOUR

High Farming and the 'Ordered' Rural Society

Less than a decade after the Swing rioting, English agriculture, with cap-italized cereal and mixed arable and livestock farming leading the way, entered a long period of settled prosperity that reached its zenith in the High Farming of the 1850s, 1860s and early 1870s. It was during this third quarter of the nineteenth century that the English model of agricul-tural capital achieved a state of near perfection. Rapid urbanization and urban population growth had guaranteed a fast-expanding market for the nation's food producers; a market that, despite the repeal of the Corn Laws in 1846 and the removal of prohibitive duties on imported grains, continued to be supplied very largely by British farmers. Expanding domestic demand meant buoyant agricultural prices, ensuring regular profits and a comfortable life for landowners and their tenants. Moreover, following the suppression of Swing and, a few years later, the introduc-tion of the New Poor Law and the threatening spectre of the Union workhouse, farmers were also able to benefit from a generally deferential and passive workforce. Only in the final few years of the High Farming age in the early 1870s, when the rural status quo was shaken by the 'Revolt of the Field' and its short-lived surge in agricultural trade-unionism, did the farmers' command over their workers come under any serious challenge. Over the period as a whole, agricultural workers – the essential human stock of High Farming – were obedient to their employ-ers and had a fatalistic acceptance of their own humble place in society. As the social historian Howard Newby has put it: 'for the most part they resigned themselves to this situation, bit their tongues rather than spoke out'.[1] There was an acceptance too of the more monotonous work rou-tines and sharper division of labour that came with the mechanization of an increasing range of farming tasks and operations.

Social discontent did exist, but by and large it was kept under the sur-face. Previously, as had happened so demonstratively in the Swing disturbances with their destruction of nearly 400 threshing machines, mechanization had been strongly resisted by those who saw their jobs

and livelihoods to be at risk. After Swing, however, apart from some isolated acts of protest such as local demonstrations against the New Poor
Law and sporadic outbreaks of rick burning in Lincolnshire and parts of
East Anglia, agricultural progress was taken more or less for granted and
attracted little active opposition. Farmers were now freer than ever to
bring in new machinery. Thus, by the 1860s, the quantity of labour
required by English agriculture had begun what has proved to be a never-
ending course of decline. As well as being a time of great prosperity
fuelled by strong investment and consistently large returns, the High
Farming age in the arable branches of farming saw the eclipse of the old,
highly labour-intensive methods of cultivation and its replacement by a
machine-dominated system. Furthermore, in applying the technology of
industrialism to the draining of marshlands and the reclamation of barren
heaths and moorland, this period also saw a substantial increase in the
aggregate cultivated area. With the ploughing up of former grassland also
contributing to the trend, the amount of arable land in England and
Wales rose from twelve million acres (five million hectares) at the beginning of Queen Victoria's reign to just short of fifteen million (six million
hectares) in 1871.[2]

Throughout its period of pre-eminence, there was always an unques-
tioning spirit of confidence in the ethos, the methods and the products of
High Farming. In particular, in those parts of the country that had the
appropriate natural conditions, landowners and farmers maintained a
complete faith in capitalized cereal cultivation and mixed farming, the
profitability of which seemed to be eternal. There was also an uncritical
belief in the permanence and the morality of the class relationships – the
rigid social trilogy of landowner, tenant farmer and agricultural labourer
– that underpinned this highly efficient and prosperous mode of farming.
The Age of High Farming, therefore, was very definitely a golden age in
the history of rural and village England, though very much more so for
the landowners and the farmers than it was for 'Hodge' and the rest of
the rural working class.

High Farming and Village England

The High Farming age had a positive impact upon the evolution of village England and the rural landscape. Arguably the most prosperous
period in the entire history of British agriculture, it brought widespread
new building which, in the cereal-growing counties, reached a scale comparable with that of the Georgian agricultural revolution and the

principal phases of the parliamentary enclosure movement. Many tenant farmhouses were rebuilt or enlarged to provide for a more affluent and more genteel lifestyle; and solidly constructed outbuildings were added, some for storing the increased quantities of grain, and others for accommodating the ever-growing assortment of new machinery. The prosperity of High Farming could also be observed in the country market towns, most noticeably in the construction of corn exchanges, warehouses, granaries and new public buildings. It was seen here too in the increasing numbers of shops, inns and commercial businesses and in the expansion of farming-related industries such as agricultural engineering, food processing and the production of artificial fertilizers.

The Age of High Farming was a time when many country houses and mansions were altered or completely rebuilt to suit mid-Victorian tastes and standards of comfort. Many of their owners favoured the now highly popular architectural style of the Gothic revival. In the design of country mansions Gothic revivalism, particularly the version that became known as 'false' or 'fantasy' Gothic, goes back to the final quarter of the eighteenth and the early years of the nineteenth century; two famous examples being William Beckford's extravaganza of Fonthill Abbey in Wiltshire and Lord Bridgewater's Ashridge House in the Hertfordshire Chilterns. However, it did not attain its highest popularity until after Queen Victoria took the throne. By then, Georgian elegance and formalism had become a fashion of the past and, following the lead of such apostles of 'true' Gothic architecture as A. W. N. Pugin and Sir Charles Barry, were seemingly everywhere being supplanted by reinventions of high medievalism with its castellated walls, dramatic turrets and spires, tracery windows and mysterious interiors. Medievalism, with its romantic imagery and connotations of feudalism, paternalism and chivalry, had a special appeal among Victorian landowners and their commissioned architects. As the tide of industrialization grew stronger and stronger, many of the landed class became more and more disenchanted with the new urban industrial culture. In their eyes industrialism was a destructive force, creating poverty, slums and social alienation in its cities and at the same time undermining the tranquillity of the countryside and the stability of rural life. As the architectural historian Mark Girouard has explained: 'a dislike of the present led them to the past, dislike of the town to the country'.[3] This mood also prompted some landowners to make efforts to foster greater integration between the hall and the estate village, as if to revive something of the protective and inclusive feudal spirit of the medieval lord of the manor. Thus, in many instances Georgian tree screens and even sections of boundary walls were removed so that the great house could now be seen from the village, and vice versa. New entrances and pathways were installed to enable villagers to enter the outer parts of the park and to provide human figures within what had previously been an unpeopled landscape; and there was a growing enthusiasm for holding (and photographing) village tea parties on the front lawn or on the terrace. By the middle of the century too, some landowners, especially those whose mansion and park were within reach of one of the new railways or could be approached by a river cruise up the Thames from London, were declaring public days and opening their grounds to the first representatives of the 'stately home' genre of weekend tourists. At a time of great prosperity among the aristocracy and the landed gentry, the desire to impress an admiring public was a much stronger motive than the small additional income that could be gained from the modest admission charges.

The affluence of the High Farming age was also reflected within the villages where, even as population stagnation and decline began to set in during the 1850s and 1860s, there was still much building activity. Indeed, the third quarter of the nineteenth century was a time of renewed interest among landowners for constructing model cottages and enlarging estate villages to accommodate extra gamekeepers, bailiffs, maintenance staff and 'living out' servants. As in the Georgian age, the best craftsmen-builders of the day were engaged in the construction of such cottages, many of which were built in a vernacular style and were designed to convey a romantic, picturesque image. Of far better quality than the labourers' hovels of open villages, these reflected the landowner's desire to demonstrate his paternal concern for his community and to present visible evidence of his good taste and his material success. This is why so many model cottages, including many almshouses too, were placed in the most eye-catching positions, typically near the entrance of the church or facing the village green.

New schools, Nonconformist chapels and commodious new vicarages were common additions to the physical fabric of the English village at this time. In many instances, but more frequently in close villages than in open ones, the wealth of the High Farming age is also evidenced in the renovation and rebuilding of Anglican churches. In expending large sums of money on church restoration, involving the appointment of such prominent architects of the day as Hodgson Fowler, John Pearson, G. E. Street and Temple Moore, parsons and their landowner patrons were driven by an urge to reinforce spiritual control over their village communities. Some indeed were influenced by the beliefs of the early-Victorian Oxford Movement, which stressed the need to promote God through stricter and more devout worship. Enhancing the aura of God's sanctuaries by restoring their interiors was seen as a means of fostering this deeper reverence. Thus, in many villages, ancient dilapidated churches were comprehensively treated, all too often at the expense of their oldest architectural features and furnishings. A considerable number were demolished entirely, to be replaced by a brand new church, usually built as a Victorian imitation of the 'early English' or 'decorated English' Gothic style. Often the interior, the aisle in particular, was opened out to make the altar and the pulpit more visible to the congregation and, one can presume, the congregation more visible to the parson and the squire. In order to achieve this, dark recesses and awkward corners were removed or reshaped, and such obscuring features as high box-pews, old rood screens and upstairs galleries were dismantled and taken away.[4] In some country churches whitewash was applied to the inside walls to give the interior what was considered to be a plainer and purer appearance.

In most of these 'improved' churches the overall effect was to make the architecture more uniform, representing just a single historical period rather than containing the incremental mixture of styles that has always been the hallmark of the unrestored English village church. The Reverend Ditchfield, who saw most Victorian church alterations as acts of 'wanton destruction', gave some details of the situation in the county of Berkshire towards the close of the nineteenth century. Here, out of 170 ancient parish churches that had existed at the beginning of the century, as many as 100 – nearly two-thirds – had been affected; and some thirty of these had been pulled down and completely rebuilt.[5] About the same time as Ditchfield was describing what was happening in Berkshire, Thomas Hardy (himself a trained architect who had once had an active professional interest in church restoration) was expressing his dismay over the extent of the trend in rural England and how its damaging effects could be seen in nearly every corner of his native Wessex. In a correspondence quoted by Ditchfield, he described the commonest forms of internal alteration:

> Its enormous magnitude is realized by few who have not gone personally from parish to parish through a considerable district, and compared existing churches there with records, traditions, and memories of what they formerly were. The shifting of old windows and other details irregularly spaced, and spacing them at exact distances, has been one process. The deportation of the original chancel arch to an obscure nook and the insertion of a wider new one, to throw open the view of the choir, is a practice by no means extinct.[6]

The 'Ordered' Rural Society

The social trilogy or natural order of landowner, tenant farmer and agricultural labourer that had taken shape with the Georgian agricultural revolution and had already become imprinted in the rural landscape in the landowner's mansion, the squire's country house, the tenant farmer's new farmhouse and, in the open villages, the labourers' humble dwellings, became even more sharply differentiated in the High Farming age. The scale of its social disproportion, however, varied geographically. It was weakest in the pastoral areas of the west and the north where farms were generally much smaller and were mostly family concerns using little or no outside labour; and it was strongest in the cereal-growing regions of eastern and southern England where the capitalization of agriculture and the division of labour had advanced the furthest. To many people the rigid stratification of rural society in the latter area seemed to be God-created and eternal; a view that is expressed very clearly, though not in fact countenanced, by Flora Thompson who, in her autobiographical *Lark Rise to Candleford*, referred to 'the supreme rightness of the social order as it then existed', and went on to confirm 'God in his infinite wisdom had appointed a place for every man, woman and child on this earth and it was their bounden duty to remain contentedly in their niches.'[7]

At the top of the hierarchy, according to Lord Derby's *Return of Owners of Land in 1873* (more commonly known as the 'New Domesday Survey'), stood a rural elite of 363 aristocratic landowners, each in possession of a great estate of over 10,000 acres (4,000 hectares). More than half of them were peers of the realm, and fifty-eight were baronets: only one out of three was untitled. In total their estates covered nearly one-quarter of the area of England, but they were distributed very unevenly over the shires. In a later landownership survey, conducted in 1883, the presence of the landed aristocracy was strongest in Rutland, Northamptonshire, Northumberland, Nottinghamshire, Dorset, Wiltshire and Cheshire, where its estates amounted to more than one-third of the county area. They were least extensive in Surrey, Essex and Middlesex, in south-eastern England, where in aggregate their share of the land was only one-tenth.[8] The individual realms stretched well beyond the bounds of a single parish: most of them included several, and the largest were spread out over entire districts. The Brocklesby estate of the Earls of Yarborough, for example, covered 55,000 acres (22,250 hectares) in north Lincolnshire in the High Farming age. In as many as eighteen parishes here the Earl of Yarborough was either the sole or the principal landowner, whilst in nine others he had more than a 25 per cent stake.[9]

Within the great estates the authority of the aristocratic landowner was virtually absolute. By means of his ownership of land he could govern the whole process of agricultural production whilst, through the operation of the tenant-farming system, he could gain the lion's share of the profits. His 'subjects' had to depend upon him not only for employment or the land that they rented, but also for all aspects of 'official' village life: the cottages that he owned and in which they lived; the great house where some villagers worked as servants or gardeners; the church in which they worshipped and listened to sermons given by the landowner's personal choice of parson; and the school that their children attended, where, even after the educational reforms of the 1870s, he could keep a strong eye on the teachers and the lessons they taught. Only in the open villages and market towns beyond his estate did the aristocratic landowner stand in the background. Yet even here members of the rural working class might eventually have to come before him in connection with his wider powers as justice of the peace or chairman of the Poor Law guardians.

Below the landed aristocracy were the landed gentry, or squirearchy, whose estates ranged from around 1,000 to 10,000 acres (400 to 4,000 hectares). They numbered just over 3,000 in the 'New Domesday Survey', and were the most widely represented in Shropshire, Herefordshire, Huntingdonshire, Oxfordshire and the eastern counties.[10] Only the larger estates of this category of landowners contained more than just a couple of villages, whilst the properties of the lesser gentry (ranging from 1,000 to 3,000 acres) rarely extended beyond a single parish. Yet within these small areas the influence of the squire could be just as pervasive as that of an aristocratic landowner. The gentry presided over a similar, if much more spatially confined, tenant-farming system; and, like the aristocracy, many of them provided livings to village parsons and became benefactors to village schools. Many too served as a county magistrate and acted as a Poor Law guardian. Within the limits of their material resources, they sought to emulate the aristocracy by enlarging and embellishing their country houses, improving their villages, and converting churches into family shrines. However, whereas most of the rural aristocracy preferred to keep themselves aloof from their tenants and servants, the squirearchy tended to have a closer relationship. These smaller rulers of the countryside, therefore, came to know the face, the name and perhaps the strengths and weaknesses of all their subjects, which, of course, was an advantage for some villagers but not for others.

Farmers – there were about a quarter of a million of them at the beginning of the High Farming age[11] – occupied the middle position within the rural social hierarchy. From the first major phase of the Georgian parliamentary enclosures to the landownership revolution of the early twentieth century, the large majority of them (around 80 per cent) were tenant farmers who, through their payments of rents, provided the most immediate, and very often the largest, source of wealth for the landed class. Though tenant farmers were always subordinate and answerable to the landowners, their standards of living, and in many cases their social standing too, increased appreciably during the High Farming age. However, farmers' incomes and material comforts did vary considerably, largely according to differences in the size and the condition of the farm-holding and also to differences in soil quality and drainage. Some tenants, usually those who worked the largest farms, achieved the rank of gentle-man farmer and employed quite large numbers of labourers and farm servants; but others were little more than rent-paying smallholders. As a class, therefore, the mid-Victorian farmers were homogeneous only in terms of their tenant status and dependence upon their landlord. Within rural England they served as a social cushion, enabling the landowners to stay beyond the reach of the agricultural workforce yet, at the same time, helping them to prosper from the fruits of its labour.

At the bottom of the hierarchy stood the agricultural labourer, or Hodge, as he was universally nicknamed. Rendered landless through enclosure and reduced to a state of total dependence upon his employer, he formed the core of the rural working class and in most cases the largest part of the village occupational community. Always vulnerable to exploitation, Hodge often found himself having to seek work by knocking on doors or presenting himself at annual or half-yearly hiring fairs. In the occupations census of 1851 there were 1.3 million agricultural labourers and farm servants in England and Wales, nine out of ten of whom were males.[12] At that time – the year in which the Great Exhibition signalled that Britain had become the world's very first industrial nation – they still represented the country's largest single employment grouping (the next three were domestic servants, textile workers and coal miners). However, despite the onset of High Farming, agriculture was falling behind other branches of the national economy in terms of output value. Moreover, due to increasing mechanization and a strengthening current of rural out-migration, the size of the agricultural labour force was about to enter a permanent course of decline. By 1871 it had fallen to around a million and at the following census it had shrunk to 830,000. Nevertheless, as the High Farming age drew to its end, agricultural labourers and farm servants still formed a very large majority among the farming population, outnumbering farmers by four times and the aristocracy and squirearchy by almost 300 times.[13] What this meant in the rural landscape were

broadly the same proportional differences in the numbers of farmworkers' cottages, the numbers of farmsteads, and the numbers of country
houses and mansions.

Whilst some historians have used the term 'the rural proletariat' as a
collective description of the nineteenth-century agricultural labourer, a
distinction should be made between regular workers, such as ploughmen,
stockmen, waggoners and shepherds who were employed over the whole
year or the larger part of it, and casual workers, seasonal hirelings and
pauper roundsmen who were paid at a daily rate or by the 'piece', usually
for the unskilled and back-breaking jobs of weeding, stone picking,
potato lifting and digging up turnips and swedes. As a rule, the regular
workers and farm servants were better housed than the rest of the agricultural workforce. Many of them lived in tied cottages, the best of which
were the ones that had been built next door to the larger and the more
isolated of the post-enclosure farmsteads. The casual labourers, always
poorly paid and as often out of work as in, were left to inhabit the worst
cottages and hovels of open villages and the crowded courts and back-
alleys of the market towns. Among their numbers were 'gang' workers –
men, and not unusually women and children too, who tramped across the
countryside in large groups to undertake periodic spells of work con-
tracted by their gangmaster. This practice was eventually brought under
some degree of control by the Agricultural Gangs Act of 1867, which
imposed a licensing system on the use of gang labour, prohibited the mixing of sexes and placed restrictions on the employment of children. Gangs
of labourers had become a common sight in the eastern cereal-farming
counties of Lincolnshire, Norfolk and Suffolk, and also in the fruit and
hop-growing districts of Kent and Surrey. George Sturt (he wrote under
the pseudonym of George Bourne) could remember seeing what must
have been some of the last of these bands of field workers – daily parties
of women in these instances – in the countryside around Farnham on the
Surrey–Hampshire border:

> Far beyond the valley they had to go to earn money at hop-tying, hay-
> making, harvesting, potato picking, swede-trimming, and at such work
> they came immediately, just as the men did, under conditions which made it
> a vice to flinch. As a rule they would leave work in the afternoon in time to
> get home and cook a meal in readiness for their husbands later, and at that
> hour one saw them on the roads trudging along, under the burden of their
> coats, dinner-baskets, tools and so on very dishevelled.
>
> (George Sturt, *Change in the Village*, 1912)

Not every working villager was engaged in agriculture. Sustained first
by the strong rural population growth of the first half of the nineteenth
century, and then by the prosperous economic climate of the High Farm-

ing age, a quite substantial sub-community of tradesmen and craftsmen had emerged in most villages, particularly open ones. A typical example was in the village of Inkpen in the Berkshire Downs, which in 1861 had 748 inhabitants and contained nineteen tradesman and craftsman enterprises.[14] As a general rule the bigger the village the larger were the numbers of these concerns. This can be illustrated by considering three open villages in the Yorkshire Wolds. In the smallest, Middleton-on-the-Wolds which had a population of 649 at the 1871 census, a county trades directory for the following year listed seventeen tradesman and craftsman businesses. In the other two villages, South Cave (948 inhabitants) had twenty-five and Kilham (1,138 inhabitants) had thirty-two.[15] These totals were mostly made up of shopkeepers, bakers, tailors and shoemakers, but all three villages also had at least one carpenter, carter, blacksmith, innkeeper and wheelwright.

If all the apprentices, journeymen and family helpers were to be included, the numbers of people working in trades and crafts in villages like these would be something in the order of three or even four times greater than the numbers of actual enterprises. Indeed, one large and very self-contained agricultural village in the Lincolnshire Wolds, Binbrook, is known to have had a tradesman and craftsman sub-community of as many as 140 people among its mid-nineteenth century population of 1,269.[16] Not uncommonly in those parts of the country where industrial out-working still lingered on in some strength, as for example in the lace-making districts of Devon and Buckinghamshire, the straw-plaiting districts of Bedfordshire and Hertfordshire, and the boot and shoe making districts of Northamptonshire, there could be found several part-farming and part-cottage-manufacturing communities in which there were at least as many craft workers, male and female, as there were people employed on the land.[17] Indeed, it was usual here for some of the out-workers to be recruited from the families of agricultural labourers; the opportunity to supplement the breadwinner's inadequate wage being a compelling incentive. Out-working continued to lie outside the scope both of rising industrial trade unionism and of the lengthening list of workplace regulations that were being applied to Britain's factories and mines. Cottage industry, therefore, was commonly associated with cramped working conditions, very low rates of remuneration and the exploitation of women and children. Such unpalatable aspects of nineteenth-century 'cottage economy' are rarely mentioned in the range of literature applauding village craftsmanship and rural self-sufficiency.

Further diversity in the occupational structures of village communities was afforded by the growth of domestic service, a trend that, in the rural

Plate 10: Heptonstall, west Yorkshire. Even before the Industrial Revolution, some villages had left behind their agrarian roots and had become more concerned with cottage manufacturing or small-scale mining. During the eighteenth and early nineteenth centuries Heptonstall housed a busy community of handloom weavers, as is evidenced by the elongated window-lights in the older cottages and the addition of an extra floor to provide additional workspace. Handloom weaving, however, was one of the first cottage industries to succumb to powered factory production, and, by the 1830s, villages like Heptonstall were in a terminal state of decline.

England of the High Farming age, was closely connected with the mounting wealth of the landed class and the growing affluence of most gentlemen and tenant farmers. Over the country as a whole, including the towns and cities as well as the countryside, the numbers of domestic servants had already risen from 665,000 in 1831 to 908,000 in 1851. But it was the next two decades, from 1851 to 1871, that witnessed the greatest increase, a large part of which was undoubtedly an outcome of sustained agricultural prosperity. By the latter date, as many as 1.4 million domestic servants, 90 per cent of them female, were recorded in the national, England and Wales, occupations census.[18] By 1871 too, domestic service had displaced farm work as the nation's largest category of employment.

In mid-Victorian rural England there were two basic types of domestic servants: firstly, there were those who resided within the village (usually a close or estate village) and made their way each day to the mansions, halls, large farms, vicarages and country villas; secondly, there were those – the more special servants – who lived in at their place of work, where their masters and mistresses provided them with sleeping accommodation and food. For living-in servants, acceptance of employment often entailed migration at a tender age and an early uprooting from one's home, family and native village. As Flora Thompson described, reflecting upon her own childhood experiences: 'they usually went on foot, carrying bundles, or their fathers pushed their boxes on wheelbarrows to the railway station in the nearest town the night before.'[19] Yet, for many hard-pressed working-class parents the departure of a daughter to take up domestic service many miles away did bring a little relief to their poverty. For one thing, it meant one less mouth to feed; for another, there was the welcome prospect of receiving postal remittances, however small and infrequent these might prove to be.

Open and Close Villages: Widening Differences

Reflecting the growing rigidity of the rural social system, the High Farming age saw a widening of the differences between open and close villages. By the 1850s and 1860s, when most agricultural villages were registering their peak nineteenth-century population figures, open villages were functioning primarily as aggregations of farm labourers, craftsmen and a rural underclass of hirelings, gang workers, and people on the verge of entering the workhouse. Most open villages were now at least twice the size of the average close village and consisted largely of agglomerations of jerry-built cottages and insanitary hovels, more often than not placed upon congested and poorly drained sites. Along the main streets, such dwellings were interspersed amongst craftsmen's and trades-men's workshops, Nonconformist chapels (there had been a resurgence in rural Methodism in the 1830s, and there was another in the 1860s and 1870s), alehouses and old, pre-enclosure, farmsteads. Often the crowding of buildings within the centre of an open village had become large enough to obstruct the view of the Anglican church that, towards the end of the High Farming age, was itself beginning to be afflicted by depopu-lation, a shrinking congregation and not uncommonly – despite all the agricultural prosperity – general neglect and disrepair.

In what many writers see as the most golden of all golden ages in Eng-lish rural history, the crowded, disorderly landscape of the open village has very little place in the popular imagery of High Farming culture. What do feature prominently in the romanticized paintings, novels and topographic literature of this period are the immaculate, aesthetically pleasing and landowner-dominated close and estate villages which, more exclusively so than ever before, served to accommodate carefully-chosen communities of regularly employed estate workers, servants and skilled agricultural specialists, all presided over by the resident landowner and his frock-coated companion, the parson.[20] Until the Union Chargeability Act of 1865 finally did away with the antiquated Settlement Laws, land-owners continued to apply them to deter or remove unwanted newcomers and social undesirables. Vagrants in particular were rudely treated: with few exceptions, they were promptly turned away and sent back to their parish of origin if this was known. Even after 1865, not many landowners changed their approach. As owners of entire villages as well as the land, they still had more than enough power to exclude all itin-erants and low-grade agricultural labour; and they continued to see that it was not in their interests to relax control over the social composition and the lifestyle of their dependent communities.

During the High Farming age not only the social make-up but also the landscape of close villages became more distinctive. Some of the wealth that was being accrued from agricultural prosperity came to be expended on a new phase of village improvement and restyling, typically involving the pulling down of poorer-quality cottages and replacing them with dwellings that were both prettier to look at and were more solidly built. In the Lincolnshire Wolds, for example, the Earls of Yarborough con-structed over 200 model cottages between 1845 and 1875, distributing them fairly evenly amongst their several close villages.[21] On some estates, for example at Somerleyton in Suffolk, East Lockinge in Berkshire, Old

Warden in Bedfordshire, Harlaxton in Lincolnshire, Ilam in the Peak District and New Wimpole in Cambridgeshire, entire settlements were rebuilt, creating a new generation of model estate villages. A prevailing fashion among mid-Victorian landowners, however, was for constructing cottages and shaping village landscapes and parks in the Romantic image, embodying ideas expressed some decades earlier by such pioneers of picturesque enhancement as William Gilpin (1724–1804), Uvedale Price (1747–1829) and Richard Payne Knight (1750–1840). Accent was placed upon the revival of rustic vernacular architecture (or rather the landowner's and landscape designer's personal notions of how this should appear) and the re-establishment of something of the quaint and informal character of the traditional English village with its winding lanes, overarching trees and clusters of picturesque cottages. This was all very much different from the orderly, formal layout of the eighteenth-century Georgian model village.[22] Victorian landowners, many of them seeking to fulfil their paternal responsibility and also wishing to infuse more variety into the appearance of their villages, built new cottages and made existing ones more charming to look at. To prettify the cottages further, their tenants were encouraged to plant flowers in the front garden and to train climbing plants round the porch and up the front wall. Allotments were often provided for the cultivation of vegetables but, since these busy plots were not part of the romantic imagination they were usually placed out of sight of the main street, either on land behind the cottages or further away on the edge of the village. Landowners normally charged small rents for the use of private allotments and insisted that each plot was kept in a good state of upkeep and tidiness.

Since most landowners discouraged Nonconformity and the building of Methodist chapels, the Anglican church was often the sole place of worship within a close village. Throughout the Victorian age it played a full part in the lives of the parishioners and, with the congregation dutifully assembling there every Sunday morning, it was the obvious place for the aristocracy and the 'old' gentry to impress upon a village community their ancient lineage, their moral authority and their generosity to the poor. Thus many close village churches became filled with such private monuments as marble tombs, family sepulchres and supine or kneeling statues; and the windows and the walls became decorated with heraldic emblems, stone tablets, brass plates, and statements of benevolent deeds and acts of charity.[23] Through his influence on the appointment of the parson and the messages that he preached, the landowner was also able to use the church as a place for conveying his paternal hold over the community and for reinforcing his social conventions and moral standards.

'Only good people were allowed to live there, her father said', wrote Flora Thompson in *Lark Rise*, as in the person of the young girl, Laura, she recollected passing through a landowner village one Sunday morning whilst travelling with her parents to visit some distant relations: 'That is why', her father had reasoned, 'so many people were going to church'.[24] Close villages and estate villages did indeed house very moral, God-fearing, and in some cases also landowner-fearing, communities. Their virtuous and respectful behaviour could hardly have been more different from the unruly and immoral lifestyle that was widely perceived to have been the norm among the concentrations of rural poor in the crowded open villages and countryside towns. These two contrasting rural cultures, and the various ways of life which existed between these polarities, did not escape Thomas Hardy's discerning eyes, prompting him to declare in *Tess of the d'Urbervilles*: 'Every village has its own idiosyncrasy, its own constitution, often its own code of morality.'

In making this comment Hardy must also have had in mind the diverse preoccupations, personal whims and material resources of the landed class, and the strong impacts that these could have both upon the built-environment of close villages and on the lives of their inhabitants. Landowners, Tory and Whig, were at one in their enthusiasm for agricultural improvement and the efficient management of their estates and tenant farms. Some, however, spent much of their time and energy elsewhere, engrossing themselves in county affairs. Others absented themselves further afield by becoming involved in the political arena at Westminster, either occupying a county seat in the House of Commons or taking a peerage in the House of Lords. Some of the landed class also devoted themselves to the patronage of painting, music and architecture, and there were those who over-indulged in such pleasures of aristocratic and gentry life as hunting, shooting, horse racing, gambling and attendances at the London season. Landowners also differed in their attitude to the people who lived and worked within their villages and estates. Many, particularly the landed families of ancient standing, were inspired by the traditional Tory ambition of fostering a practical and moral balance between material needs and philanthropy: stewardship and the accumulation of wealth on the one hand, and the undertaking of paternal responsibility for the welfare of their villagers and tenant farmers on the other. However, whilst this was the prevailing vision, especially so in the High Farming age, there were also some less enlightened and less humane landowners. Drawn mainly from the 'nouveaux riches' or 'new gentry' of the industrial and commercial classes, these people were imbued with the Whig or liberal spirit of material self-interest and undivided faith in the capitalist ethos and the operation of unrestrained market forces. According to the landscape historian Nigel Everett, this type of landowner tended to see his mansion and landscaped park more as an expression of his personal wealth and power than as a private leisured environment.[25] As a general rule, villagers who had to depend upon this 'new breed' of landlord found life harder and less secure than did those who lived under an old-fashioned Tory squire. Whichever the case, the inhabitants of close villages always had to be mindful of how their whole way of life could be abruptly changed, either for the better or for the worse, by the death of their master or the selling of the estate. The accession of his heir, or alternatively the arrival of a complete outsider, could well bring a much different ideological outlook and, with this, a new set of priorities and social imperatives.

High Farming, with its wealth and affluence at one end of the social spectrum and deference and poverty at the other, was underpinned by highly functional village communities in which the agricultural population was organized into a steadily hardening class system. At a time when religion still played a prominent role in country life, this rigid ordering of rural society, in which every person knew his or her precise place, was nowhere more clearly symbolized than inside the churches of the landowner villages. Here, as described by the rural historian Pamela Horn, the seating was often deliberately arranged: 'with the families of the squire and the clergyman sitting in special pews, carefully segregated from the rank and file of the congregation. Even these humbler beings were graded so that the farmers and tradesmen were kept apart from the cottagers who were pushed into the lowliest places of all, in the side aisles or at the back of the nave.'[26]

Village England in the High Farming age still consisted of a multitude of little self-contained worlds, and, as Hardy remarked in *The Mayor of Casterbridge* (written in 1886, but for the most part set in the High Farming age) 'the England of those days was a continent, and a mile a geographical degree'. Even by the third quarter of the nineteenth century, this very inward-looking way of life was only just beginning to be broken down through the combined forces of improved education, the increasing use of the railways and country carriers and a greater incidence of population migration. Migration, which among the younger generation was usually followed by letters back home and periodic return visits, brought for those who stayed behind some knowledge of other places and an awareness of the existence and location of villages, towns and perhaps even a dream city somewhere beyond the distant line of hills or sweep of downland. Yet for most inhabitants of village England, including the still very large numbers of the rural working class who worked long hours and either lived beyond reach of a railway or could not afford its fares, such horizons continued to represent the geographical bounds of their existence – limits that could be penetrated only by migrating themselves, spending some time in the army or the navy, or despairingly trudging off to a Union workhouse. Richard Jefferies in *Hodge and his Masters* wrote of the typical rustic labourer in 1880: 'He stays in the same cottage and on the same farm all his life, his descendants remain and work for the same tenant family. He can trace his descent in the locality for a hundred years.' Indeed, for the residents of many a close village, localism – a deep sense of belonging to a particular place and being anchored to a homeland – was deliberately fostered by landowners in their desire to sustain for themselves unchallenged spheres of authority over clearly defined domains or 'little kingdoms'.[27] Moreover, attachment to locality, and with this a clear understanding of one's geographical place as well as one's social position, helped to encapsulate villagers and keep them away from any malign external influences, especially those that were deemed to be potentially corrupting and had the capacity to undermine social stability and traditional home-bred virtues.

With the Swing rioting becoming just a distant memory and the worst of poverty now being shut out of sight behind the doors of the Union workhouses, the social system of the High Farming age reached something approaching a perfected state from the standpoints both of capitalist agricultural production and the governing of the countryside. Though a few more outbreaks of rural unrest did occur, most notably the eruption of agricultural trade unionism in the 1872–4 Revolt of the Field, these were seen just as ephemeral happenings rather than shocks of lasting significance. In effect, there was no serious challenge to a social order and rural culture that seemed to be underpinning eternal agricultural prosperity. However, in the markedly different economic climate of the final quarter of the nineteenth century, this prosperity and the confidence that it generated did come to an end, and it did so with calamitous consequences for rural and village England.

CHAPTER FIVE

Villages in Decay: Rural England in the Agricultural Depression

The contrast between the High Farming age and the final quarter of the nineteenth century could hardly have been any greater. Following the 'last good year' in 1874, agricultural prosperity and optimism quickly gave way to a new, and increasingly dismal, age of plunging profits, farm failures and rural decay, with the worst of it coming during the years from 1875 to 1884 and from 1891 to 1899.[1] Although there was some quiet improvement in certain branches after the turn of the century, farming as a whole remained in a generally depressed state until the food crisis of the First World War and the onset of a brief period of government protection brought some respite. But difficult economic conditions returned soon after this war ended, and they persisted until shortly before the next one, the Second World War, broke out. The historical geographer P. J. Perry, in his book *British Farming in the Great Depression*, summarized the long period from 1875 to the late 1930s as 'more than half a century of decline and decay, broken only by the emergencies of the First World War.'[2]

Even before the end of the High Farming age and the swift transition from agricultural prosperity to agricultural depression, a large majority of English villages were in a state of demographic stagnation or decline. According to one set of calculations, the rural population of England and Wales had reached a nineteenth-century peak of 9.1 million in 1861.[3] Thereafter, the trend for the rest of the century, continuing into the early decades of the next, was one of unrelenting decline, with the numbers of rural dwellers falling to 8.7 million in 1871, 8.3 million in 1881, and 7.5 million in 1901. Within four decades their share of the national population had almost halved, from 45 per cent to less than 25 per cent. Throughout rural England, villages were decaying and shrinking as farmsteads were being abandoned and cottages were being left uninhabited and derelict. The historian F. M. L. Thompson describes the scene:

> The countryside has seldom looked more dejected than at the turn of the present century: neglected and overgrown hedges, weed-infested meadows

and pastures, decaying thatch, dilapidated buildings, untidy farmyards; everywhere examples of lack of attention, misfortune or despair.[4]

Such neglect, decay, dilapidation and despair differed in every respect from the prosperous, progressive and self-assured rural England of the High Farming age.

Rural Depopulation: the Flight from Village England

These families, who had formed the backbone of village life in the past, who were the depositories of the village traditions, had to seek refuge in the large centres; the process, humourlessly designated by statisticians as 'the tendency of the rural population towards the large towns', being really the tendency for water to flow uphill when forced by machinery.

(Thomas Hardy, *Tess of the d'Urbervilles*, 1891)

Movements of people, predominantly young adult agricultural labourers and their families, from the countryside to the expanding towns and cities were by no means new to the history of rural England. Earlier in the nineteenth century, acceleration in the growth of urban population and expansion of the nation's industrial labour force had been fuelled by rural migrants seeking a better future and a higher material quality of life. By the 1840s, decennial migration losses from rural England and Wales were approaching half a million.[5] Yet a flow even of this size was insufficient to outweigh a high rural birth rate and a very large excess of births over deaths, which explains why, over the country at large, the rural population continued its upwards trend between 1841 and 1851. It rose by 302,000 during this intercensal decade; a slower growth than in preceding decades but, nevertheless, an appreciable increase in absolute terms. Indeed, it was not until after the census of 1861 that the numbers of people leaving the countryside at last began to exceed the natural reproduction of the rural population. During the years 1861–71, rural England and Wales lost 684,000 people through migration, marking the onset of a process of general rural depopulation that persisted for well over half a century. There were, of course, differences from region to region and from district to district. In some rural counties, such as Huntingdonshire and Rutland, a falling population trend had set in a decade or so earlier; and in Wiltshire, where in several villages what had once been a flourishing cottage cloth-weaving industry had entered its final phase of decline, it had commenced in the 1840s. On the other hand, mostly in the pastoral west, there were regions and localities where rural population growth persisted right through the High Farming age. Dorset, Herefordshire, Shropshire and Westmorland are four predominantly rural counties in which the highest nineteenth-century population figure was not reached until the census of 1871.[6]

There was even greater diversity of demographic experience *within* each rural region, county and district, with any general pattern being disturbed in many parishes and villages by such localized events as the building of a railway line and the success or failure of an important rural industry. As a rule, close parishes had a steadier population trend and tended to register later peaks. Usually decline did not commence here until several years after agricultural depression had set in and landowners had started to feel the pinch. Rather different from this was the situation commonly recorded in open parishes and their villages. With their accumulations of agricultural labourers and their quite sizeable sub-communities of tradesmen and craftsmen, these tended to have earlier population peaks, mostly in 1851 or 1861. Having sustained much the stronger population growth during the first half of the nineteenth century, they endured the heavier losses in the latter.

There is no single explanation for the drift of people from the country-side and the persistence of this trend well into the twentieth century. Whilst the large and constant disparity between agricultural and industrial wages was always a powerful influence, it should be noted that in proportional terms the gap was no greater – rather less in fact – in the final quarter of the nineteenth century than it had been in the earlier decades when the migration flow had been much weaker. Widespread agricultural mechanization with its relentless displacement of manual labour was a potent push factor, particularly in the cereal-growing districts; and it goes a long way towards clarifying why the depopulation of much of village England began some years *before* High Farming and its prosperous conditions came to an end. The numbers of agricultural workers (including farm servants and shepherds as well as agricultural labourers) in England and Wales had reached an all-time peak of 1.3 million in 1851, just a decade before the onset of general rural population decline. By 1871, there were 270,000 fewer regular farmworkers; and, by 1901, through a combination of further agricultural mechanization, a quarter of a century of depression and an even longer period of rural depopulation, their numbers had dwindled to 733,000.[7] During the latter half of the nineteenth century, the agricultural workforce shrank to little more than one-half of its former strength.

The backward state of what stood for an agricultural engineering industry, still mainly in the hands of village blacksmiths and wheelwrights, was one reason for the slow progress of agricultural mechanization in the days before High Farming. Another reason was the cheapness and abundance of agricultural labour, which, for the farmers and landowners, lessened the need for investing in machinery. In the case of the threshing machine – the one major mechanical device that did make an early appearance and was being widely used some decades before the High Farming age – an additional disincentive had been the hostile opposition of the agricultural labourers. By the 1850s, however, weakening resistance against technological progress and the beginnings of the transformation of agricultural engineering from a workshop craft to a fully-fledged urban factory industry were stimulating a revolution in farming mechanization. This included universal adoption of mechanical threshers and widespread implementation of winnowing machines, mechanical reapers, and more efficient versions of the horse-drawn sowing drill. Then, towards the end of the High Farming age, steam-power in the forms of the steam thresher, the traction engine and the steam plough, started to make an appearance, although it became a common sight only on the larger and most prosperous arable farms.

Very little of the profitability of High Farming had been expended on improving the living conditions of the mass of the rural working class, though many new farmhouses and model cottages were constructed. The former, however, were mostly built for well-off tenant farmers whilst the latter were provided for just a small minority of rural workers and were rarely built anywhere else than within the landowner villages. In other villages, if any model or improved cottages did exist, they were usually easily outnumbered by the cramped and often insanitary dwellings of the agricultural labourers and the rest of the rural poor. A survey and report on *The Sanitary Condition of the Labouring Population of England*, conducted for the Privy Council and published in 1865, highlighted the worsening condition of agricultural labourers' dwellings and revealed the extent of overcrowding within them. In a sample of 5,375 'typical' rural cottages, distributed amongst several English counties, the survey counted 8,805 bedrooms and lofts serving as sleeping accommodation for 13,432 adults and 11,388 children. Only 250 of these cottages had more than two bedrooms, whilst more than one-third of them had just one.[8] Such findings call to mind Thomas Hardy's description of the humble abode of the Durbeyfield family in the Blackmore Vale village of Marlott (Marnhull), where Tess – Hardy's tragic female symbol of the final eradication of the English peasantry – had lived with her impoverished parents and her six little brothers and sisters, and had slept each night 'underneath her few square yards of thatch'.

Whereas housing conditions in the towns and cities were gradually being improved through urban public health reforms, those of most open villages and small countryside towns steadily worsened as the agricultural depression wore on and the period of neglect and decay lengthened. Thus, whilst the thatched cottages of late-Victorian village England were being heavily romanticized in contemporary paintings, such as those of Helen Allingham, Myles Birket Foster and Stanley Wilkinson, the reality was that many were anything but idyllic to live in. Indeed, behind their picturesque exteriors, with their rose-festooned porches and clematis-clad walls, there was nothing but squalor inside. The rooms were small and dark, the roofs let in the rain, and often the only sanitation was an outside privy shared by neighbouring families. Moreover, such dwellings had become a source of growing unease among clergymen and social commentators concerned about the harmful effects that slum conditions and overcrowding could have upon the physical and moral well-being of the inhabitants. Not only was it a common practice for parents to share their bedroom with at least one of their children, but very often the cottages were structurally unsound; and, because of their rotting window-frames, leaking roofs and earth or uneven stone-flag floors, were always damp and cold in the winter months. Typical of these rural slums were the ramshackle cottages that Rider Haggard encountered when he visited a decaying village, deep in the Somerset countryside at the beginning of the twentieth century:

> In this Arcadian retreat the walls were falling down, the thatch was rotting on the roofs, the windows and doors were loose and unpainted. In short, the settlement which, from its position and natural advantages ought to have been both healthy and beautiful, was a scene of unwholesome desolation. Yet people lived in these ruinous homes, and children are bred there, for I saw them standing about the sodden gardens.
>
> (H. Rider Haggard, *Rural England*, 1902)[9]

And very similar to these were the cottages that the novelist Francis Brett Young described in his fictional village of Monk's Norton in the heart of the Worcestershire countryside in the 1930s. Interestingly, he was writing at the time when rural local authorities were about to embark upon their first extensive programmes of rural slum clearances:

> Their domestic water-supply must be drawn laboriously, bucket by bucket, from shallow wells, the purity of which is not above suspicion. Their thatched roofs, if they do not leak, become in winter, half-sodden sponges of rotting straw exhaling odours of mildew, while the slate-slabbed floors which are laid upon clammy clay are always cold and darkened here and there by patches of damp which show where water is lying. The threads of the stairs are worn into holes and warped to disclose crevasses with rat-gnawed edges. Ventilation they have in plenty, for no door fits and no window is watertight, though the chinks in the casements and frames are stuffed with brown paper; but the sanitary virtue of airiness (if perpetual

draughts deserve that euphemism) is heavily overbalanced by the dungeon darkness to which their inmates are condemned not merely by the inadequate window-space of their small-paned lattices but by the greenery that envelopes them, and the pallid pot-plants set to catch the sun on the sills. There are corners in those low-ceilinged living-rooms and in the dank lean-to sculleries that no direct light save that of lamp or candle has ever illuminated.

(F. Brett Young, *Portrait of a Village*, 1937)

Few labourers' cottages were actually owned by the people who lived in them. The large majority were tenanted, with the poorest dwellings being rented from small proprietors within the village, and others, usually of better quality, being leased out as tied cottages by farmers and landowners. The system of tied cottages, in which occupancy depended upon the tenant staying in his or her agricultural employment or domestic service, had become a special focus of grievance among the rural working class. Indeed, as the rural reformist Frederick Green described in his impassioned outcry, *The Tyranny of the Countryside* (1913),[10] vulnerability to unaffordable rent rises and the ever-present possibility of eviction (which could be enforced with very short notice) weighed heavily on the minds of cottage dwellers, and in many cases continued to do so long into the twentieth century. Not surprisingly, such conditions often became the final straw when it came to a question of deciding whether or not to turn one's back on village England and seek a new life somewhere else.

Moreover, for the new generation of the rural working class, the late nineteenth century was a time of widening aspirations. The Education Acts of 1870, 1876 and 1880, which introduced the principles of universal elementary education and compulsory school attendance, played a significant part. New and better-equipped village schools were built and professional teachers were appointed. Education of village children was broadened beyond the narrow confines of memorizing passages from the Bible, performing the simplest of sums and learning very elementary reading and writing, to include subjects such as general knowledge, history and the countries of the world. To each new class of village children these brought visions of far-off lands, exciting capital cities and the wide-open territories of the British Empire, all of which must have made strong impressions upon young and receptive minds. At the same time, the townsman was making his first incursions into the countryside and village England. Some villages, particularly in the Home Counties, were also seeing the arrival of 'pioneering' suburbanites, whilst others were beginning to witness invasions of weekend excursion parties making use of the extending rural railway network. Intruding into what was very much a decaying, dispirited and still highly rustic village England, such people were bound to convey messages of a hugely different and seemingly far more rewarding way of life. Later, in the early twentieth century, battery radios added a further dimension to this positive perception of urban living, with broadcasters frequently giving it a comfortable, middle-class and distinctly modern flavour. The power of the radio was often commented upon by the popular travel writer H. V. Morton. In an interesting passage in his most widely-read book, *In Search of England* (first published in 1927), he wrote about a small group of people sitting down inside a remote Cornish cottage on the Roseland peninsula: 'the new picture of rural England: old heads bent over the wireless set in the light of a paraffin lamp. London coming to them, out of space.'[11] The welcoming urban images that were presented in radio broadcasts, whether they were of fact or of fiction, contrasted strikingly with the cheerless view of muddy lanes and rain-sodden fields that, in the winter months, would have confronted any youthful and ambitious villager gazing out through a cottage window on a typically drab and cold weekend afternoon.

Whilst many inhabitants of village England were moving to the towns and cities, others, attracted by the prospects of a better life in America, Australia, New Zealand and imperial Africa, were choosing to migrate much further afield. According to Armstrong's calculations,[12] just over 100,000 people from rural England and Wales (including countryside towns) emigrated overseas during the intercensal decade 1851–61. The numbers of rural emigrants then rose to 148,000, or around one-fifth of all rural out-migration, during 1871–81, before soaring to over half a million in the next decade and establishing a very definite high-tide mark in the emigration flow. As with the internal rural to urban current of population movement inside England and Wales, the labourers' contribution to this exodus was driven by new advances in farming mechanization and, after the 1871 census, worsening agricultural depression. The exceptionally high emigration of the 1880s, however, owed much also to the agricultural trade unions and their policy of encouraging members and their families to protest with their feet. The idea behind this was to eliminate the labour surplus and thereby strengthen the wage-bargaining power of those who stayed behind. In pursuit of this strategy Joseph Arch's National Agricultural Labourers Union (which, just before it was broken by the lockout of 1874, had a membership of nearly 100,000 and had branches in nearly every English county) was the most active, though it provided rather more in the spheres of moral support and publicity than it did by way of financial backing. Emigration of rural people, especially estate workers, farmers and skilled craftsmen, was further encouraged by assisted-passage schemes operated by various colonial governments and arranged by local agencies that, with business booming, were sprouting up in most sizeable market towns. It was supported too by the Poor Law Boards, which saw the emigration of able-bodied paupers as a convenient way of easing pressure on workhouse accommodation and of reducing the Poor Law Rate; and it was promoted by bodies such as the Colonial Commissioners of Land and Emigration, which had a vested interest in facilitating the transfer of men and women from over-populated rural Britain to the under-settled colonies and dominions. After the 1880s, however, most assisted-passage schemes and other forms of subsidized emigration came to an end, whilst the embattled agricultural trade union movement, now with a much-reduced membership and an acute shortage of funds, quickly withdrew its interest. The intercensal 1891–1901, therefore, whilst seeing no let up in internal migration from rural Britain to urban Britain, witnessed a very sharp reduction in overseas emigration. During this decade, only 54,000 rural people left the shores of England and Wales, which was just a small fraction of the very large numbers who had departed in the 1880s.

Rural depopulation and the flight from the land had an enervating impact upon village England and its social fabric. Few villages were unaffected, and many experienced a continuous sequence of population decline over the entire period from around the time of the 1861 census to the outbreak of the First World War. Even before the end of the High Farming age, cottages were becoming untenanted and some, to save their owners the costs of upkeep, were already being pulled down. Moreover, in many villages the older and less energetic inhabitants were beginning to outnumber the younger and more ambitious. Then, from the early 1870s onwards, this demographic weakening of village England – gradual and scarcely perceptible at first – became overshadowed by the grip of agricultural depression and the decline of most remaining rural trades and crafts. By the close of the nineteenth century, the traditional economic mainstays of the English village were in a ruinous state, and the rural optimism and self-confidence of the High Farming age had irretrievably given way to pessimism and despair.

Agricultural Depression

The 1870s were very much a turning point in the economic history of rural England, for it was during this decade that the agricultural implications of the Industrial Revolution and of developments in the overseas trading of farming commodities at last began to present themselves within the historical heartland of capitalized agriculture.[13] Having for long been in the forefront of the British domestic economy, accounting for nearly half of national economic output at the beginning of the nineteenth century, farming had now fallen well behind industrial production. Indeed, by 1880, its contribution to the gross national product had fallen to just 10 per cent, and it was employing only one-eighth of the total working population. Furthermore, with food imports rising steeply, Britain's farmland was also ceasing to be the nation's principal source of food supply. Britain had become emphatically an industrial country, leading the world in manufacturing and commerce.

At first, it was thought that a run of wet summers and poor harvests between 1875 and 1882 was the main reason for the steep decline in the profitability of British agriculture, particularly cereal growing. Wet weather, of course, meant waterlogged soils and an abundance of weeds, which added substantially to the costs of arable farming. Damp conditions also had adverse affects on cattle and sheep farming, contributing to a higher incidence of diseases such as cattle pneumonia and liver rot. However, although there did come some amelioration of weather conditions after 1882, including a series of dry summers in the late 1880s and the 1890s, profits continued to fall and agricultural depression persisted. Poor weather, therefore, could hardly be blamed for what, by the final years of the nineteenth century, had clearly become a long-term agricultural crisis.

The root cause of what many historians refer to as the 'Great Agricultural Depression' was the intensifying competition placed upon British farmers by an ever-increasing flood of food imports from overseas. Most striking was the huge rise in grain imports – a quadrupling in volume between 1870 and 1908 – principally from Canada, the United States, Australia and South America. In all save the last few years of High Farming, Britain had been nearly self-sufficient in food production, with the nation's farmers providing more than four-fifths of domestic needs. However, by the beginning of the twentieth century, as much as 85 per cent of bread grain and 60 per cent of all food was being brought in from overseas.[14] The impact of this upon prices and agricultural profitability was quite catastrophic: between 1873 and 1895 wheat prices were halved, cattle prices fell by one-third and wool prices dropped by one-quarter.[15]

A question which arises here is why were overseas producers able to undercut British farmers so easily? The answer is not to be found in lower per-capita labour costs in the competing parts of the world, since agricultural wages in England, though rising, stayed well below those of the labour-hungry farming regions of Australia, Canada and the post-bellum United States. The explanation instead lies in the prime advantages there of much more favourable climatic conditions, vast reserves of land, and highly productive soils. Bearing in mind that, ever since the repeal of the Corn Laws in 1846, overseas cereal growers had enjoyed unrestricted access to British markets, this leads us to another question: why then was it not until the final quarter of the nineteenth century that they were able to properly exploit these advantages? The answer to this rests in the huge improvements in bulk transport in the 1860s and 1870s. These two decades and the rest of the nineteenth century saw the vast agricultural resources of the mid-west of the United States, the prairie provinces of Canada, and the lowland plains of New South Wales being opened up by railway development, whilst major improvements in shipping and the handling of cargoes were greatly reducing the economic distance to British ports. Perry presents some revealing information on this for the United States where the railway network was expanded from a rather modest 9,000 miles just before the outbreak of the Civil War in 1861, to an impressive 53,000 miles by 1870. Just as emphatic was the massive reduction in transatlantic shipping costs, which was made possible through increased usage of steamships and a trend towards much larger vessels. This is why, to take one example, the costs of transporting wheat from Chicago to Liverpool fell by as much as three-quarters during the period from 1870 to 1900.[16]

To a large extent British agriculture in the final quarter of the nineteenth century became the victim of its own great success in the period of High Farming. Most English farmers, even after several years of trying to cope with increasing overseas competition and falling agricultural prices, still kept faith in the products and methods of that mid-Victorian golden age. High Farming had encouraged over-investment in machinery, new farm buildings, model farms and ambitious reclamation and drainage schemes; and in too many cases there was a reluctance to adapt to new types of farming after economic conditions had changed for the worse. Indeed, for some considerable time after the onset of depression, agricultural investment – especially in labour-saving machinery – continued very much as before. There was also an obstinate unwillingness, particularly among wheat and barley farmers, to face up to the new economic realities. Nobody, it seemed, was prepared to believe that the depression was going to last much longer, and few people thought that there would not be a return to agricultural prosperity. Moreover, even when it did become obvious to everyone that economic circumstances had altered for ever,

many landowners and gentlemen farmers still clung on to their extrava-
gant lifestyles. Instead of adjusting to a more frugal standard of living,
they retained their servants and continued to run carriages, send their
sons to public schools, and participate in county society at fox hunts, race
meetings and country-house parties. And, rather than withdraw their
support, and thus signal that they were falling on difficult times, they
kept on providing for village charities and making generous donations
towards the upkeep of village institutions.

The intensity of agricultural depression varied considerably from
county to county and from one district to the next. This is evidenced in
Perry's analysis of the geography of farm bankruptcies during the years
1881–8.[17] His findings demonstrate that the highest incidence of agricultural failure was in central and eastern England, and most notably in
Essex, Suffolk, Cambridgeshire and Hertfordshire – counties in which the
prevalent soils were clays and heavy loams, where conditions were generally on the marginal side for wheat cultivation. When prices were high, as
they had been in the High Farming age, cereal growers could prosper
here: but when prices fell, as happened so dramatically after 1874, they
were the first to suffer. Bankruptcies, however, were much less common
in northern and western England (especially the pastoral and upland
counties of Cumberland, Westmorland and the North Riding of Yorkshire) and the dairying and mixed-farming counties of Cheshire, Devon
and Somerset. The type of agricultural specialization was one determi-
nant of the geography of depression: variations in the scale of farming
were another. As a normal rule, small family-run farms, using little or no
hired labour, had a greater chance of survival, since these were more
adaptable to changing economic circumstances and were much less
encumbered with the legacies of High Farming. It was the once highly
prosperous large-farm counties that suffered the worst. Here, heavy
dependence upon wheat and barley growing, and thus the greatest vulnerability to overseas competition, was often compounded by a stubborn
refusal to abandon the increasingly outmoded High Farming culture.

Agricultural depression had a deleterious impact upon the rural landscape. One very noticeable effect was the marked reduction in the acreage
of cultivated land, much of which was grassed over or was left to become
overgrown with thistles, nettles and patches of scrub. Over the period
1873–1939, the total area of arable landuse in England and Wales
decreased by 39 per cent from 14.7 million to 8.9 million acres (6 million
to 3.6 million hectares). In this, the decline of the wheat acreage was the
most acute, falling very steeply from 3.5 million to 1.3 million (1.4 million to 0.5 million hectares). However, chiefly as a result of the running

down and grassing over of former cereal land, the acreage of permanent grass increased by one-third; and, over the shorter period from 1892 to 1939, the area of rough grazing doubled from 2.8 million to 5.6 million acres (1.1 million to 2.3 million hectares).[18] The latter trend gives a measure of the full extent of what, to all intents and purposes, was complete agricultural dereliction.

The desolate state of much of rural England in the latter years of the Victorian age and in the early twentieth century is portrayed in some of the contemporary literature. The Reverend Ditchfield, for example, in his extensively illustrated *Vanishing England* (published in 1910 after more than three decades of agricultural depression and rural decay), complained about the increasing frequency of old cottages being left to crumble away and disappear from the landscape through a combination of long-established rural depopulation and neglect by their owners.[19] Throughout rural England, but particularly in the hardest-hit areas, villages were becoming smaller as more and more farmsteads and cottages became derelict, some of them sinking into ruins and others being quickly pulled down. Indeed, it was not unusual for even the church, the spiritual focus of the traditional English village and a prominent symbol of its antiquity and stability, to fall into a ruinous condition. Ditchfield described such a state of affairs in East Anglia where, a few years before the First World War, he counted some sixty dilapidated churches: 'many of which have been lost, many that are left roofless and ivy-clad, and some ruined indeed, though some fragment has been left secure enough for the holding of divine service.'[20] Later, in the 1930s, just before government intervention and the imminence of the Second World War at long last brought agricultural depression to an end, Thomas Sharp, a leading town and country planner at that time, wrote:

> Village Greens, roadside streams, ponds and a score of pleasant features that seemed once to be the very essence of the rural scene, all now seem ownerless and unvalued. Even the fields in many parts display the same characteristics. The land itself has deteriorated. Vast areas of once valuable and productive land have gone back to bracken and gorse, and rank marsh. … The English countryside to-day, to those who can read its meaning, is indeed a disturbing and a melancholy place.
>
> (Thomas Sharp, *English Panorama*, 1936)[21]

H. J. Massingham, one of the most prolific of the inter-war generation of countryside writers, described the dismal scene in the Cotswolds, arguably the most venerated of all of village England's heartlands: '… we saw more gates open than shut, more gates that could not be shut than could, more gates broken than whole, tousled heaps of straw, dishevelled combined fields, tumbled or gaping drystone walls, ivy-covered trees, indifferently ploughed fields, weedy pastures, dilapidated farm buildings, even barbed wire sagging or twisted.'[22] Unkempt and tumbledown land was indeed the most striking feature of the depression landscape. Often entire farmholdings and, as for example in the Essex claylands and parts of the Chiltern chalklands, even whole parishes had been reduced to such a state.[23] The contrast between this and the tidy, highly prosperous land-scape of the High Farming age could not have been starker.

New Directions in Farming

The Great Agricultural Depression and the re-emergence of depressed conditions after the First World War set the stage for an era of great diver-sity of agricultural experience in rural England. For over half a century, most regions, localities and even parishes contained a mixture of unprof-itable and quietly remunerative farming; a landscape of failure on the one hand, but one of survival and adaptation on the other. Indeed, by the beginning of the twentieth century, a bird's-eye view of the English countryside had become one of a mosaic of perseverance in depressed cereal farming in some places, run-down and derelict land in others, and in certain favoured areas the appearance of some new specialization or new direction. Later, a clear picture of this diversity of agricultural prac-tice and farming landscape was presented in Dudley Stamp's largely self-financed *Land Utilisation Survey of Britain* with its detailed 'County Reports'[24] and colourful, one inch to the mile, landuse maps (published by the Ordnance Survey). The survey work, which was performed by teams of volunteer geographers recruited from universities, teacher-training colleges and school sixth-forms, was carried out between 1931 and 1936, significantly just a few years before the plough-up campaign of the Second World War. The results demonstrated that, over the country at large, some six decades of almost unbroken agricultural depression had been accompanied by a sharpening of regional and local differences in agricultural landuse. Furthermore, through greater geographical speciali-zation, within every region there had emerged a closer relationship between the type of farming and the local natural and economic condi-tions. In achieving this and also by using the widening network of rural railways to reach the fast-expanding urban markets, British agriculture was able to show some positive developments and a general shift towards farm products that were either too bulky or too perishable to be moved across the seas.

The most widespread of these developments was the expansion of dairying, with many farmers changing from traditional cheese- and butter-making to the production of milk for the urban masses. Such a trend had already become established within the pastoral regions of western and northern England before the onset of agricultural depression. However, the strongest growth and geographical spread of this branch of farming came after the 1870s. By the end of the nineteenth century, not only had it become more strongly entrenched within such traditional butter, cheese and milk strongholds as Cheshire and Somerset; but also a number of new, or partly new, dairying areas had emerged, some of which (for example the Vale of Pewsey in Wiltshire, the claylands of east Leicestershire, the Vale of the White Horse in north Berkshire and south Oxfordshire and the Holderness Plain in east Yorkshire) included localities where cereal cultivation and mixed, cereal and livestock, farming had formerly prevailed.[25] Here the growth of the rural railway network in the latter half of the nineteenth century was the crucial factor. Railway companies, in particular the Great Western Railway which provided special trains travelling through the night from south-west England to London, Bristol and Birmingham, invested quite heavily in the running of milk trains from pastoral England to the major cities. One such train features in a symbolic passage in *Tess of the d'Urbervilles*, where Tess and Angel Clare, one autumn evening whilst conveying some pails of milk from Talbothays farm to the nearest railway station, came to a spot within the Vale of the Great Dairies where: 'by day a fitful white streak of steam at intervals upon the dark green background denoted intermittent moments of contact between their secluded world and modern life.' From here the couple moved on and eventually:

> They reached the feeble light, which came from the smoky lamp of a little railway station: a poor enough terrestrial star, yet in one sense of more importance to Talbothays Dairy and mankind than the celestial ones to which it stood in humiliating contrast. The cans of new milk were unladen. … Then there was the hissing of a train, which drew up almost silently upon the wet rails, and the milk was rapidly swung can by can into the truck. … 'Londoners will drink it at their breakfasts to-morrow, won't they?' she asked. 'Strange people that we have never seen.'
>
> (Thomas Hardy, *Tess of the d'Urbervilles*, 1891)

Another important development or new direction in British agriculture was the expansion of horticulture, a branch of farming which is taken here in its broadest sense to include vegetable growing, fruit cropping, and the cultivation of flowers and bulbs. Horticulture shared some of the advantages of dairying, particularly its capacity to make good use of the railways and to profit from expanding urban markets. Until the first major advances in the technology of refrigeration and canning in the 1890s and the early years of the twentieth century, it was also almost completely immune from overseas competition. Furthermore, most branches of horticulture could succeed on land such as clayland and tracts of sandy soils that were marginal for cereal cultivation. In certain parts of England, therefore, the growing of vegetables or the planting of soft fruits and orchards on abandoned wheat and barley fields became a logical course of action for many farmers, especially those who were short of capital and worked only a small acreage. During the period 1873–1939, the area under orchards and soft fruits in England and Wales increased from 187,000 acres (76,000 hectares) to 302,000 (122,000 hectares); and during the shorter period from the late 1860s to the late 1890s, the value of the nation's fruit and vegetable harvest increased by 21 per cent.[26]

In the same way as the growth of dairying, the expansion of horticulture took place, not only within old-established locations (such as west Lancashire, north Kent, the Biggleswade and Sandy areas of Bedfordshire and the Lea valley in Hertfordshire and Essex), but also in some largely new areas further away from major urban markets. A well-known example of the latter is the Vale of Evesham, though in some places here fruit and vegetable growing, usually in combination with dairy farming or small-scale cereal cultivation, does have a longer history. It was, however, towards the end of the nineteenth century, following the opening of the Evesham to Worcester railway, that the 'Vale' emerged as one of the country's leading specialist market-gardening locations,[27] bringing a new lease of life to several of its villages. Another interesting example is the Lincolnshire and Cambridgeshire fenlands where once again the economic distances to urban markets were greatly reduced by railway development. In this region, what had formerly been just a few pockets of market gardening (bulb growing did not come into its own here until the 1880s), mainly within the vicinity of Spalding and Wisbech, became much more extensive as the depression wore on and as more and more farmers moved out of cereal cropping.[28]

It was indeed in areas and regions like the Vale of Evesham and the fenlands that the expansion of horticulture created a new kind of agricultural landscape, very much different from that of the large and tidily arranged tenant farms of the High Farming age. Though (following the 1892 Small Holdings Act) increasing numbers of new horticulturists were accommodated in specially constructed, council-financed, small-holder cottages, it was the simple self-built dwelling and its improvised out-buildings that became the norm in many places. Small bungalows, fragile-looking greenhouses, old railway waggons, wooden huts and corrugated-iron sheds, more often than not occupying sites on the edges of a village or the outskirts of a market town, peppered the landscape here and reflected the very limited capital resources of their owners.

A third new direction was the increasing popularity of poultry farming, with the total number of poultry birds in England and Wales doubling between 1890 and 1914, and then, after suffering from shortages of feed during the First World War and its aftermath, doubling again between 1924 and 1934.[29] Poultry products, however, were difficult to transport, particularly by railway. This branch of farming, therefore, tended to take root within fairly close reach of its main markets, which – as with dairying and horticulture – were the principal urban centres and their large food-consuming populations. The most notable example was the extensive concentration of poultry farming that had emerged in the unremarkable countryside of west Lancashire, not far from the big cities of Liverpool and Manchester, and near enough to several of the county's fast-growing cotton towns and seaside resorts. Like horticulture, poultry farming gave rise to a distinctive type of agricultural landscape; a landscape which, around some villages, was even more improvised and disorderly than that of the new market-gardening districts. Thomas Sharp, with unrestrained distaste, described the scene between Southport and Preston: 'In the daytime one passes through what seems a gigantic, unending garden-city for pigmies, with one's whole horizon broken by hundreds of detached wooden houses of all sizes and in all conditions from perfect newness to ancient dilapidation.'[30]

The Smallholder Movement

Until the agricultural depression, support for an alternative to capitalized farming had been largely confined to certain radical political and social movements, namely the Chartists and their National Land Company in the 1840s, the Co-operative Movement in the following decade, and the agricultural trade unionism of the 1870s. However, as the depression lengthened and showed no signs of easing, some of their ideas were taken up by a growing body of independent reformist thinkers who now saw the ethos of agricultural progress and constant capitalization as a failed doctrine. In its place they advocated the re-establishment of smallholdings as the best means of adapting to the new economic climate and arresting what was threatening to become overwhelming rural decay. Indeed, in the words of one very active and enthusiastic advocate of

smallholdings, C. H. Gardiner, this seemed to be 'the only stabilizing factor in an unsettled national atmosphere.'[31]

Horticulture and poultry-keeping were particularly well suited to
smallholdings, since these two branches of farming required only a modest amount of capital and could be undertaken quite effectively by an
average family on just a few acres of land. By the early years of the twentieth century, support for smallholder farming had come to include
politicians, agricultural advisers and influential writers such as Rider
Haggard, Lord Ernle and, in the latter years of his life, Thomas Hardy.
To these people, intensively capitalized farming had fallen into a disastrous state and its economic difficulties seemed to have become
insuperable. Any lasting recovery from depression and any reversal of
rural decay would require not only fundamental changes in agricultural
methods and products, but also the settlement of more, not less, people
on the land. What became known as the 'smallholder movement', therefore, became part and parcel of a wider 'back to the land' ideology.
Smallholdings offered a means of entry into farming – the first rung onto
the agricultural ladder – for the enterprising 'small man'; and recreating
them was seen as a practical way of reversing rural population decline and
reinvigorating rural England and its village communities. Massingham,
writing in 1945 and looking back to the vanished age of peasant England
before its 'ruination' by the parliamentary enclosures and the agricultural
revolution, saw the smallholder movement as 'the road back to craftman-
ship and a true husbandry'.[32] What he meant by this was, first of all, an
end to the long and destructive history of engrossment of land and
uprooting of countrymen from the soil; then, as this was being accom-
plished, the reconstruction of rural and village England through the
restoration of the lost culture of self-sufficient peasant cultivation that had
been swept away by agricultural modernization and the relentless march
of agricultural capital. Carefully managed, this 'way back' could enhance
the rural landscape and not cause the sort of unsightliness that had been
allowed to become commonplace in such market-gardening and poultry-
farming areas as the Vale of Evesham and west Lancashire.

The smallholder movement and the idea of rural resettlement being
used as a means of arresting rural decay, stemming the population drift
from the countryside and perhaps bringing some relief to urban overcrowding had its first political victory in 1892 when the first Small
Holdings Act was passed through parliament. This legislation gave the
newly constituted county councils the powers to acquire land for the specific purpose of providing smallholdings for agricultural labourers and
other landless villagers to purchase by instalments. The state carried the

burden of any financial losses, and the county councils, with the co-operation of Rural District and parish councils (after their formation two years later), were encouraged to arrange local schemes for the preparation of smallholding land and the construction of smallholders' cottages. At first, only a handful of counties – Worcestershire, Lincolnshire, Norfolk, Cambridgeshire and Hampshire – actively responded, but eventually most other counties followed their example. Further Small Holding Acts were placed on the Statute Book in 1908, 1919 and 1926. These served to speed up the whole process and provided government subsidies to the authorities concerned. In response to criticism of the 1892 Act, there was also a change in policy from one of encouraging owner-occupancy of the holdings to one of renting them out to selected tenants.

By 1908, some 14,000 council smallholdings had been prepared and occupied.[33] These ranged in size from just a couple of acres (0.8 hectares) to a maximum of about fifty (twenty hectares), with most of them coming close to the lower of these limits. The large majority were to be found in open parishes where they were taken up mainly by agricultural workers and the sons of poorly-off tenant farmers. Additionally many more small-holdings, in these cases commonly displaying an untidy clutter of sheds, huts and cheaply-built glasshouses, were created by private individuals and local associations, taking advantage of the depressed prices of agricultural land and the willingness of landowners to part with some of their untenanted and run-down fields. In certain parts of the country much older (and to the observer often quite picturesque) smallholdings and smallholders' farmsteads, established centuries ago through encroachments into ancient commons and wastes, had survived parliamentary enclosure and had resisted all the pressures of agricultural progress. A small cluster of such settlements and a typical example of how their occupants might respond to a new market opportunity, are described by Flora Thompson in her reminiscences of the countryside around Grayshott, a straggling village set amongst the heathlands and woodlands of the Hampshire–Surrey border, where she had lived for a short while at the turn of the nineteenth century:

> There, tucked away in the long narrow valleys of the heath, were small ancient homesteads, each with its two or three fields, where the descendants of the original inhabitants of the countryside farmed on the smallest possible scale … and sold butter and eggs and garden produce to the newcomers.
> (Flora Thompson, *A Country Calendar*, 'Heatherley', c. 1947)[34]

Provision of council smallholdings and smallholders' cottages was stepped up again soon after the First World War, as rural local authorities sought to establish new enterprises and homes in the countryside for

Plate 11: County council smallholder cottages and sheds, Dunswell, east Yorkshire. Towards the end of the nineteenth century, the state began to take an active interest in the 'smallholder movement' primarily as a means of arresting the rural decay and depopulation of the Great Agricultural Depression. The photograph shows a pair of council smallholder cottages, built after the 1892 Smallholdings and Allotments Act. Purpose-built cottages like these, with their plain exteriors and use of modern building materials, looked out of place in the romanticized imagery of the late-Victorian and Edwardian countryside, as did their unsightly sheds and ramshackle huts.

those 'returning heroes' who had a rural background and some previous agricultural experience. By 1926, the number of council-promoted small-holdings in England and Wales had risen to 30,000, many of which were now occupied by ex-servicemen. However, the decision that year to shift the financial burden from central government to the county councils meant that far fewer new schemes were introduced after this date.[35] Until then, the construction of smallholders' dwellings, some laid out in small detached colonies and others built on their own alongside the roads lead-ing into and out of a village, had been virtually the sole means of public supply of rural housing. After 1926 this role was taken over, and indeed substantially augmented, by the construction of village council housing.

Some county councils were more enthusiastic than others in pro-moting smallholdings. Appropriately the horticulture counties of Worcestershire, Bedfordshire, Cambridgeshire and the Holland division of Lincolnshire were amongst the most active. Worcestershire, one of the first counties to make a positive response to the first Small Holding Act, is an illuminating example. Most council smallholdings here were estab-lished in the districts of Evesham and Pershore, right in the heart of the main fruit-cultivating and vegetable-growing area. Significantly, Evesham Rural District, during the intercensal 1911–21, was one of just a small proportion of predominantly rural and still strongly agricultural localities in England to have witnessed a reversal of population decline and a halt to the drift of people from the land. Moreover, within the wider area of the Vale of Evesham a clear distinction had emerged between, on the one hand, the smallholding and horticulture parishes that all experienced pop-ulation growth; and, on the other, parishes that were dominated by cereals and livestock farming and could register nothing other than a con-tinuance of rural depopulation. Just after the Second World War, Gardiner, himself a small farmer and a local inhabitant, counted 395 hor-ticulturists in the Vale, occupying holdings which averaged just seven acres.[36] Smallholders, romantically described by Massingham as 'the new peasantry', played a leading role in the expansion of horticulture here and elsewhere in rural England during the long depression. 'And how is the new peasantry to be created?' asked Massingham: 'Only by fostering the small holder and small owner, and by opening up new opportunities for them' came his immediate reply.[37] Yet the smallholder movement never really attained the momentum and the degree of success that its advocates had hoped for. Indeed, many of the new enterprises, both public and pri-vate, were unable to survive the very difficult farming conditions of the 1920s and early 1930s; and the numbers of holdings under five acres in England and Wales declined rather than increased during this time. Sadly, by 1935, there were 25 per cent fewer of them than there had been on the eve of the First World War.[38]

Decline of Village Trades and Crafts

The end of the High Farming age not only brought a farewell to agricultural prosperity, it also saw the onset of a long and ceaseless history of decline of village trades and all that remained of traditional craft industries. Farm failures, plummeting profits and diminishing agricultural investment meant much less custom for village carpenters, builders, carters, hurdle makers, saddlers, wheelwrights and blacksmiths. Moreover, depopulation, which had been afflicting most rural communities since the 1850s and 1860s, was now taking its full toll. Whereas the rural population growth and village expansion of the first half of the nineteenth century had brought increased scope for their businesses, population decline in the second half (once it had become well established) had the opposite effect. It aggravated the fall in demand for tradesmen's services and craftsmen's products, and it undermined the resolve to carry on. The persistent departures of agricultural labourers and other villagers meant that, year after year, there were fewer people wanting their cottage doors and windows to be mended, clothes to be made, shoes to be resoled, bread to be baked or ale to be served.

Not only did they have to face a climate of unrelenting agricultural depression and long-term rural depopulation, the tradesmen and craftsmen of village England were also confronted with an unequal struggle against the concentrating effects of technological and organizational change in manufacturing industry. Thus more and more traditional rural handicrafts finally succumbed to mechanized factory production. Cottage wool-spinning, handloom weaving and 'framework' knitting had already almost completely disappeared from the countryside as a consequence of earlier phases of rural de-industrialization. However, it was the final quarter of the nineteenth century that saw the beginning of the end for such ubiquitous village craftsmen as wheelwrights, hurdle makers, saddlers and corn millers; and it was this period too that witnessed the dying out of such survivals of cottage out-working as straw plaiting in Bedfordshire and Hertfordshire, boot and shoe making in Northamptonshire, chair making in the Chilterns, lace making in Bedfordshire and Devon and glove making in Oxfordshire, Somerset, Dorset and Wiltshire. In these, and in several other instances, competition from the new urban factories proved to be the decisive blow. As an indication of the speed with which some rural crafts fell into obscurity, Pamela Horn refers to the experience of female lace-makers in Buckinghamshire and Bedfordshire, whose numbers plunged from 14,000 in 1871 to just 2,000 in 1901; and the fate of shoemakers in Devon whose numbers dwindled from nearly 6,000 to under 3,000.[39] Yet, by changing to new products and new services, some craftsmen, especially blacksmiths, did manage to survive for at least one more generation. In Devon, for example, the numbers of smiths fell by a quite modest 20 per cent over the same period, whilst in Norfolk, where 2,522 smiths were recorded at the former date and 2,386 at the latter,[40] their decline was hardly noticeable.

Because they had been so strongly rooted within the village occupational community, and in many cases had become social leaders among the rural working class, the departure of tradesmen and craftsmen – often they were among the first to leave in the population exodus – had a particularly damaging effect upon village self-sufficiency and community cohesion. Due to the nature of their work – 'a thing of evolution and inheritance' according to the countryside writer, Adrian Bell[41] – such people had always played a vital part in village life and its folk culture. They had been indispensable to the farmer who required his waggons, ploughs and agricultural implements to be repaired; to the parson who wanted his church to be furnished, and even to the humble labourer who needed his boots to be mended and his bread to be baked. In their heyday they had performed a unifying role within the English village, usually occupying a social position somewhere between the labourers and the farmers. Moreover, their ancestors – past generations of masons, blacksmiths, carpenters and thatchers – had been the very people who had fashioned the village and its building-fabric in the first place. When they closed their small workshops and bid farewell to their villages, craftsmen took with them not only their handed-down occupational skills. Echoing the thoughts of many other nostalgic rural writers, Massingham saw their disappearance as the final act in the long, and often painful, disintegration of the traditional organic village and its self-contained, closely-knit, communal way of life:

> Their sons rarely now stay at home to learn their fathers' trades; there is either too great or too little demand upon their services; the village life to which they contributed so much is the ghost of itself and they are survivors into an alien new world which takes no account of them at all, or if it does, only as museum pieces.
>
> (Hugh Massingham, *The English Countryman*, 1942)[42]

Changing Control of the English Village

The age of High Farming had brought with it the culmination of land-owner power and the class system that it presided over. Thereafter, the Great Agricultural Depression, with its much-diminished returns from the land and its heavily reduced rents, put this authority under increasing economic strain, and in the worst years did lead to some increase in the incidence of disposals of landed property. However, deeper inroads into the rural *ancien régime* (and its eventual replacement by democratic institutions) came from two developments that were unconnected with the worsening economic climate. The first of these was the reform of village schooling: the second was the democratization of local government.

The foundations for the former were laid by the Gladstone government's Elementary Education Act of 1870 which decreed that every child who was not receiving a private education had to be provided with a place in a local elementary school. After further legislation in 1876 and in the 1880s, full-time attendance was made compulsory for all children aged between five and eleven; every pupil had to take a standard leaving test, even if this meant having to stay on for an extra year; and the system of inspection was strengthened in an effort to ensure an acceptable national standard of education and literacy. Moreover, schools were required to teach something more substantial than the religious indoctrination, basic reading and writing, and very simple arithmetic that had been all that most villagers had been taught in former times. Unlike their parents and grandparents when they had been young, village school-children were now given the opportunity to broaden their minds and widen their horizons. Thus, as each cohort of school-leavers grew into adulthood, slowly but surely landowner and parson authority came to be taken less and less for granted.

In most villages, what had served as school accommodation in previous years could not fulfil the requirements of the 1870 Act. Many had been nothing more than a very inadequate and cramped 'dame' school, typically comprising of just a room in a cottage or a loft above a workshop. An earlier government decision in 1833 to distribute annual grants for the construction of new school buildings had brought some improvement. Outside industrial and urban Britain where the Nonconformist British and Foreign School Society also played an important part, these grants were administered almost entirely through the Church of England National Society for Promoting the Education of the Poor in the Principles of the Established Church, and did lead to many villages being provided with a reasonably comfortable church school. However, whilst this was certainly a considerable advance on the average dame school, in the larger villages it proved to be too small for the additional numbers of places that were required to be available under the new legislation. The 1870 Act, therefore, was followed by a nationwide wave of construction of new, purpose-built, village schools and enlargement of existing structures, paradoxically at a time of quickening rural depopulation. At first, in rural England the greater part of this investment was organized by the National Society; but as time passed an increasing share of it (initially in the countryside towns and the more heavily populated of the open villages, where there had been the greatest deficiency of school accommodation) was promoted by a new institution – the local School Board which was elected by ratepayers and in many cases had authority over more than just a single parish. In the smaller villages, where there were fewer children, the original church or landowner-endowed school usually sufficed and needed little, if any, modification. Here, unless a School Board took over, it retained its independence and the squire and parson could still pull the strings for several more decades to come. Meanwhile, in all save the most neglected of villages, the dame school had disappeared.

For a long period after 1870, the large majority of rural children were given their education at one or the other of two basic types of village schools: the new rate-supported Board schools that normally served the larger communities; or the older church and endowed schools that were typical of the close and estate villages. In both types the teaching had to comply with the requirements of each successive Education Act, but many schools of the latter type continued to be permeated by the spirit of religion and were still subject to landowner patronage. This difference in the mode of control was reflected in the design of school buildings. The Board schools were mostly purpose-built and were designed to a standard functional plan (see Plate 12). Typical architectural features were their distinctive tall windows, with sills high enough to ensure that children, sitting at their desks and attempting to look outside, could see nothing but the sky to detract them from their lessons. Widespread use was made of bricks and roofing slates, whilst everything inside was arranged for the efficient running of the school and the fostering of Victorian standards of discipline. The headmaster's room was placed in an all-seeing position, and in some of the larger versions there were separate entrances and playgrounds for boys and girls. There was, however, some variety in the architecture of the other schools, especially those that had been founded by a wealthy landowner. Most of these had been built earlier in the century, often using local stone and local roofing material; and, by

Plate 12: Village Board school, Langham, north Norfolk. The Education reforms of the 1870s were followed by a great improvement in village schooling, including the construction of new 'Board' schools in villages where existing facilities were deemed to be inadequate. Note the characteristic tall windows and the use of non-vernacular building materials (bricks and slate roofing), in contrast to the flint walls and pantile roofing of the neighbouring buildings. There are still two entrances from the street; the nearer one originally for girls, and the further one for boys.

incorporating such ecclesiastical features as Gothic lancet windows, arched porches and miniature steeples, they resembled a church both from the outside and the inside. Such schools have been well described by the educationist H. M. Burton in his book, *The Education of the Country-man*, published in 1943.[43]

> ... these schools looked like small chapels. They have a steeply pitched roof, tall lancet windows beginning some five to eight feet from the ground, little Gothic porches and a bell turret. ... Inside, these buildings most often contain one large room and a small additional class room. The roof is so lofty that one or two blazing fires are seldom enough to warm the air in winter until well into the afternoon.

An important administrative change was made in 1902 when the running of Board schools – by then accounting for nearly two-fifths of all village schools – was transferred to the county councils. Henceforth, teachers in these establishments were appointed by the county education committee instead of being selected under the shadow of the village parson and the principal landowner. Moreover, even in the places where it had survived the earlier educational reforms, church and squire influence over the minds of village children eventually ebbed away as more and more of the remaining 'voluntary' schools came to depend upon the public purse and were put into the hands of the county authority.

The creation of county councils, following the Local Government Act of 1888, represented the first official step towards the democratization of village England and the transfer of power from the private to the public domain. Until then, the administering of county affairs had been conducted by the county magistrates, or justices of the peace; influential men who were nominated by, and chosen from, the rural establishment. After 1888, the county councils took over their role (apart from the dispensing of justice) and later assumed responsibility for a growing range of new administrative functions, including the provision of smallholdings, the management of state schools, and the development and upkeep of county highways. From their inception, the county councils were elected institutions and had to be responsive to a wide spectrum of opinion. Further progress towards democratization was made after a second Local Government Act was passed in 1894. This finally did away with the archaic parish vestries, and established two new tiers of local government: first, parish councils which were made obligatory for parishes with over 300 inhabitants, and were intended to look after rural communities at the most local of levels; and, secondly, Rural District councils whose functions included provision of water supply and sanitation, and were later extended to the construction and management of rural council housing.

In a large majority of cases the areas of the new Rural Districts were co-extensive with the post-1834 Poor Law Unions, and were centred on a countryside town.

The Local Government Acts of 1888 and 1894, coming just a few years after the third Reform Act had widened the franchise to include most of the rural, adult male, working class, aroused high hopes of a much more equitable rural society. In practice, however, these two pieces of legislation proved to be not as revolutionary as many had first thought. For a long time after their passage through parliament, landowners continued to exert some leverage upon county councils and Rural District councils through their wide social connections and their membership of advisory committees. For many years too, elections of parish councillors in some villages were nothing more than a show of hands in a crowded schoolroom or a newly-built parish hall. In such instances any challenge to the traditional rulers or their representatives was all too visible. It was not in every village, therefore, that a member of the rural working class had the courage to stand and had a fair chance of winning a seat. Indeed, people had to wait until after the Second World War before secret ballots were made obligatory in parish elections; and they had to wait just as long before smaller rural communities, with under 300 inhabitants, were able to have their own council.[44] It was not until then that the whole of village England was given the opportunity to acquire this lowest tier of local government.

CHAPTER SIX

Village England in the Inter-War Years

It was after the War [the First World War] that cheap motor cars and motor omnibuses, and later coaches, began to transform the English road; and this period I remember well. Few of us realize how complete was the transformation; how colossal the sums expended on the upkeep of roads and the provision of new ones; how quickly a network of bus routes opened up deserted hamlets and linked remote villages with the nearest towns ... Inevitably the country has changed.

(H. V. Morton, *I Saw Two Englands*, 1942)[1]

The period between the two world wars was a transitional time in the evolution of village England. It saw the shoots of economic and demographic recovery emerging in some villages, representing islands of rural regeneration: but it also witnessed the persistence of population decline and economic decay in many others. There were progressive villages and there were backward villages, often coexisting within the same locality and not uncommonly next to each other.

With few exceptions the former had emerged from the larger and more viable open villages, especially those that were suitably positioned for the development of a dormitory function and new economic activities. Access to a main road, closeness to a railway station or halt and nearness to a focus of employment, such as an urban centre, a large rural factory, or a military airfield, were the favoured locations. At the same time, coastal villages, 'beauty spots', literary and artistic shrines, and any other villages with a special tourist attraction were 'discovered' and frequented in an age when motor transport – the car, the bus and the charabanc – was beginning to make its mark. However, it is important to bear in mind that this process of opening up rural and village England was imposed upon a predominantly depressed and decaying countryside, rather than one that was prosperous and energetic. In the 1920s and 1930s, therefore, there was a clear contrast between the poverty and sleepy backwardness of the old village life and, with its motor cars, bustle and insensitivity to traditional rural values, the energy and modernity of the new.

The Retreat of the Landowners

> Most people have experienced the feeling of sadness and incompleteness in a village in which the 'big house' is derelict, demolished or turned into an institution. It is not only the sign of a devastated park, grass-grown drives and broken fences that depresses us, but a feeling deeper and more spiritual, a sense of intangible loss which probably even the village socialist will share.
> (Ralph Dutton, *The English Country House*, 1935)[2]

Despite the weakening of their social power and having to face the economic effects of four decades of agricultural depression, most landed families with something to spare were still managing to hold on to the things that mattered the most – their land, their landscaped parks and their splendid mansions – when war broke out in 1914. It was not the Great Agricultural Depression that put these to the ultimate test, but the harrowing experiences of the First World War and its eventful aftermath.

At a time when the ancient custom of primogeniture (first-born male succession) to landed property was still a normal rule among the rural aristocracy and old-established gentry, for numerous landowning families the traumatic loss of an only son in the First World War brought a sudden end to the lineage, with no natural heir to succeed to the great house and an intact estate. But this was not the only reason why many of them now decided to part with portions or, in some cases, all of their estates. Only a few months after the armistice, landowners were confronted with the steep rises in inheritance and land taxes presented in the Lloyd George government's first post-war budget. Moreover, two years later, the effects of these were compounded by the repeal of the wartime Corn Production Act with its guaranteed minimum prices for home-produced wheat and oats. Depressed agricultural conditions promptly returned, and once again income from the land fell sharply. Thus, with many male lines having become extinct, with taxation soaring, and with land and other rural property proving to be more of a liability than an asset, inter-war England witnessed an emphatic retreat of landlordism, with widespread disposals of former parklands and tenant farms, particularly those that had belonged to small and medium-sized estates ranging from 1,000 to around 10,000 acres (400 to 4,000 hectares).

Previously there had been a moderate flow of disposals in the wake of Lloyd George's pre-war 'People's Budget' of 1909, with its proposals for a near doubling of death duties and extension of other taxation ('incremental value' and 'undeveloped land' duties) on what he had famously denounced as the 'land monopoly'. Then, during the war years, many country houses had been requisitioned for military hospitals and convalescent homes, some of which were never reoccupied by their owners. As soon as the war ended, the trickle of land sales quickly grew into a flood. Initially this was principally a matter of land and farmsteads being sold off to tenants wanting to become owner-occupier farmers. Later, however, an increasing proportion of disposals involved conversions of former parkland and farmland into new uses such as golf courses, holiday camps and military training grounds. Within just four years, from 1918 to 1922, around 7 million acres – approximately one-quarter of rural England – changed hands, representing a scale of land transference comparable to that of the dissolution of the monasteries in the reign of Henry VIII.[3] The countryside writer and broadcaster John Moore, flying over the Cotswolds in a Tiger Moth aeroplane on a clear day in the late 1930s, had a bird's-eye view of the impacts of this process upon the rural landscape:

> I could see quite clearly how a great estate was being gradually 'whittled away' at the edges, like an island being eaten up by the tide. Some hard-pressed landlord had sold a few acres, perhaps to a Local Authority, then a few more acres to a jerry-builder, then a wood to a timber merchant, a hillside to a golf club, a strip beside the main road to a garage proprietor.
>
> (John Moore, *The Cotswolds*, 1937)[4]

The crisis afflicting the landowners was reflected in the increasing incidence of overgrown parklands, notices of sale and the neglect and dereliction of many country mansions. Of those that did not fall into ruins, many were purchased by the nouveaux riches, especially wealthy urban industrialists and city financiers, whilst others were converted into private boarding-schools or hotels. Later, following the introduction of the 'Country House Scheme' in 1937, some stately homes and their grounds were handed over to the National Trust, sparing them from any further deterioration and opening them for visitors at weekends and holiday times. More commonly, however, they were sold outright to an increasing range of public institutions, including those that formed a part of the embryonic welfare state. Thus, such public functions as hospitals, colleges and government research stations became present in the midst of the English countryside, in places where private authority had formerly prevailed.

As a rule it was the smaller landowner – one of the lesser gentry – who, because his interests and incomes were more exclusively tied to the land, suffered the more severely from the new taxation and renewal of agricultural depression, and was the more likely to part with his mansion and estate. Although it was now quite a common practice for the largest land-owners to dispose of the odd tenant farm and a few of their tied cottages, most of them were able to survive quite comfortably. Indeed, some of the aristocracy had enough wealth at their disposal to engage in such new 'spirit of the age' pastimes as flying aeroplanes, rekindling village festivals and collecting small fleets of motor cars. A few, impressed by its capacity to heighten patriotism and to stem what they saw as an accelerating descent into national economic and social disintegration, leant towards fascism.[5]

The greater resilience of the aristocracy owed nearly everything to their greater accumulations of wealth and their having economic interests that extended beyond land and farming into such vastly more remunerative spheres of investment as the stock market, overseas enterprises and urban development. Accordingly, they had built up a strong stake in the profits of industrial and commercial Britain, which perhaps explains why few among the younger generation of aristocratic landowners were unduly concerned about surrendering agricultural and rural leadership. Such leadership, especially in the promotion of agricultural knowledge and the construction and management of estate villages and model farms, had been at its zenith in the Age of High Farming. Thereafter, it had subsided gradually and quietly during the Great Agricultural Depression; then, in the aftermath of the First World War, what remained of it was taken over by the state with its new agricultural colleges, research institutions, mar-keting boards, Forestry Commission and government advisory boards.

One more nail in the coffin of the traditional rural social order was the decline of churchgoing, a trend that became more pronounced after the First World War. Flora Thompson, writing shortly before her death in 1947, was one of those who had noticed its impact on village life:

> On Sundays village churches were no longer as well filled as they had been. … very few of the clergy preached to full churches or had much influence over their parish as a whole, for a common faith no longer knit old and young, rich and poor, into one family and the church was no longer the centre of village life. The new centre for surrounding villages was the near-est town.
>
> (Flora Thompson, *A Country Calendar*, 'Heatherley')[6]

The increasing numbers of vacant pews at Sunday church services and the tendency for parsons to become less central figures in village life owed much to the upsurge in weekend recreation, but it also owed something to people's realization of the huge magnitude of the carnage of 1914–18. With this (after a brief revival in attendance during the war itself and in

the first year or so of peace) there had come some widespread disillusion-
ment with the rural establishment including the Anglican Church. Rural
Britain had sent to the trenches the greater part of its manhood and male
youth, large numbers of whom had been encouraged to enlist by the
prospect of a more exciting life as well as by their sense of patriotic duty.
Many returning servicemen, however, did not forget that the village parson had been among those who had urged them and their fallen
comrades to answer the call to fight for 'God, King and Country'. Landowners too had played a prominent part in stirring up patriotic feeling,
sending their sons to lead the nation's crusade against the 'Hun' and
exhorting their male servants, estate workers, and the younger of their
tenant farmers to follow them to the front. Of the half a million or so
rural men and youths who served, nearly one-quarter were killed or
wounded.[7] The social impacts of this vast scale of death and maiming
were far-reaching, and were felt in virtually every English village. Moreover, the casualties of the First World War were spread fairly evenly
among the rural classes, so that there was a unity in village England in its
grief and mourning. After four years of continuous military slaughter,
and with some of the survivors deciding to spend the rest of their lives in
a town or a city, villages had become places where there was a scarcity of
young men and male life-blood. Young women, therefore, had to look
further afield for prospective husbands – beyond the traditional meeting
place of church or chapel. The First World War indeed was to affect all
aspects of village life. In the uncomplicated, but very fitting, words of
H. V. Morton it was 'the thing that was to change all our lives'.[8]

One very tangible statement of the human sacrifice of 1914–18 was
the erection of public war memorials in prominent positions – on the village green, in the middle of the main street, or in front of the church – in
virtually every village, listing and honouring those who had given their
lives.[9] There are many versions of these solemn monuments, the size and
quality of which were not always commensurate with the population-size
of a village and the numbers of bereaved relatives and friends. The less
expensive ones – a stone cross standing upon an inscribed block was the
most widely adopted structure – were affordable through the normal
channels of public subscription, house-to-house collections and local
money-raising events. However, the more elaborate types of village war
memorial, such as the ones that were embellished with decorative carving
or carried a life-size 'soldier with rifle' statue, were usually beyond the
scope of ordinary communal funding. Erecting one of these often hinged
upon a substantial donation or a legacy from a wealthy benefactor, which
is why in rural England they are more commonly found in landowner vil-

lages. Despite being pressed by increasing taxation and the prospect of renewed agricultural depression, many patrons of close and estate villages saw it as a prime duty to ensure that their own communities were provided with the finest of monuments – a dignified final curtain on 'the war to end all wars' – to pay proper homage to the heroes who did not return. Many landowners too, in commemoration of a lost son, also placed a private memorial inside the village church, usually in the form of a simple tablet on a wall or an inscription in a stained-glass window.

Plate 13: Village war memorial, Ashbury, Berkshire. Village war memorials, with their solemn statements of the human sacrifice of the two World Wars, are symbolic of a major watershed in the history of rural life – in many villages the transition, around the time of the First World War, from the *ancien régime* of landowner and parson control to a democratic society. Always placed in a prominent position such as the village green, each memorial displays a list of 'those who gave their lives'. Ashbury 'lost' twenty men and youths in the First World War, representing around one-tenth of its male population and a much higher proportion of its 'life blood'.

Today, there will soon be no one left of the proud generation that fought and lived through the martial horrors of 1914–18; and the numbers of Second World War veterans are dwindling rapidly. Yet village war memorials remain as an immutable part of the English village scene, and they are still visited each November by congregations of Remembrance Day devotees, each listening to the last post being sounded, and watching the wreaths and poppies being laid. At these sombre ceremonies, and indeed throughout the year, not only do these stone crosses and granite blocks honour a generation sacrificed; but they also evoke something of those lost virtues of comradeship and social unity that are perceived to have been endemic qualities of the unmodernized village community.

Modernity and the Inter-War Village

Reading the signs of the times, energetic parsons strive to keep spiritual and social balance among the villagers. Motor 'bus services connect almost everywhere, gaily painted petrol devices have displaced the old parish pumps, roadside inns and tea-gardens are busy, village stocks now make resting-places for tired hikers and white lines on the roads point to an outer world beyond.

(Sidney Jones, *English Village Homes*, 1936)[10]

The inter-war period was a time of markedly differing experiences in village England. On the one hand, there occurred a stronger and more pervasive erosion of traditions, including faster decline of landowner and parson influence, further depletion of the agricultural population and the disappearance of many rural trades and crafts. On the other hand, the period did witness the materialization of various new features of village life, including the appearance of new enterprises, modern infrastructure, village halls and council housing. Moreover, in some parts of the country it also saw a growing momentum of rural suburbanization. Each of these developments played a significant part in the revitalization of many, though not yet a majority, of English villages by the time war broke out again in 1939.

Prominent in this revitalization was the emergence of several new village trades, each of them stimulated by the technological and social changes of the inter-war years. With the numbers of private cars on British roads rising from just 109,000 in 1919 to the million mark in 1931 and over two million in 1939,[11] the motor car was arguably the most important single influence, creating promising opportunities for such new enterprises as petrol stations, repair garages, fruit and flower selling and countryside tea rooms. For the latter, the spread of bus services and the increasing popularity of charabanc outings provided additional custom, as did the growth of cycling and organized 'rambling'. This upsurge in mass outdoor leisure and exploration of rural Britain – what the philosopher and ramblers' spokesman C. E. M. Joad disparaged as 'the untutored townsman's invasion of the country'[12] – also rescued many a struggling village publican whose trade had been falling away as a consequence of rural depopulation and demographic ageing. The 'outdoors movement' and the increasingly popular craze for 'discovering England' also breathed some fresh life into those village shops whose owners were prepared to respond to the new potential by selling such wares as ice-cream, souvenirs, local guidebooks and picture postcards.

Another stimulus for the nurturing of new village enterprises came from the Rural Industries Bureau (RIB), an institution that was set up by the Ministry of Agriculture and Fisheries in 1921 principally to encourage the revival of village crafts and workshop industries. Influenced by the broader messages of the Arts and Crafts movement which saw such a revival as a vital step in the restoration of villages once again as organic folk communities, the RIB provided technical and advisory services for small endogenous entrepreneurs and showed how surviving craftsmen could stay in business by diversifying their operations and adapting to modern technology. Perhaps its most noteworthy achievement was the support given to blacksmiths and wheelwrights, two very old village crafts that had been losing out through their inability to compete with engineering factories or to come to terms with the declining use of horses and horse-drawn vehicles. The RIB promoted new skills here, in particular the application of electrical power to arc welding and machine-tool work. In the 1920s and 1930s several new outlets for blacksmiths and wheelwrights emerged, the most important of which were the servicing of tractors and the repairing of bicycles, motorbikes, and motor cars. In turning to these new activities, many blacksmiths and wheelwrights, particularly in villages that lay astride a main road, converted their antiquated premises into makeshift garages and repair shops. In these, and similarly in the hundreds of small building firms and road-haulage businesses that were established by village carpenters and carters, one can see an interesting evolutionary link between tradition and modernity.

Reversal of several decades of economic and demographic decline depended very much upon whether or not a village became equipped with modern infrastructure. Until the 1930s, most villages were without piped water and lacked mains electricity, telephone lines and a proper system of sewage disposal. Pumps, wells, water carts, earth closets and oil lamps were still normal, if rarely publicized, features of daily life in village

Plate 14: Blacksmith's workshop and inter-war garage, Binbrook, Lincolnshire. A new village trade emerging from an old village craft. The nineteenth-century blacksmith's and wheelwright's workshop is now derelict: the garage next door was constructed in the 1930s and has seen little alteration since. In pre-war times buildings like the latter were widely condemned by rural preservationists.

England. Provision of public infrastructure was a principal function of the Rural District councils, especially after the 1933 Local Government Act which enhanced their powers for this and granted them larger financial resources. Following this Act, there began a wave of infrastructure investment in rural England which continued until the outbreak of the Second World War. However, much the greater part of this was focused on the largest and the most accessible villages, leaving countless numbers of more remote and smaller settlements, including many picturesque close villages, still unsupplied. Indeed, the 'Scott Report' in 1942 indicated that one out of every three villages in England was still without any piped water, and only one-quarter of farms were connected to mains electricity.[13] Two years later, the Agricultural Economics Research Institute, in a comprehensive survey of a rural area in the Oxfordshire Cotswolds, reported in more detail:

> Houses themselves are too often damp, dark, ill ventilated and ill found. Piped water is almost unknown in most cottages, and in hundreds of villages there are no supplies even to stand-pipes in the streets. It follows, of course, that internal sanitation and arrangements for sewage disposal are equally rare. Slops are emptied in the garden, baths are non-existent, and the outside privy-vault is universal.[14]

The inter-war period with its new spirit of rural self-help saw a nation-wide enthusiasm for constructing village or parish halls; institutions which played an important role in resuscitating thousands of rural communities and broadening their way of life. The 'parish hall movement' of the 1920s and 1930s, however, was not an outcome of active state involvement, though the governments of the day were certainly concerned about the backward condition of rural Britain and were well aware of the need for its social as well as its economic reinvigoration. Some halls, mostly in close villages, where a surviving squire or a larger landowner had provided generous financial backing and had perhaps also paid for the services of a professional architect, were built to a high standard and blended in with the existing building-fabric. Most, however, were assembled through collective initiative and voluntary labour. Much of the money needed for the purchase of building materials, internal fittings and furnishing was raised from local collections and individual donations, whilst welcome assistance could be provided by the National Council of Social Service and its affiliated, county-based, Rural Community Councils. These bodies offered advice on the construction of the halls, and administered small grants and interest-free loans from such fund-donating bodies as the Rural Development Commission and the Carnegie Trust. The first Rural Community Council was formed in Oxfordshire in 1921, and, by 1934, they had been set up in thirty-five English counties.[15] Their main aims were to infuse new life into villages and to recreate something of their old community spirit. However, in supporting the parish hall movement, the Community Councils unintentionally also contributed to the final eclipse of the church and the chapel as the principal gathering points of English village life.

Unlike the parish halls founded by a landowner or some other wealthy personage, those that were established through community self-help often had to be built under the tightest of budgets. This was necessitated by the smallness of their financial resources, but perhaps it was also a reflection of an underlying lack of rural confidence at the time of their construction. Although there has been a trend towards improvement and gentrification in recent years, many inter-war parish halls have yet to be treated and have retained their original corrugated iron, timber or prefabricated concrete walls and their plain interiors. Whereas the church and the chapel had been the normal meeting places for most inhabitants of Victorian and Edwardian village England, it was unpretentious buildings like these, with their growing range of communal activities, that became the new 'headquarters' of rural life as the twentieth century moved into its second quarter. It is in these and in the other, less utilitarian, types of parish halls where the parish council, the scouts and guides, the Women's Institute, the drama club and the youth club still regularly meet; and it is here too where events such as village dances, vegetable and flower shows, jumble sales, Christmas parties, adult education classes and amateur dramatics have always been held.

Some further broadening of the scope of village life, particularly for the younger generation, came with the rise of organized village sports and games. One stimulus for this was the nationwide 'fitness campaign', or 'National Efficiency' drive, which had stemmed from the recruitment reports of the First World War and official concern over the physical inadequacy of much of the nation's future military and economic manpower resources. Another stimulus came in 1919, with the introduction of a Saturday half-day off for agricultural workers, giving them more time to play football in the winter months and cricket in the summer. Further encouragement for village sports came from the Rural Community Councils which provided funds for acquiring playing fields and the construction of simple pavilions. Organized village football and cricket, and greater participation in them, helped to widen horizons. With the formation of 'district' and 'county' leagues in the 1920s and 1930s, closer links were forged with neighbouring rural communities, and contacts were made with some of the more distant villages and market towns.

Plate 15: Inter-war village halls. Village or 'parish' halls played an important part in the reinvigoration of rural life in the inter-war years. In most villages they were built through communal self-help, usually with very limited funding. Two typical examples are shown here: in the upper photograph, a makeshift corrugated iron structure; in the lower photograph, a wooden hut placed upon brick and concrete supports. Both types are now beginning to disappear as one by one they are pulled down and replaced by more substantial and more comfortable buildings.

A very noticeable and widely criticized addition to the landscape of most English villages in the inter-war years was the advent of rural council housing. The Tudor Walters Report in 1918 and the Addison Housing Act in 1919 had set the stage for the nation's first large-scale programme of council-house construction. However, for several years this was almost wholly urban in application. In rural Britain, where farm workers and their families still predominated in many localities, authorities were reluctant to undertake the building of dwellings for households whose low incomes meant that there was little chance of them being able to pay an 'economic' rent. Accordingly, until the late 1930s, few villages were allocated anything more than just a handful of council houses. Indeed, for much of the inter-war period, rural housing policy in several counties and in many Rural Districts continued to place more faith and resources on the provision of smallholder dwellings and (under the terms of the 1926 Housing of Rural Workers Act) giving subsidies for property owners to recondition old cottages that were judged not bad enough for pulling down but fell some way short of an adequate standard of habitability. The turning point eventually came with a further piece of housing legislation, the National Government's Housing Act of 1936, which offered rural local authorities subsidies of up to 80 per cent on the costs of constructing new homes for agricultural workers. This Act was followed by a higher incidence of rural slum clearances, nearly all of which were in open villages and in the courts and back streets of countryside towns. However, it also led to the removal of many run-down but, nonetheless, historically valued old cottages. Such actions provoked strong reproach from preservationists and ruralist writers who saw them only as acts of 'state vandalism' and bureaucratic insensitivity.

> ... old houses and cottages in the villages are diminishing rapidly. A heritage of unique value is in danger of being destroyed. Modern acts and by-laws, and the interpretation of them, weigh heavily against the preservation of work which, of its kind, is not likely to be equalled again.
>
> (Sidney Jones, *English Village Homes*, 1936)[16]

By 1939, some 159,000 council homes had been constructed in the Rural Districts of England and Wales, most of them coming after the 1936 Housing Act.[17] The earliest rural council housing took the form of small-scale development within the core of the village, often on or adjoining the sites of the first cottage clearances. After 1936, however, it became more usual for new council housing to be built on the periphery of the village either in standard terrace blocks of four to six dwellings, or as semi-detached housing grouped around a short cul-de-sac access street. The Agricultural Economics Research Institute in its 1944 treatise, *Coun-*

Plate 16: Sydling St Nicholas, Dorset. An interesting group of cottages: in the centre, a craftsman's cottage and workshop; on the left, an example of traditional Dorset thatching and chalk-with-flint walling; and, on the right, a pair of labourers' cottages, reconditioned after the 1926 Housing of Rural Workers Act.

try Planning, described such developments as 'council colonies' – a fitting reference both to their peripheral position and their intrusive appearance. It went on to declare:

> The common practice ... is to select sites on the edges of villages – a field, or the village allotments – upon which to execute their housing schemes. The new houses, raw as most new houses must be, stand out stark and staring on the bare site, with no setting, no background, their gardens mere pieces of land fenced off from the field, without a tree or a bush or even a hedgerow to suggest a natural boundary. Inevitably, the new houses are the most remote from the shops, inns, schools, and places of worship.[18]

This type of development became the norm for open villages in the late 1930s and again in the next surge in rural council housing construction that began soon after the Second World War. Though village council estates are usually very modest in scale when compared with their urban counterparts, the style of building and the internal standards of comfort are not dissimilar. Despite the characterless appearance and peripheral positions of most post-1936 rural council dwellings, they were certainly popular as far as their first occupants were concerned. With their minimum of 750 square feet (70 square metres) of living space and their standard three bedrooms, bathroom, living room, kitchen-cum-scullery, and internal toilet, the new homes were in all material respects a great improvement on the crowded, damp and often insanitary cottages in which rural working-class families had had to spend their lives in former times. Moreover, the rents were unlikely to be raised unreasonably, and households, unless they fell into serious arrears, were at long last able to enjoy some security of tenure.

Very little inter-war council housing was built in the close villages where in many cases landowners were still able to oppose anything that smacked of modernization and extra expense. Most of them also saw it as a threat upon the visual qualities and social virtues of their charming, well-kept villages; and there was the additional burden on the rates to consider too. For these reasons landowners, with some exceptions, actively opposed the construction of council homes within their own parishes and demonstrated an unwillingness to part with land for this purpose. Those who eventually did permit council houses to be built usually insisted that this was to be modest in scale, discretely positioned and did not infringe upon the aesthetic quality of the village. To ensure such demands were properly met some landowners managed to persuade the Rural District council to consult with a panel of architects operating under the auspices of the Council for the Preservation of Rural England.

Village England and Inter-War Suburbanization

Suburbanization of village England – the conversion of former agricultural communities into residential 'dormitories' – has a long history, going back far into the nineteenth century in London's rural fringes and in such popular scenic areas and middle-class retirement retreats as the Sussex coast, the Windermere–Grasmere area of the Lake District, and the Berkshire and Buckinghamshire stretches of the Thames valley. By the early years of the twentieth century, in the Home Counties and within reach of the largest provincial cities it was beginning to spread out over wider areas, transforming village landscapes and challenging traditional rural values. A graphic illustration of the process is contained in George Sturt's *Change in the Village* in which the author, the son of a village wheelwright, described what was happening in the countryside to the south of Farnham on the edge of the Surrey Weald. Here, some thirty miles away from the centre of London (but within walking distance of a mainline railway station), suburbanization was already fairly well entrenched by the time he began writing this book, a few years before the outbreak of the First World War. Rustic cottages and old farmhouses were being 'snapped up' and occupied by affluent city incomers, whilst speculative new residential development for weekday railway commuters was becoming a familiar sight. As was happening elsewhere in the Home Counties, the new suburban housing was spreading over former common land and heathland which in living memory had succumbed to the final 'mopping up' phase of parliamentary enclosure. Sturt describes the scene:

> And now, during the last ten years, a yet greater change has been going on. The valley has been 'discovered' as a 'residential centre'. ... No sooner was a good water-supply available than speculating architects and builders began to buy up vacant plots of land, or even cottages – it mattered little which – and what never was strictly speaking a village is at last ceasing even to think itself one. The population of some five hundred twenty years ago has increased to over two thousand; the final shabby patches of the old heath are disappearing; on all hands glimpses of new building and raw new roads defy you to persuade yourself that you are in a country place.[19]

Fuelled by the widening rural aspirations of the urban middle classes, increasing car-ownership, and cheaper and speedier public transport (including the expansion of electric train services in London's 'Metroland'), the suburbanization process quickly grew in strength after the First World War. In the intercensal decade of 1921–31 several counties, in addition to the Home Counties, recorded fairly substantial increases in their rural populations, despite the return of agricultural depression and further depletion of the agricultural workforce. Reversal of rural

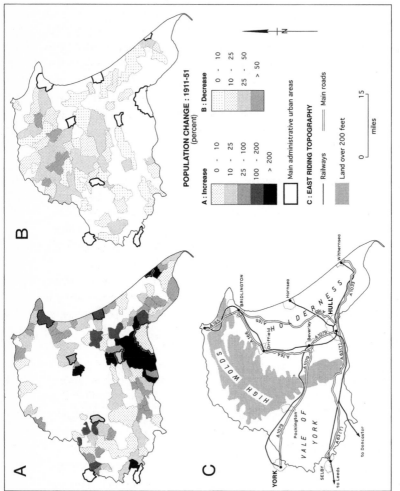

Figure 6: Population change in the parishes of Yorkshire East Riding, 1911–51. Map A shows parishes which recorded increases in numbers of inhabitants; Map B shows those which recorded decreases; and Map C shows the railways and main roads as they existed in 1951. Maps A and B are based on the parish population counts published in the East Riding county volumes of the 1911 and the 1951 census.

depopulation became more widespread after 1931, although it was not until after the Second World War that population growth took place in a *majority* of Rural Districts, including some that were a quite considerable distance away from a city or large town. Within each rural county there emerged a patchwork pattern of demographic revival in some parishes and ongoing decline in others. This is illustrated in the example of the East Riding of Yorkshire, which is presented in Figure 6. The East Riding was one of several administrative counties to have experienced an upturn in rural population in the 1920s, following more than half a century of decline.[20] However, as elsewhere in rural England, there was a wide range of local trends. Between 1911 and 1951 (there was no census in 1941) some parishes recorded a doubling or even a trebling of population, but many endured continued demographic stagnation, with several suffering a heavy loss. As the first map (Map A) in Figure 6 shows, the population upturn was the strongest and the most extensive within the vicinity of Hull, east Yorkshire's single major urban centre. Elsewhere the distribution of parishes in which population growth occurred is much more patchy, and is complicated by the existence of several small towns dotted randomly within the East Riding countryside. The largest of these – Beverley ten miles to the north-west of Hull, Driffield in the centre of the county and Bridlington on the coast – were expanding with enough momentum to exert their own localized suburban effects within adjoining parishes. A number of 'growth' parishes, however, do appear beyond the environs of Hull and other urban centres, mostly in linear groupings astride one or other of the main transport axes leading out from the port city. The most continuous of these can be seen extending westwards, following the A63 trunk road and the mainline Hull–Leeds railway; and another is quite easily identifiable, stretching between Hull and York where the Hull–Beverley–York railway and the A1079 had stimulated the revival of several decaying villages. A third line of 'growth' parishes had emerged along the coast. Some of these were experiencing population increases as a consequence of the residential development of a nearby coastal resort spreading across the parish boundary. Others, however, were gaining population through the erection of plotland settlements – clusters of makeshift shacks and huts that were springing up in many places in coastal England in the inter-war years.

Nevertheless, more than half of the parishes and villages in the East Riding of Yorkshire experienced continuance of population decline between 1911 and 1951. As the second map (Map B) shows, the most extensive area of this depopulation, including some parishes that suffered more than a halving of numbers of inhabitants, was in the High Wolds in the higher and remoter northern and central parts of the county. Agricultural depression was particularly severe here, since each village community was still heavily dependent upon agricultural employment, with capital-intensive wheat and barley cultivation dominating the farming economy. However, notwithstanding the demographic consequences of agricultural depression and of machines displacing manual labour, it was more the isolation of the High Wolds villages – most of them situated off the beaten track and well out of reach of suburbanization – that accounts for the persistence of heavy depopulation here throughout the period. Elsewhere in the East Riding, rural depopulation was also prevalent in the Vale of York in the west of the county and in the Holderness plain in the south-east. Here, as in the High Wolds, most of the depopulating parishes were in out of the way locations, away from any transport artery and any positive urban influences.

The inter-war period saw the construction of 865,000 new dwellings in rural England and Wales, of which 706,000 or 82 per cent were owner-occupied.[21] To provide the space for all this development, conversion of agricultural land accelerated sharply, with yearly acreages of new building averaging around 30,000 (12,000 hectares) between 1918 and 1939, and reaching as much as 60,000 (24,000 hectares) in the housing boom of 1936–9 at the end of the period.[22] Interestingly, the latter figure measures an intensity of rural suburbanization that has never since been surpassed. In the sphere of private housing, speculative building dominated, assisted by the cheapness of rural land and its easy availability. The virtual absence of planning controls in rural areas and the prevalence of small builders with little capital meant piecemeal development, some of it taking the form of sporadic infilling of vacant plots inside villages, but most of it materializing as disorderly, straggling settlements or 'ribbons' alongside any road that led towards a sizeable urban centre or a railway halt. Because of its disorganized and 'restless' appearance, ribbon development was widely condemned by inter-war preservationists and town and country planners such as Clough Williams-Ellis, Patrick Abercrombie and Thomas Sharp, who saw it not only as a growing threat upon the rural landscape but also to be entirely out of keeping with the cohesive and 'enclosed nature' of the traditional English village. Ribbon development, however, was certainly the cheapest and the most convenient means of providing new suburban houses with direct access to a transport route for car and bus travel. Moreover, in rural areas the verges of main roads entering and leaving villages were now being used for the first lines of modern infrastructure, which made it easy and inexpensive to connect ribbon housing to existing electricity and water mains and to equip it

Plate 17: Inter-war 'ribbon development' between Hull and Beverley. Note the typical straggling form, the housing diversity and, for some of the dwellings, the croft-like gardens. Ribbon development was much criticized by inter-war preservationists and town and country planners, but it offered house buyers a front view facing the way into a town or a city, and a rear view of open country-side. In this part of east Yorkshire this open countryside contains a scattering of market gardens and smallholdings, most of which were established on former cereal-growing land abandoned during the worst years of the Great Agricultural Depression. With kind permission from Getmapping plc.

with up-to-date sewage disposal. Such sites also offered two comforting vistas – the best of both worlds – for the house buyers: a front view facing the road and the way into the town or city; and a rear view of open countryside, reassuring occupants that they had indeed achieved their ambition of living in rural Arcadia. The reasons for the popularity of ribbon development, both from the speculators' and the residents' points of view, are ably summarized by the architectural historian Arthur Edwards in his *The Design of Suburbia*:

> Ribbon-development was, however, the natural consequence of motor-transport, of a depressed agriculture, and of weak planning control. To the farmer, bungalows were often a more profitable crop than corn. For the developer, it was often easier to build along an existing highway than to lay out roads of a new estate. To the householder, ribbon-development seemed to provide the ideal combination, easy access at the front and a view over open countryside at the back.[23]

Within the ribbons the new housing was typically heterogeneous, reflecting the multiplicity of individual tastes, lifestyle aspirations, and income levels of inter-war England. The rather modest 'pyramid roof' bungalow (denounced as a foreign import by some of its many critics) was ubiquitous, whilst 'mock Tudor' and 'Tudorbethan' detached and semi-detached houses of various qualities and sizes were also widespread, especially in the affluent Home Counties and around the prosperous midlands cities of Birmingham, Nottingham and Coventry. The reinvention of Tudor and Elizabethan domestic architecture, which is very much an identifying characteristic of inter-war private suburbia, had its roots in the late nineteenth- and early twentieth-century vernacular revival and 'Olde English' style made fashionable by such prominent architects as Norman Shaw, C. F. A. Voysey and Edwin Lutyens. The larger and more expensive versions of Tudorbethan houses, with their steeply pitched roofs, tall chimneys, sweeping gables, and black and white half-timbering, were indeed suburban replicas of rustic manor houses and yeomen's farms in which imitations of traditional materials and craftsmanship, such as leaded window lights, 'blacksmith' ironwork and 'Colly Weston' tiles, had stemmed from the popular appeal of the Arts and Crafts movement. In contrast, the domestic architecture of the inter-war 'modern movement', with its flat roofs, horizontal lines, steel-framed windows, white concrete walls and conspicuously positioned garages, found little acceptance as a style appropriate to rural-suburban life. Thus, despite its wide publicity in the housing and architectural manuals of the day and its strong influence on the design of new offices, railway stations, cinemas and blocks of flats,[24] this particular architectural fashion made only a sporadic and subdued appearance outside urban Britain.

The larger ribbons – those that stretched from the edges of cities and large towns to the nearest villages – consisted of more than just housing development. As Thomas Sharp described in his *Town and Countryside*, published in 1932, they contained a 'semi-suburbia of personal houses, poultry farms, refreshment shacks, petrol stations, wide roads, and linking wires that stretch from pole to pole'.[25] Moreover, by the 1930s, suburbanization of the countryside and village England was not limited to the accessible parts of the Home Counties, the environs of the big cities, and the more sought-after of rural retirement havens. It was now (as we have seen in east Yorkshire) encroaching along certain coastlines and around smaller urban centres. John Moore, in the same bird's-eye view in which he had observed the 'whittling away' of a landed estate, could observe the effects of rural suburbanization even in the Cotswolds and the Vale of Evesham some considerable distance away from any large city: 'I could see the towns and even some of the villages nibbling their way outwards, not wisely and orderly, but as haphazard and casually as caterpillars nibbling at a leaf; I could see the mess creeping along the sides of all the roads that radiated from the [market] towns.'[26]

Despite the protestations of writers such as Thomas Sharp and John Moore, 'suburban sprawl', with its intrusive ribbons, bungalows and pseudo Tudorbethan housing, had been imposed upon only a minority of villages when the outbreak of the Second World War brought a sudden halt to the entire process. With very few exceptions, these were the larger and the most conveniently located of rural settlements, especially ones that had been amongst the first to have acquired modern infrastructure. From the outset, open villages were much more likely to experience suburban development than were the still fairly substantial numbers of close villages, although the selling of tied cottages in the latter often led to abrupt social change as wealthy incomers quickly arrived and displaced the former occupants.

To rural preservationists – the growing body of people who became involved in trying to prevent what they thought would eventually become a universal defacement of the rural landscape – the inter-war period was a time of ever-widening threats and pressures upon the countryside and its villages and hamlets. The assault, driven by the forces of modernity and the 'new metal age', seemed to be coming from every direction, and, unless the state took firm action, was unstoppable. That it was taking place in an age when rural depopulation still prevailed in many areas and the old rural way of life had become no more than a folk memory, could only deepen their mood of pessimism and alarm. The countryside and its charming sleepy villages were being invaded by strangers – 'townsmen' – who brought with them alien forms of behaviour, disturbed rural tranquillity and quietness, and undermined traditional rustic values. Above everything else there was the rising spectre of the suburban 'beast' and the dismal prospect of a 'ruination' of rural England well beyond the vicinities of town and suburb. The architect Clough Williams-Ellis, author of *England and the Octopus* and editor of *Britain and the Beast*, described it all as 'a planless scramble';[27] and C. E. M. Joad, one of the most outspoken defenders of the countryside, looked out in horror over 'a ravished landscape'.[28] Moreover, much of the destruction of the countryside was happening within parts of Deep and 'Deepest' England – the Thames valley, the Chiltern hills, the Sussex coast and rural Warwickshire and Worcestershire – just where it could cause the greatest harm. Witnessing what was happening in areas like these, Massingham saw the connection between the long-term 'internal decay' of rural England and the whole modernization process: '… it expels the native population, pulls down its cottages or puts them in fancy-dress, builds houses of its own as characterless and innocent of design as are all its acts, debases the neighbouring countryside and suppresses its crafts and husbandry.'[29] Similar thoughts are expressed in J. B. Priestley's conclusion (warningly carrying the heading 'Britain is in Danger') to an anthology entitled *Our Nation's Heritage* and written just before the outbreak of the Second World War. In it he wrote: 'It took centuries of honest workmanship and loving craftsmanship to create the England that was renowned for its charm and delicate beauty. In twenty years we have completely ruined at least half of that England.'[30] Priestley here was blaming rural suburbanization not only for destroying much of the English countryside, but also for offending against what, in the insular spirit of the late 1930s, had emerged as a predominantly *rural* national identity, cultivated largely from idealized images of rural life and reassuring visions of timeless village scenes. With the clouds of war once again looming large, he, along with many other writers and broadcasters of his generation, regarded the suburban tide as unpatriotic; a sort of 'enemy within' and an act of national vandalism that could be compared with the huge might of the Luftwaffe in its destructive capacity. Not only was suburbanization reaching further and further into the countryside and devastating more and more of the rural landscape, it was also causing irretrievable damage to village culture, breaking down all that was left of traditional rural virtues and indeed undermining what to many people had become the metaphorical embodiment of 'Englishness' and national character. Priestley and other preservationist writers, however, had nothing to say about the positive benefits that rural suburbanization might bring for native villagers; in particular the welcome, if poorly paid, new employment opportunities that it could offer to the menfolk as gardeners, chauffeurs, house decorators and building workers, and to the womenfolk as house cleaners, nursemaids and child minders.

Many preservationists were unable to conceal their contempt for unchecked private enterprise and those people – the bungalow owner, the garage proprietor, the poultry farmer and the demonic 'jerry-builder' – whom they deemed most responsible for the desecration. The farmer and novelist A. G. Street spoke for most ruralists when he rebuked the unthinking townsman: 'In his desire to get away from his hideous town and live in more pleasant surroundings he has let loose a swarm of red brick and drab concrete locusts, which has spread over thousands of acres of God's own England and destroyed all the beauty and charm which once graced them.'[31] In a similar tone Thomas Sharp pointed his finger at the 'little' man and his seemingly unrestricted freedom to live more or less wherever he pleased: 'Every little owner of every little bungalow in every roadside ribbon thinks he is living in Merrie England because he has those "roses round the door" and because he has sweet-williams and Michaelmas-daisies in his front garden.'[32] According to the planning historian, John Punter, what was really at stake in reproaches like these was the threat that widening suburbia and mass enjoyment of the countryside presented to the 'culturally selfish' – those privileged and well-off people who, in terms of where they lived and where they spent their leisure, were already 'in possession' of rural Britain.[33] Viewed in this light, the 'defence' of the English countryside may be seen as a class resistance.

As the inter-war period unfolded, countryside preservationists were confronted with a lengthening list of 'outrages' and 'national disgraces'. Suburbanization, with its ugly ribbons and intrusive bungalows continued to be the prime concern, but other 'horrors' were making their presence felt and were seen to be contributing to the ruination of the rural landscape. Roadside petrol stations and garages, many of which had evolved from a blacksmith's or a wheelwright's workshop, were strongly condemned. Clough Williams-Ellis, betraying a distaste too for the economic opportunism of their owners, described their motley enamel advertisements and unsightly concrete or corrugated-iron sheds as 'bludgeoning importunity' and 'destroyers of highway amenity'.[34] Market gardens and poultry farms, two of the much-needed new directions in British farming during the long period of agricultural depression, were likewise widely disparaged. John Moore, having observed the disorderly scattering of market gardens along the northern edge of the Cotswolds where the Jurassic escarpment eases out onto the Vale of Evesham, claimed that these 'can devastate a beautiful landscape as thoroughly as a mushroom suburb', and complained about their owners having a tendency to 'erect horrible little sheds and shelters at the sides of the roads and stick up scrawled notice boards about the price of asparagus or plums.'[35]

Electricity power-lines carried by 'arms-stretched, steel giants' – in rural Britain the most striking of all monuments to inter-war modernity – began to stride across the countryside soon after the Electricity Supply Act of 1919 gave the go-ahead for the construction of a national transmission grid. S. P. B. Mais, a prolific writer of topographic and 'open air' books, described them as sprawling 'wantonly across our noblest landscape like a lunatic's slashings across the face of an old master'.[36] Noise too was seen as a growing menace, especially at weekends when in many places the traditional tranquillity and quietude of the countryside and its peaceful villages were often rudely disturbed by loud and unfamiliar noises. The chugging and grinding of motor-car engines could be heard along every main road; speedboats roared across beautiful lakes such as Windermere and Coniston; parties of ramblers sang lustily as they tramped across the hills and meadows; and people on charabanc outings, with their blaring gramophones and radio sets, congregated on many a village green or outside many a village pub. Thomas Sharp gloomily predicted that rural England, whose 'essential silence is already broken by the roar of motor traffic, by speed boats on rivers and lakes, by mechanical music from gramophone and portable radio, and by the personal music of exuberant hikers', was about to receive 'the full fury of the horror'.[37]

Plotland Settlements

To some preservationists the most offensive spectacle of all was the eruption of 'plotland' settlements, most commonly on the cliff tops and shingle shores of coastal England, but also appearing inland on river banks, in secluded chalk denes and along the margins of woodlands and heaths. Sites for such settlements were easily acquired by speculators, able to take advantage of depressed prices of agricultural land and the absence of planning controls. The land was then divided into small rectangular or square plots that, after they had been advertised, were sold off randomly to individuals who were left free to develop them according to their own particular aspirations and resources. The purchasers, or 'plotlanders', came from various walks of life: they included ex-servicemen, actors and actresses, 'Bohemians', unmarried mothers, casual workers, the unemployed and people seeking recuperation from respiratory diseases such as bronchitis and tuberculosis. What these people all had in common, however, were their urban roots, their low incomes and a yearning for a simple and healthier life. As Denis Hardy and Colin Ward, the co-authors of *Arcadia for All?*, concluded: 'It was from the growing pool of the economically disadvantaged, sharing the desires of the period for holidays and outings, but who were unable to buy a villa or stay in a boarding house, that many of the plotlanders emerged.'[38] Plotland settlements, therefore, provided an opportunity for the urban poor to take their own place in the sun and in rural Arcadia, at first just at weekends and holiday times, but later more commonly as permanent places to live. Some plotlanders perhaps were also guided by deeper, subconscious motivations: a primitive impulse to claim back just a tiny piece of what had been taken from their forefathers by parliamentary enclosure; a reassertion of the ancient squatting tradition; and a rediscovery of peasant proprietorship in what the social historian John Lowerson has described as 'a half-remembered countryside'.[39]

Plotland development became instantly recognizable as a ramshackle landscape, 'put together on the cheap ... a colourful kaleidoscope of shacks and shanties'.[40] Each settlement contained a curious collection of personalized 'architecture' – a clear reflection of the plotlanders' freedom and spirit of independence. Very typically the plotland landscape consisted of cheap, improvised dwellings, including 'army surplus' huts, old railway carriages, converted buses and 'kit-built' wooden chalets. More often than not these makeshift homes were painted in the brightest of colours, with pink, primrose yellow and sea blue predominating; and the cheapest of building materials were used, especially asbestos, corrugated iron, plywood and old railway sleepers. As far as public utilities were concerned, plotland settlements were usually ignored by local authorities until after the Second World War. For a long period, indeed until quite recently in many cases, they were without mains electricity and street lighting: many too lacked a sewer-line and were considered to be a threat to public health. Access lanes and streets were rarely surfaced, most of them quickly degenerating into rutted, mud-filled tracks; and access to essential services, such as schooling, a food shop and a doctor's surgery or a health clinic, very often involved a bus journey or a time-consuming walk to and from the nearest 'proper' village or small town.

No assessment has ever been made of the total numbers of plotland dwellings that were built in rural England between the two wars. Though some settlements, such as Peacehaven on the Sussex coast, the Isle of Sheppey in Kent, and the Essex plotland communities of Canvey Island,

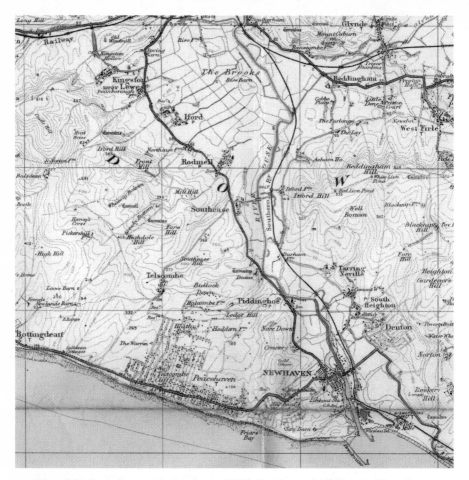

Plate 18: Peacehaven plotlands, *c.* **1935.** By the mid-1930s, the Peacehaven plotlands had become one of the largest and the most maligned of inter-war plotland settlements. Perched on top of the symbolic Sussex white cliffs and stretching for nearly three miles on either side of the Newhaven–Rottingdean main road, they formed a stark contrast with nearby 'normal' villages and hamlets such as Telscombe, Southease and Piddinghoe. Anarchistic settlements like Peacehaven were seen to be despoiling many rural localities prior to the Second World War and the 1947 Town and Country Planning Act.

Reproduced from Ordnance Survey, One Inch to the Mile, *Revised Popular* edition, sheet 134, published in 1935.

Pitsea and Jaywick Sands, may well have had upwards of 2,000 shacks, huts and self-built chalets in their heyday, it is unlikely that any nation-wide figure would have been much greater than 100,000 or around one-eighth of all new rural dwellings in this period. Yet, despite its fairly modest quantity, plotland development (and in some instances the plotlanders and their unconventional lifestyles too) provoked a dis-proportionately large outcry from rural preservationists and members of the growing profession of town and country planning. Mais, alarmed at its intrusion into some of the choicest spots in south-east England, described plotland dwellings as 'hideous shacks, thrown haphazard like splodges of mud';[41] and Joad, who kept coming across them on his countryside rambles in the Home Counties and elsewhere, saw them as the very worst excesses in a general process of rural desecration. At Mar-low Bottom, where one of the Chiltern chalk denes opens out into the Thames valley, Joad observed a typical scene: 'To my horror I found not an empty valley but a muddy road running through an avenue of shacks, caravans, villas, bungalows, mock castles, pigsties, disused railway car-riages and derelict buses, scattered higgledy-piggledy over the largest possible area of the Chiltern hillsides.'[42] It was, however, the 'shanty town' of Peacehaven, perched for all to see on top one of the most scenic and symbolic stretches of the nation's natural defences – the Sussex 'white cliffs' towering above the English Channel between Newhaven and Rot-tingdean (see Plate 18) – that came in for the strongest condemnation. Sharp called Peacehaven 'a national laughing stock',[43] whilst the broad-caster Howard Marshall went even further, describing it as 'a monstrous blot on the national consciousness'.[44]

Denouncements like these went beyond expressions of outrage against specific disfigurements of the rural landscape. Plotland settlements, wher-ever they existed, were regarded as nightmarish places that only the 'arch-fiend' speculator could devise and only the townsman could inhabit or spend his holidays and weekends. In all respects they stood out as the very antithesis of normal, old-fashioned, village England and the values that it represented. Plotland complexes were ephemeral, unsightly, anar-chistic, and an affront to good taste: in complete contrast, the long-established English village, despite several decades of depopulation and an increasing momentum of social and cultural change, was still seen as ancient, cohesive and aesthetically correct.

Most plotland settlements reached their fullest size during the darkest days of the Second World War when their resident populations were heavily swollen by friends and relatives seeking refuge from the blitzing of cities such as London, Southampton, Bristol, Plymouth, Hull and

Plate 19: Plotland dwellings, Humberstone Fitties, Lincolnshire. The two wooden chalets shown here are of better quality than most plotland dwellings, and have survived the test of time. Their self-built structures and use of cheap building materials are clearly in evidence, as is the small size of the individual plotland spaces.

Liverpool. Since then, many plotland landscapes have disappeared or have changed nearly beyond all recognition. Some were taken over by the military to be incorporated into coastal artillery or bombing ranges; some were devastated by 'act of God' in the form of the east coast floods of January 1953; and, more recently, a number (including parts of Peacehaven) have been subjected to gentrification by their owners or in conjunction with a local-authority improvement scheme.

Defending Village England

The protection of rural England and its villages, however, needed much more than aggressive rhetoric and denigration: it required a national mood for countryside preservation and active intervention from the state. Some paving of the way for this had been made in the latter part of the nineteenth century, with the formation of the Commons, Open Spaces and Footpaths Preservation Society (subsequently shortened to the Commons Society) in 1865 and, twelve years later, the creation of the Society for the Protection of Ancient Buildings. The former, which sought to prevent the enclosure and loss to the nation of its last surviving commons, heaths and ancient forests, had some notable successes, especially in the strongly contested countryside of southern and south-eastern England. These, as well as the famed 'saving' of the New Forest, Epping Forest and Hampstead Heath, included the less well-known preservation of Berkhamsted Common in the Chilterns, Chobham Common in Surrey and parts of Ashdown Forest in the Sussex Weald. The Society for the Protection of Ancient Buildings, founded by William Morris who served as secretary in its early years, pressed the government into passing the Ancient Monuments Act of 1913. Designed to protect the country's rich heritage of ancient buildings and archaeological relics, this Act established a national 'Office of Public Works' with the authority to designate specific sites and to enforce Preservation Orders upon them and their immediate surrounds. Amongst its early designations were Stonehenge and the Avebury Circle in Wiltshire, Maiden Castle in Dorset and some of the most impressive sections of Hadrian's Wall in Northumberland. The list was periodically lengthened and, by 1933, as many as 273 ancient sites and around 3,000 historic buildings were included. However, this still left hundreds of less valued sites – lynchets, round barrows and the smaller Iron Age hill-forts – vulnerable to tractor ploughing, Forestry Commission tree planting and construction of military airfields.

Another preservationist institution which dates back to the late nine-teenth century is the National Trust or, to give it its full title, The National Trust for Places of Historic Interest or Natural Beauty. Founded by Octavia Hill in 1895 and incorporated by Act of Parliament in 1907, this organization was constituted to serve as a custodian for places of high scenic value and for buildings of national cultural importance. Land and buildings bequeathed to the Trust and made accessible to the public carried exemption from inheritance taxes, a concession which encouraged many landowners to hand over parts or all of their properties. By 1938, the Trust held nearly 300 separate estates, covering a total area of 46,000 acres (18,600 hectares) and comprising diversely of parklands, wood-lands, historic buildings, stately homes, coastal headlands, hilltop viewpoints, ancient sites and places of strong literary interest. Seven years later, at the end of the Second World War, the extent of its holdings had risen to 110,000 acres (44,500 hectares), with a further 40,000 acres (16,200 hectares) of properties being guarded by restrictive Trust cove-nants.[45] By then, the neat, green and grey 'oak leaves' signs of the National Trust had become familiar sights in rural England, although the regional distribution of acquisitions was very uneven. As is still the case today, they were generally fairly thin on the ground in north-east England and in the rather unremarkable countryside of the east midlands and the fenlands; but they were strongly represented within the more scenic and heritage-rich areas, especially the Lake District (the spiritual home of the English Romantic movement), the Cotswolds, the Peak District, the North Downs and, forestalling such disfiguring development as plotland settlements and holiday camps, the coastal headlands of Devon and Cornwall.

However, whilst such voluntary bodies as the Commons Society, the Society for the Protection of Ancient Buildings and the National Trust did help to curb some of the worst excesses of development pressure on the rural landscape and its historic heritage, they did not explicitly cham-pion the protection of village England. With few exceptions, preserved commons and heathlands, romantic castles, ancient hill forts and stone circles and many of the stately homes and gardens of the National Trust lie well outside villages, not within them. In the most threatened parts of the countryside there was very little that the inter-war preservationists could really do to arrest the growing menaces of ribbon development, roadside petrol stations, anarchistic plotland settlements and unsightly market gardens, which very often were either attached to a village or were plainly visible from it.

It was the Council for the Preservation of Rural England (renamed in 1969 as the Council for the Protection of Rural England) which became the first national organization to extend the scope of landscape and historic buildings protection into village England. Formed in 1926 and including such eminent constituent bodies and affiliated societies as the Town Planning Institute, the Royal Institute of Architects, the National Trust and the Country Landowners Association, the CPRE quickly emerged as the co-ordinating body of the entire preservation movement. With such influential figures as Patrick Abercrombie and Clough Williams-Ellis serving on its executive committee, the membership was drawn from a wide range of professions and callings, but consisted almost exclusively of a middle- and upper-class cultural elite. It included academics, town and country planners, writers, broadcasters, landowners and even a few Fabian socialists; people who, despite their different occupational backgrounds and political convictions, had a shared belief that the protection of the rural landscape, supported by strong government regulation, was of paramount importance. This is indeed endorsed in the opening page of the CPRE's *Aims and Objects of the Council*,[46] which significantly also includes a specific declaration to safeguard 'the artistic and historic features of country towns and villages'. From its very inception, therefore, the CPRE was concerned with the protection of village England as well as the preservation of the open countryside and its historic legacies.

The CPRE used its influence to help persuade the government to bring in measures to combat the mounting pressures on the rural landscape. The threat of wider proliferation of badly designed petrol stations was met head on by the Petroleum Consolidation Act of 1928, a piece of regulative legislation that enabled county councils to have a strong say in the location and the appearance of new petrol-selling premises. In some rural counties, such as Devon and Warwickshire, one outcome of this Act was for new filling stations to become more visually acceptable and to have less obtrusive signs and advertisements. Many were built in a pseudo-rustic style,[47] the more fanciful versions of which sported incongruous thatched roofs or were adorned with mock black and white timbering.

The Town and Country Planning Act of 1932, unlike the earlier Planning Acts of 1909 and 1925 that were very largely urban in their application, recognized the need for *country* planning, especially the protection of the rural landscape and the control of suburban sprawl. It gave county councils powers to institute by-laws and local Acts to check the most unsightly forms of development, particularly plotlands and 'ribbons', within acknowledged beauty spots and other pressurized tracts of countryside. However, since they were still obliged to compensate property owners and had insufficient financial resources to pay for this, few councils were prepared to risk exercising this legislation. Moreover, only a minority of councils made full use of the 1935 Restriction of Ribbon Development Act which enabled authorities to control frontage development alongside arterial roads.

Despite the combined weight of the countryside preservation movement, increasing state intervention and the emergence of town *and country* planning, the shadow of the 'suburban beast' loomed larger and larger over village England in the inter-war years: specific preservationist victories, whilst always strongly applauded, were modest in scope and were too few and far between. Ribbon development, although in some counties it had to be more orderly after 1935, continued to spread; and plotland settlements, poultry farms, rural petrol stations and roadside cafes continued to spring up. Then, suddenly, in September 1939, the outbreak of the Second World War brought all of this to a standstill. The suburban beast now had to lie dormant; but new 'monsters' quickly emerged as the English countryside became engulfed with Nissen huts, airfields, pill-boxes, tank ranges, army-training grounds and all the apparatus of the national military effort. When the war ended, for several years the building industry had to concentrate upon the rebuilding of the blitzed city centres, the construction of new factories and a huge programme of council-housing provision. Moreover, before the market for owner-occupier housing was re-established and before building firms were once again able to turn their attention towards private suburbia, the draconian 1947 Town and Country Planning Act was passed through parliament. This, as we shall see in the following chapter, underpinned a new era in the physical evolution of village England and became instrumental in shaping what was to become its second social transformation.

Plate 20: Aldbourne, Wiltshire, in the 1930s. Note the absence of motor vehicles and the group of rustics sitting facing the village pond and green. At the time this photograph was taken, Aldbourne, like so many workaday English villages, had endured over half a century of agricultural depression. The photograph conveys something of the atmosphere that this had created.

Reproduced from a photograph taken by Will F. Taylor and published by Batsford in H. J. Massingham, *English Downland* (1936).

Plate 21: Aldbourne today. Rather unusually for countryside pubs and inns, the 'Crown' has not been extensively altered. The village, however, is now filled with cars, the rustics have gone, the village green has been manicured, the posts and railings have been removed, and the pond has been tidied up. One other sign of the times is the 'For Sale' notice outside the little shop on the street leading up to the church.

— CHAPTER SEVEN —

The Second Transformation:
Village England in the Post-War Era

Town should be town, and country country; urban and rural can never be
interchangeable adjectives. If this polarity is grasped there should be no
danger.

(Patrick Abercrombie, *Town and Country Planning*, 1943)

Prior to the 1947 Town and Country Planning Act, controls on village
expansion had been confined to private regulation in the diminishing
numbers of landowner-controlled close villages and, in certain locations,
the application of the 1935 Restriction of Ribbon Development Act and
operation of county zoning policies aimed at preventing some specific
excesses of the 'suburban beast'. Indeed, at the time of the Scott Report
in 1942, little more than half of landuse in Britain was subject to official
'Interim Development Control', and less than one-tenth of rural England
was covered by a functioning statutory planning scheme.[1] Following the
1947 Act, however, the whole country, including every village and indeed
every piece of land, came under a comprehensive system of compulsory
development control imposed by the state and managed by the municipal
and county authorities. With only agricultural buildings (under 465
square metres of floor space) and military installations carrying exemption, all new development, large or small, had to gain the consent of the
local planning authority. In rural areas this meant that it had to comply
with general directives on landuse policy and also with county development plans once these had been drawn up and given authorization. Until
a general loosening of controls by the Thatcher government in the 1980s,
'country' planning was highly restrictive, since it had to comply with the
national priorities of curbing suburban sprawl, maintaining a clear distinction between town and country, imposing defined physical limits on
settlement growth and preserving agriculturally productive land. The Act
of 1947 ensured that there would be no post-war return to ribbon

development and proliferation of plotland settlements. Henceforth, in rural England all new residential development had to conform to a statutory standard of planning and had to be contiguous with existing settlements. No longer could it take place within open countryside and wherever market forces might dictate.

Village England in the Early Post-War Years

It is wrong to assume that, with the suburbanization process coming to a sudden and quite lengthy halt, nothing happened to the physical and social make-up of village England during the Second World War and the first few post-war years. A few villages and the countryside around them, for example Imber on Salisbury Plain, Tollington in the Norfolk Breckland, and more controversially Tyneham in south Dorset,[2] were commandeered by the military for artillery and tank training, and were reduced to rubble or left to ruin. A much greater number of villages, mostly in east Yorkshire, Lincolnshire, East Anglia and south-east England, were greatly affected by the construction of an RAF airfield and the building of accommodation for airmen and ground staff. In many cases the opening of an airfield was accompanied by a doubling or even a trebling of the parish population, bringing a new lease of life to village services and creating the opportunity for local agricultural workers to earn appreciably better wages on government contract work. Some of these airfields are still in operation today, but many were closed soon after the war ended, leaving their runways, hangars and prefabricated huts to crumble away whilst the villages nearby reverted to something like their former state.

Many villages and countryside towns were designated as 'safe places' for the reception of evacuee children from urban England. Over 800,000 children, some of the youngest being accompanied by their mothers, were moved out of the threatened cities and industrial areas in September 1939.[3] Many rural settlements also became retreats for longer-term urban migrants – mostly elderly couples and women with young families – escaping from the Blitz, and staying with a relative or occupying a vacant cottage, bungalow or plotland dwelling. By no means all of these wartime incomers returned to their towns and cities after the war ended. Having gained a taste of the rural way of life, some decided to remain where they were, either securing (or building for themselves) a home of their own or waiting to move into one of the new village council houses.

Pushed by the modernizing spirit of the Attlee Labour government, the building of rural council dwellings was quickly resumed after 1945. Indeed, in some rural areas work on the first post-war council housing schemes was well under way or had already been completed prior to the 1947 Planning Act, and was not affected by this legislation. Between 1945 and 1951, as many as 186,000 new council homes – considerably more than the numbers built during the whole of the inter-war period – were completed within the Rural Districts of England and Wales.[4] In order to rationalize the distribution of council homes and to ensure that this was in accordance with other forms of investment, rural local authorities focused their construction within what, in most early post-war County Development Plans, were defined as 'key settlements' or 'rural growth points'. As a rule these were the larger and better-positioned villages that already provided schooling and could offer a reasonable range of other services. Some had the additional 'advantage' of being situated near a rural factory or a quarry, either of which could make a substantial contribution to local employment opportunities.

The increased amount of rural council-housing construction, together with the policy of concentrating it in the more populated and more viable settlements, led to the building of larger versions of 'council colonies'. These, like much of the post-1936 inter-war council housing, were normally positioned on the periphery of the village. Here it did not mingle with private property, and it was easier for the authorities to install underground sewage pipes and electricity and water mains without having to incur the expense of running them underneath the streets and congested spaces of the old village core.[5] Many post-war council colonies were built in the form of small compact estates rather than as simple terraces. In their typical uniformity and dullness of appearance, they are not dissimilar to their urban counterparts. It is in their much smaller scale and, of course, their rural location that they differ.

Rural council housing construction declined steeply after the mid-1950s when it became clear that the emergence of a new and very capital-intensive phase of agricultural mechanization – heavy tractors and combine-harvesters in particular – meant that far less labour would be required for the nation's 'healthy and well-balanced farming' than had first been forecasted at the end of the Second World War. By the end of the 1960s, most rural local authorities were building only a small fraction of the numbers of homes that they had been completing in the early post-war years. Moreover, much of this reduced quantity was being constructed on the edges of countryside towns rather than within and around village settlements. Eventually provision of new council housing came to a virtual standstill in most villages, never to be revived again on any appreciable scale. Significantly, the main phase of decline in rural council-housing construction coincided quite closely with the first post-war boom in private house building (from the late 1950s to the early 1970s) and, having been held back by government restrictions and general economic austerity, the re-emergence of rural suburbanization in quickly growing strength. These trends were interconnected, and were underpinned by rising incomes and the ability of more and more people to buy their own homes. Two other stimuli were the idealization of rural and suburban life in an increasingly image-influenced society and, boosted first by the end of petrol rationing and then by easier access to hire purchase, a sharp rise in car-ownership.

The re-emergence of rural suburbanization was reflected in the general rural population trend. During the first post-war intercensal decade, 1951–61, the numbers of people living in rural England and Wales increased by 9.6 per cent, which was more than twice as fast as the now faltering urban demographic growth rate. The rural trend accelerated to 12.6 per cent during 1961–71, before easing somewhat to 10.3 per cent in the 1970s. Between 1951 and 1981 (due to widespread changes to administrative areas and census districts, there are no comparable figures after the latter date) the population of rural England and Wales increased by over one-third, from 8.4 million to 11.4 million, and from 18.7 per cent of the total population to 23.8 per cent. At first, this growth was largely confined to the 'accessible countryside' within easy reach of the larger towns and the urban agglomerations. After the 1950s, however, rural suburbanization, responding to the advent of mass car-ownership and extensive improvements to the road network, spread much more widely. In coastal locations and scenic rural areas inland another impetus came from the increasing numbers of comfortably-off retired people who, from their savings, their private pensions and the sale of the family house, now had the means and the freedom to achieve their ambitions of a rural existence well beyond commuting range of a place of work in a town or city. By the 1970s, strong population growth was being recorded as far away from urban and industrial England as Cornwall, Devon, Dorset, Norfolk and Herefordshire.[6] However, within these and other rural counties, population trends still varied substantially from district to district and from one parish to the next. Interestingly in many cases these differences now had as much to do with county planning policy as they had with travel distances to and from large urban centres.

Today population trends at national, regional and local levels are no longer regarded as accurate indicators of the need and the market for new housing. This is because social changes, including demographic ageing, much higher divorce rates and the tendency for couples to have fewer children, have brought a marked reduction in average household size, from 3.2 persons in 1961 to just 2.2 in 2001. Most significant here has been the steep rise in the proportion of single-person households, which in England and Wales has risen from 18 per cent in 1971 to more than 25 per cent in 1991, and is expected to reach 36 per cent by the year 2016.[7] Thus the modest slowing down of the rate of rural population growth since its high point in the 1960s has not been accompanied by any commensurate lessening of housing demand. In fact, according to a government directive at the end of the millennium, between 4.4 million and 5.5 million new homes will be required in Britain by the year 2020, with nearly one-half of these having to be built in rural and outer-suburban locations.[8] Rather than slowing down, it may well be that the strongest phase in the residential expansion and suburbanization of village and rural England has yet to come.

The Planning Framework

The categorization of villages into a minority of 'key settlements' or 'rural growth points' and a majority of non-growth settlements (some county authorities also included an intermediate category) established a basis for the location of new private housing development as well as influencing the allocation of council housing and public services. Settlements that were not designated for expansion in County Development Plans became places where the full weight of restrictive, or 'negative', planning could be applied. With few exceptions these were the smaller and less viable villages that were deficient in services and infrastructure but in most cases had a building fabric which happened to be worth conserving. Until the 1970s, when some inroads were made into the rigidity of post-war town and country planning, little or no new residential development was permitted here, though the system could not intervene against what in the more picturesque villages often became emphatic social change. Different in all important respects, settlements scheduled for expansion were selected on the basis of their larger population size, stronger infrastructure, good road connections and better services (especially schooling and public transport). In a large majority of cases they had evolved historically as open villages, which explains their typically workaday appearance. By focusing new residential development in such settlements, and thereby relieving pressure on others, rural local authorities not only tried to make it complement the existing distribution of services and modern infrastructure but, perhaps as much by accident as by design, also ensured that it did the least harm to the wider rural landscape and environment.

This selective approach to rural settlement development was reinforced by the Town and Country Planning Acts of 1968 and 1971, which compelled planning authorities to replace their County Development Plans by comprehensive County Structure Plans indicating the pattern of future settlement expansion, industrial and transport development and landscape conservation phased over a time-span ranging from ten to twenty years.[9] Introduced throughout England in the late 1970s and early 1980s, the new plans revised the designations of growth villages and renamed them 'selected settlements' or 'main villages'. Most County Structure Plans also obliged market towns and other small urban centres to accommodate larger shares of new housing development. Indeed, it is upon this particular policy change that blame has to be laid for the 'residential swamping' of many countryside towns, including some of the most historically and architecturally valued.

The Acts of 1968 and 1971, followed by the reorganization of local government in 1974, also created an operational role for district-level 'Local Plans' in the management of landuse and building development, which in many instances led to the compilation of blueprints for individual villages. Hitherto these had been few and far between, and were not very effective. The ones that were drawn up after the early 1970s, however, did have a major effect on the extent and the shaping of subsequent settlement growth. The key feature here was the defining of a boundary line around the village, representing the physical limits of permissible housing development. Such limits or 'envelopes' were drawn more liberally around some settlements than they were around others. As a general rule, however, they were designed to make the form of an expanding village as symmetrical and compact as possible.

As well as restricting the supply of land to developers, the highly regulative planning regime of the earlier part of the post-war era meant that nearly all new housing development in village England at that time had to be built at low densities, not exceeding the standard guide-line (for rural settlements) of a maximum of eight dwellings per net residential acre. Builders had to ensure that there was no overcrowding, that every new house had sufficient natural light, and that building-lines were undisturbed and set well back from the road or street. Such stipulations inevitably led to some under-utilization and wastage of development land. Another outcome was the tendency for builders – always mindful of the disproportionately high costs of installing infrastructure on land that at the best could be used for only a handful of houses – to leave aside the smaller crofts and paddocks which lay within or adjoining the village cores. Very often, development upon this type of site had to await the 1980s and the emergence of a more flexible approach to settlement planning. Until then, estates of low-density, standard-size and uniformly designed housing on the peripheries of villages continued to be the norm. Piecemeal housing construction by small local builders, which had been so characteristic of inter-war rural suburbanization, played a much smaller part.

The prospect of a revival of rural suburbanization on an extensive scale moved the Ministry of Housing and Local Government in 1955 to urge for a widespread adoption of green belts around major cities, conurbations and towns of special quality, following the example of the London Green Belt which had been first devised in 1938 and had been incorporated into Patrick Abercrombie's 'Greater London Plan' of 1944. The idea of green belts, with their ambitious objectives of containing urban sprawl, retaining agricultural land and maintaining clear visual and functional breaks between the city and the countryside, goes back to the thinking of Ebenezer Howard in his pioneering book *Tomorrow: a Peaceful Path to Real Reform*, first published in 1898 and subsequently reissued under the more specific title of *Garden Cities of Tomorrow*. Since 1955, green belts have been drawn around various provincial cities and industrial agglomerations, including Manchester, Nottingham, Southampton and the whole of Birmingham and the Black Country (Figure 7). In each case the overriding concern was to prevent any further spread of suburbia into the surrounding countryside. The firmest of planning controls were, and still are, enforced, with only essential new infrastructure and buildings for agricultural use carrying exemption. However, authorities responsible for the first generation of green belts did not foresee how vigorous the post-war suburbanization tide was to become. For the most part, the planning system has succeeded in keeping the zones 'green' (though less and less agricultural); but it has been unable to prevent the 'leap-frogging' of new development to localities and villages beyond these protected spaces. Thus, to take the most controversial case as an illustration, the London Green Belt has been instrumental in the retention of a broad band of open countryside around the entire circumference of the city. However, rural suburbanization has tended to spread out further and further into the Home Counties and south-east England, eventually intruding into such formerly secluded parts of Deep England as the Vale of Aylesbury, the Middle Thames valley, the fringes of the Berkshire Downs, and the inner Weald.

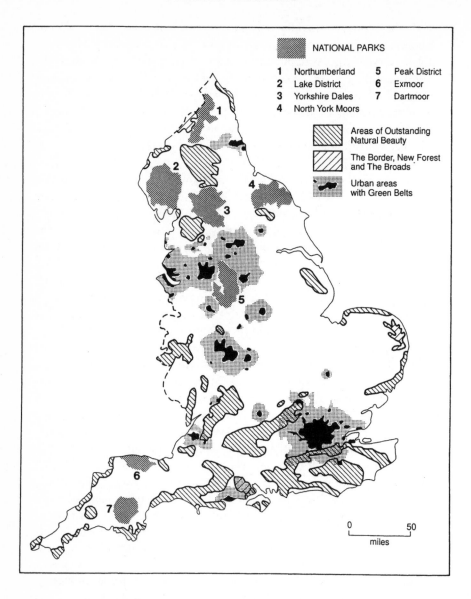

Figure 7: Specially protected areas in post-war England. Not shown are the two recently announced new National Parks of the New Forest and the South Downs.

Strong development controls, including some restrictions on the design and the scale of new agricultural buildings, are also enforced in the National Parks that were designated after the National Parks and Access to the Countryside Act of 1949. Aimed at protecting the nation's most beautiful natural landscapes and providing access and open-air recreation for the general public, the seven National Parks in England[10] – the Northumberland, Lake District, Yorkshire Dales, North York Moors, Peak District, Exmoor and Dartmoor parks – are all located in the hillier and (with the exception of the Peak District park which is quite centrally situated) remoter northern and western parts of the country. Each contains large tracts of high moorland and also some extensive sparsely populated areas in which the only settlements are hamlets and scattered farmsteads. Most of the parks, however, do include localities that have a higher rural population density and a more nucleated pattern of settlement. The pleasant limestone villages of the White Peak in Derbyshire and the string of tidy Jurassic-stone villages on the southern margins of the North York Moors, for example, make rich contributions to the English vernacular landscape. And the same can be said for other National Park villages in Wensleydale and upper Wharfedale in the Yorkshire Dales, the Porlock district on the eastern side of Exmoor and the Windermere–Furness Fells area of the Lake District.

Within the National Parks, and more recently in certain other scenic areas such as the Cotswolds, the north Norfolk coast, the Dorset Downs and the Lincolnshire Wolds, which have been designated as 'Areas of Outstanding Natural Beauty' (Figure 7), policy on village development is strongly in line with the environmental priorities of protecting the landscape and preserving its architectural heritage. Developments that do gain planning approval here, unless there are special circumstances, are almost invariably small in scale. Even minor modifications to existing buildings are subject to tight controls, with National Park authorities and local authorities administering an Area of Outstanding Natural Beauty (AONB) insisting that any alterations and additions are unobtrusive and are not out of keeping with the local vernacular style. Very often an important condition is the incorporation of traditional building and roofing materials or at least an acceptable imitation of them. This usually adds to the expense, though hardly enough to deter the more determined and the more affluent of owners.

The Middle-Class Ascendancy

The treachery of the English village is to have turned its back on its own people. Rich men now live in poor men's cottages.
(Caroline McGhie, 1989)[11]

Nationwide restrictions on the extent and the density of new, extra-urban, residential development, together with additional controls within the various areas designated as green belts, National Parks or AONBs, have meant that the supply of rural housing has constantly lagged behind the demand. This is one reason why rural house prices have risen faster than urban house prices for most of the post-war era. Another reason has been the tendency for builders, some of them exclusively so, to focus on the middle-class, owner-occupancy, sector of the housing market, which has proved to be much more profitable than the construction of cheaper priced or rented dwellings for local inhabitants. Developers, therefore, have paid little or no heed to the needs of native villagers who, with fewer and fewer council houses being built, have had to face a growing shortage of affordable dwellings and ever-diminishing prospects of being able to continue living within the village of their birth and upbringing. With most of them living on low to average incomes, what they needed from the building industry was for it to supply a diversity, not a uniformity, of new rural housing.

Whilst the bulk of the post-war middle-class invasion of village England has been accommodated in new residential developments, wealthier and more adventurous incomers have bought up and taken over the best of the older properties – the pretty cottages and pre-enclosure farmhouses – which give character to every historic village core. In doing so they have not only achieved their ambition of attaining what they see as the 'good life' of village England, but they have also managed to take into possession a piece of its quaintness and its architectural heritage. This process is not new, especially in the London countryside. As long ago as the early nineteenth century, Cobbett had been complaining about 'stockjobbers' taking over ancient country homes in the villages and hamlets around 'the great Wen'. Further away from the metropolis, writers such as E. M. Forster in *Howard's End* (1910) and George Sturt in *Change in the Village* (1912), had observed how wealthy city businessmen were buying up 'suitable' old cottages and farmhouses in the period of commercial prosperity just before the First World War. And we know from the comments of such staunch upholders of traditional rural values as H. J. Massingham, John Moore and Clough Williams-Ellis that the trend was becoming more pervasive, indeed 'rife' in some places, in the inter-war years. What is different in the post-war era is its much wider geographical incidence, to the extent that today it has become nearly universal.

The new inhabitants of cottage and farmhouse England were able to acquire their Arcadian retreats by virtue of their appreciable financial resources. In the first two to three post-war decades, however, they were greatly helped by the large numbers of old properties that were being placed on the market, some as a consequence of the out-migration of native villagers and the demographic ageing of those who remained, and others through landowners disposing of estate cottages to meet a tax debt or to help fund some new investments outside the spheres of land and agriculture. In some cases, mostly in the aftermath of the Second World War, entire estate villages were sold off, though quite often the sitting tenants were given an option for purchase. After the 1970s, however, with the enthusiasm for 'cottage hunting' becoming stronger than ever but the numbers of unrestored old dwellings rapidly diminishing, what for long had been a buyer's market turned very much in favour of the seller. By the 1980s, a large and increasing proportion of cottages coming up for sale had already been subjected to costly renovation and internal conversion to suit the comforts and fancies of earlier incomers. The effect of this was to drive up the prices of all old and 'desirable' rural properties – large and small – and to put them out of reach of all save a small minority of native village households.

The upsurge in prices for 'traditional' cottages and old farmhouses meant that the fashion for buying, refurbishing and gentrifying them spread wider and wider, eventually reaching almost every part of rural England. Indeed, few villages today have not been affected. The process, often accompanied by a change from tenancy tenure to owner-occupancy, has caused many of the native rural population to be pushed out from the cores of the villages where they, their parents and their forefathers had always lived. Whilst some of these displaced people have managed to stay within their home community by renting a council house, this was not possible in some rural settlements, especially close and estate villages where there was very little, or in some cases none at all, public-sector housing. Here, once a landowner decided to sell his cottages, the tenants (unless they were given an offer of purchase and had enough money to accept it) had to leave. Some villagers also lost their job at the same time as they were uprooted from their home. When this happened, migration was pressed perhaps just as much by the need to gain new employment as it was by the urgency of having to find a new place to live. Indeed, in post-war rural England it was not unusual for a landowner village to be sold off so quickly that, within less than a decade, what had once been a

Plate 22: Cottage renovation, East Hendred, Berkshire. One more small piece of old village England is being subjected to comprehensive refurbishment and gentrification. Note the centuries-old 'wattle and daub' in the wall of the cottage in the foreground, and the breeze blocks that have been installed in the one next door.

close-knit community, in many ways more in keeping with the nineteenth century than with the modern age, became almost completely overrun by wealthy incomers. Many people from these 'disbanded' communities moved to the council-house colonies of larger villages and the market towns where there existed some affordable housing.

Due to their attractive trim appearance, their picturesque surrounds, and the protection or 'fossilization' afforded to them by the post-war planning system, former landowner villages have become the most desirable of all habitats in rural England, and have become so despite their paucity of services. Although these rustic showpieces have undergone far less physical alteration than have other villages, in terms of their social make-up they are the most unbalanced of English rural settlements. To the casual observer they may indeed look like idyllic perfections of village England, but as places to live in they are inaccessible to households on low incomes and most have become dominated by the new rural rich – high-earning professionals, company directors, well-off retirees and perhaps one or two wealthy celebrities – few of whom have roots within the locality. Other villages, however, have a more heterogeneous social structure which is reflected in a differentiated pattern of housing. They still accommodate quite sizeable native populations, though many of these people now reside in council housing on the periphery of their village rather than, as used to be the case, in the cottages and farmhouses within the core.

Whilst most incomers travel to their jobs and occupations, a quite sizeable proportion of the native rural population still work within their village or in sight of it. Some of this indigenous 'occupational community'[12] are members of the ever-diminishing band of agricultural workers; others make a living as an assistant in the village shop, a cleaner in the village school, a mechanic in the local garage, or a home-help. However, increasing numbers are now being employed further afield, typically as factory workers, road menders, lorry drivers, supermarket employees, or hospital workers. It is not just because of the incomers that most English villages have become residential dormitories.

In the expanded villages, especially those for which the designation of a 'key', and later a 'selected', settlement has meant extensive post-war residential growth, two distinct groupings of incomers have emerged. One, the more affluent of the two, consists of those who have taken over the village core and its old dwellings (though the middle-class invasion here has tended to be slower and less complete than in former close and estate villages). The other grouping, which is usually the more numerous, are the people who have come to live in the new private residential development. However, in the composite social geography of these villages there are always exceptions to the general rule: some native villagers who have managed to hang on to their cottages or farmhouses within the centre of the village; some wealthy incomers who prefer an ordinary modern house on a new residential estate, even though they can afford the higher price for an older and more 'desirable' property of historic value; and some occupants of council housing who are not from the locality. Moreover, in villages that have experienced a longer history of suburbanization there are the residents of the pre-1947 ribbon-housing to consider too. Few of their original occupants are alive today, but in many cases their homes have been handed down to one of their sons or daughters who (along with the next generation of offspring) qualifies as a native villager by birth and upbringing. They add an interesting dimension to the social composition of their villages. Partly as a reflection of the diversity of this type of housing development, and partly also because of the tendency for the fortunes of families to change as one generation succeeds to the next, the present-day occupants of inter-war village ribbons come from various walks of life. It is here where we are the more likely to find a wealthy household living next door to one that has seen better times; incomers living among long-established residents; and a smallholder, a garage proprietor or a village shopkeeper having a solicitor, university professor or local-government officer as a neighbour.

Population growth in village England and the influx of large numbers of affluent ex-urbanites have not been accompanied by a regeneration of rural services. On the contrary, these have diminished relentlessly in the post-war era; their seemingly terminal decline representing the 'final act' in the long historical process of the breaking down and elimination of village England's traditional self-sufficiency. In the pursuit of rationalization and economy of scale, the trend has been for village schools, police stations, doctors' surgeries and now even post offices too to be withdrawn in favour of concentrating them within larger and better-located settlements.[13] In the private sector, closures of village shops (or in tourist areas their conversion into such enterprises as 'craft' boutiques, delicatessens and antiques outlets) have been a constant feature of recent decades. Indeed, due principally to competition from the fast-increasing numbers of 'out-of-town' and country town supermarkets, they have become so widespread that as many as 70 per cent of parishes in rural England now have no general store, and 42 per cent of them have no shop at all.[14] Villagers, therefore, are being forced to make a journey even for the simplest of needs; and, if they do not have their own car and if bus services are not available, have come to depend upon friends and relations to give lifts or do the shopping for them. The planning system is powerless to stop this trend and the deprivation that it can aggravate. Closures of village shops and other services cause little discomfort to most of the 'car-rich' incomers, who are easily able to undertake and afford the necessary travel to other places. However, they do cause hardship to some, predominantly native, inhabitants who, because they do not have sufficient income to run a car or are too old to drive one, are much more confined to the village. It remains to be seen how far recent improvements in rural bus services in some areas (after more than a quarter of a century of decline) will reduce their isolation.

The New Landscape of Village England

> Into our delicate old villages have come swaggering new executive housing estates. Identically dressed dwellings line up around a cul-de-sac like grey-suited managers around a conference table. Double-glazed, double-garaged, double income houses have elbowed their way past church and cottages and eased their bulk on to little infill sites that might once have been a garden or a paddock.
>
> (Clive Aslet, *Countryblast*, 1991)[15]

The post-war period has seen a transformation not only in the social composition of most English villages but also in their physical appearance. Today only a small proportion of villages bear a close resemblance to what they looked like half a century ago. The most widespread and most conspicuous feature of this physical transformation is the large quantity of new private residential development, much of it built in the form of trim-looking housing estates located on the periphery of the village. Rising costs of development land, together with the need to engage professional advisers to deal with the complexities of the post-1947 planning system, meant that large-scale nationwide building companies came to dominate, bringing with them standardized, mass-produced, construction materials and bequeathing to village England a universal ordinariness of housing design.

During the 1950s and 1960s a plain functional design prevailed, providing modern comforts for the house buyers. Underpinned by the first (and the longest) post-war economic boom and what at the time was a great faith in all things modern, it made no reference to past architectural forms. Instead, it was typified everywhere by its box-like shapes, plain walls, gently sloping roofs and absence of decorative features. Semi-detached and detached housing was the norm, grading from roomy 'executive' homes at the higher end of the market to bungalows and chalets at the lower. This, however, is just about as far as variety went in the suburban residential development of the earlier post-war years. The bulk of it was constructed in the form of orderly arranged estates, with rigid building-lines set back from a circulatory public road and branching streets. The houses themselves incorporated a standard range of modern industrial technology. Throughout the country extensive use was made of artificial roofing tiles, plate-glass windows, concrete breeze-blocks and drainpipes and guttering made out of reinforced plastic. Garages, which (in the days before people were happy enough to leave their cars outside) had become indispensable for the middle-class commuter, were fitted with steel doors and placed in a conspicuous position at the head of the drive or protruding out from the front of the house. All of this was far removed from the pre-war predilection for historical architectural styles. Yet to prospective buyers the competitive price and modern internal features, such as insulation and central heating, could outweigh everything that older suburban housing could offer.

Architectural fashion changed again in the 1970s and 1980s, in response to the emergence of a very different spirit of the age and perhaps also as a reaction to over-familiarity and growing boredom with modernity and functionalism. Whereas almost the whole of the third quarter of the twentieth century had seen sustained economic growth and low levels of unemployment, the final quarter proved to be a time of much economic instability and job killing, with two major recessions and the spread of job insecurity into middle-class white-collar occupations. Such conditions and the global forces that underlay them led to growing disenchantment with the modern world and increasing anxiety about the future; a mood which has contributed much to the so-called 'post-modern' aesthetic. In the spheres of suburban architecture and the landscape of village expansion, 'post-modernism' departs radically from the monotony of functionalism. Building companies and their house designers have fostered this difference by creating an impression of diversity of new housing and by applying an assortment of historical architectural motifs. In what they see as responding to new consumer tastes, they have not been short of ingenuity. Although they still built to just a small range of standard designs and sizes, and continued to use mass-produced materials transported from all over the country, they have managed to create an illusion of heterogeneity either by mixing two or three styles together within each development or, as in many recent housing developments, by varying their decorative features and historical references. The purist may well pour scorn on this 'bogus' architecture that, with apparently little concern for authenticity, in some cases tries to resemble a Georgian town house or a Victorian villa, and in others attempts to reproduce a country cottage of no determinable period. Yet, however unreal and ill-fitting these 'toy town' homes may seem to their critics, their owners find them a good deal more interesting and more attractive than the unimaginative structures that the building industry had produced in the earlier part of the post-war age.

The advent of post-modern style in village England came more or less at the same time as some very noticeable changes in the form of new residential development. Most prominent has been the trend towards higher densities, which first became evident in the more pressurized areas of the country in the 1970s, following the relaxation of rules on building-lines and some easing of the long-standing 'eight dwellings to the acre' maximum-density guideline for new rural housing. Release from these and other planning constraints was carried a stage further by the deregulating reforms of the first Thatcher government, each aimed at reducing the powers of planning authorities and giving private developers greater freedom from 'red tape' and 'local bureaucracy'. Moreover, with pressures on rural England's finite resources of development land becoming stronger and stronger, it was now a matter of urgency at all levels of government to maximize the utilization of new residential space. Higher-density housing, therefore, has come to find favour not just solely with the building companies.

Since the 1970s, much of village England's new residential development has indeed been constructed at a density appreciably higher than that of the first two to three post-war decades. Under today's more flexible planning regime, building companies often claim that in constructing to a higher density they are simply reacting to the shortages and inflated costs of development land. They are, however, also taking the opportunity to enlarge their profits by producing considerably more houses to the acre and providing for what they recognize as a much changed, and increasingly individualized, suburban lifestyle. A large and increasing proportion of the new generation of village incomers are single persons or partners without children, who initially do not require much living space nor ask for much, if anything, by way of a garden. Unlike previous ex-urbanites, who took something of a puritanical pleasure in whiling away their weekends and summer evenings digging flower beds, pruning the roses and mowing the lawn, today's new villagers see 'gardening' as a time-consuming task to be undertaken as speedily as possible and seemingly always accompanied by the din of noisy garden machinery. Their way of life, which in many cases is dedicated to bringing work home, gazing for hours at a computer screen, the internet and the video, taking frequent holidays abroad and devoting weekends to shopping and travelling about everywhere, gives them far less time to spare – just enough perhaps to tend a small patch of grass and to grow the odd shrub and climbing plant. A symptom of the new leisure priorities is the common tendency, on the small pieces of land that are attached to the new housing, for paved patios or gravel surfaces to take precedence over garden space. Patios, provided that they are properly laid, need only a few minutes of sweeping and tidying up, and they provide somewhere to install a seat and a tub of flowers. Moreover, in today's age of very high usage of private motor vehicles (especially by the suburban and rural middle class) the front patio has become essential as a place for the parking and the manoeuvring of the household's second car or 'off road' four-by-four.

Once they were allowed to build at higher densities developers saw that, by squeezing in more houses to the acre, they could make handsome profits from virtually any available site – not just the larger and the better-positioned ones. At the same time, they were faced with a growing shortage of good-quality building land on the peripheries of villages. Since the 1970s, therefore, residential infilling has become the prevailing form of village growth, and generally speaking has tended to be countenanced rather than opposed by planning authorities. Some of it has taken place on former vacant spaces lying between the village cores and existing post-war housing estates, but more noticeable (and often more harmful to a village landscape) is the cramming of new housing within the centuries-old crofts and closes stretching back from either side of the main streets. Before the builders and the bulldozers arrived here, some of these ancient plots of land had been occupied by small orchards, giving natural colour to the village scene especially at blossom-time and when the fruit ripened in late summer and early autumn. Other crofts and closes, with their mature hedges, tumble-down sheds and outhouses and moss-covered fences and gates, were used for keeping poultry and pigs, wintering a small flock of sheep, pasturing cows, or paddocking a few horses. The infilling process is not only removing these rustic spaces, it is also destroying some of the best and most familiar sights looking into and out from the village. There had once been a time when people could gaze across such spots and admire a good view of the medieval church, an interesting old farmhouse or a favourite group of cottages. One by one, however, such visual pleasures are now being taken away by the intrusion of infill housing and its incongruous post-modern architecture.

Different too is the way in which this housing is laid out. Previously the very first stage in a new residential development was for the road pattern and the building-lines to be defined; and it was these that deter-

Plate 23: Walkington, east Yorkshire; a suburbanized village. The old linear village can be seen on the left-hand side of the photograph. The bulk of Walkington's post-war suburbanization has taken place in the middle and on the right-hand side where two main phases of residential expansion can be observed: in the top half, the orderly layouts of housing development in the 1960s and early 1970s, with its lower densities, rigid building-lines, circulatory roads, and front and rear gardens; and, at the bottom, some typical 1980s and 1990s residential infilling, with its higher densities, miniature gardens, driveway access systems, and absence of building-lines. In the latter almost every croft has been filled with new housing, but the boundary between the built-up area and the open country-side is still rigidly maintained. With kind permission from Getmapping plc.

mined the positioning of each house and garden. Now, however, it is common practice for the arrangement of the housing to be decided upon first, and it is the access roads that have to be fitted in. The flexibility of the new approach, often accompanied by dispensing with building-lines, is much better suited both for incorporating higher-density housing and for making optimum use of smaller and more confined sites. Entrance into a modern infill estate is normally provided by a cul-de-sac access lane, since a circulatory road takes up too much space and is often impossible to place inside the narrow and elongated configuration of a typical village croft or close.

Very common in recent infill development is the informal clustering of housing, typically in groups of a dozen or so dwellings focusing upon a short driveway or 'mews-court' branching off from the access lane. Unlike the roads and cul-de-sacs of the earlier estates, which had been built and are maintained by the local authority, these driveways and courts in many cases are privately owned, initially by the developers on behalf of the residents, then by the residents themselves. There is no distinction here between communal and private space, a characteristic that is reflected at the front of the houses by the absence of fences or any other visual demarcation between personal patio and shared court. Absent too in this so-called 'soft landscape'[16] are pavements and kerbs, since the road surfaces are intended to be used jointly for vehicle and pedestrian movement, with the former not having priority over the latter. Very wisely their design often incorporates a variety of traffic-calming devices, including rumble strips, ramps, chicane-like 'gateways', and deliberate twists and turns. Efforts are also made to proclaim to incoming drivers and pedestrians that they are no longer moving along a public road and have in fact entered an entirely private domain. Thus, instead of the dull grey tarmac that one is accustomed to see everywhere else in the village street pattern, the infill driveways, and the courts and patios too, are given a much different colouring and texture. In this, the current fashion for using pink or orange-red-brick paving gives anything but a rustic air to this boundary-free new residential landscape.

The infilling of ancient crofts and closes is not confined to the 'selected settlements' and 'main villages' of County Structure Plans. Due to the increasing flexibility of the planning process and the tendency for developers to look wider and wider for new rural building sites, it has become quite ubiquitous. Moreover, faced with the prospect of many 'non-selected' settlements dying away as a consequence of continued planning restriction, authorities now see the need to permit a certain amount of new housing development here as a means of arresting, if not reversing, this trend. Residential infilling, therefore, is now to be seen in some of the prettiest and most secluded villages in the country. In places like these, however, the planning system is still able to rule that this is modest in scale and in harmony with the older buildings nearby; and, in the National Parks, AONBs and village conservation areas, authorities still insist that the new buildings are unobtrusive and are built in a style in harmony with the traditional local vernacular. Quite often infill development in these locations is restricted to just one or two small groups of 'local needs' houses, with a preference for housing association 'starter' homes and 'social rent' dwellings that can be afforded by native inhabitants.

New lifestyles and new architectural fashions, which have been exerting such a strong impact upon the landscape of recent infill development, are also being imprinted on the housing estates of the 1950s, 1960s and early 1970s. In the private estates many of the once dutifully-kept front gardens have now been paved over or surfaced with gravel to create a place for parking an extra car and perhaps a caravan or small boat. At the same time, increasing numbers of residents here, aided by their rising incomes and easy availability of financial loans, are having their homes enlarged to provide a larger kitchen, a conservatory or a room above the garage. Building-lines are still enforced in these older estates and, to ensure that they are not infringed, authorities insist that any extensions are at the rear or the side of the house, not at the front. However, when they are undertaken for several properties along the same street or stretch of road, the estate loses its open character and takes on a more crowded appearance. One other trend here is for householders, dissatisfied with the plainness and uniformity of their houses, to personalize and embellish them with their own particular choice of decorative statements. Particularly noticeable, since they are normally considered as 'permissible development' for post-war housing and are allowed to be attached to the front of a dwelling, are the mass-produced 'rustic' porches, 'classic-style' front doors, and 'Dickensian' bow windows, that seem to be proliferating everywhere and are visual testimony to the power of modern advertising and the persuasive skills of door-to-door salesmen.

The same degree of freedom to adorn their homes applies to the owners of privatized council houses. Since the Thatcher government's Housing Act of 1980, which gave tenants the legal right to buy their homes, large numbers of village council dwellings (now exceeding one-third of the total rural stock) have become owner-occupied. Certainly for those who can afford the outlay, the 'right to buy' option has a strong appeal. For one thing, under the generous terms offered by this Act, it

Plate 24: Village 'clutter'. The centres of many villages today are becoming cluttered with road markings, street lighting, and advertisement signs. The scene here is quite typical of a village that does not have the special protection afforded to places in National Parks and Areas of Outstanding Natural Beauty. The zebra crossing, the zigzag road markings, the railings and the 'state of the art' street lamps have been installed to provide pedestrians with some protection against the constant stream of traffic. Here, in the centre of the village, there are advertisements everywhere, each designed to catch the eye of the passing motorist.

was quickly seen as a sound investment and a chance not to be missed. For another, in ceasing to be a council tenant and in becoming an owner-occupier, the buyer immediately achieves a new social status: no longer is he or she one of the rent-paying and council-dependent rural working class.[17] And, as if to proclaim this new status, many who have taken up the 'right to buy' have made special efforts to individualize their homes, eradicating their impersonality and making them appear as different as possible from the council homes that are still tenanted. Once they have become owner-occupiers they are free (unless there are any restrictive local by-laws) to 'face-lift' their properties in the same way as are the residents of the private estates. Thus, the dull uniformity of many village council colonies is being broken up as, in one house after another, the original windows and front porch are replaced, the outside brick walls are covered by stone-cladding, and the once ubiquitous privet hedge, wire-mesh fence and concrete path are ripped up. The selling of council homes, however, is having a disruptive effect on village England's poorest inhabitants. In countless villages, council-house sales and the subsequent rise in the value of the privatized properties to the market level are substantially reducing the stock of affordable housing. Before the 1980 Act, the growing imbalances in the rural housing market had been excluding native villagers from the historical accumulation of old cottages and small farmsteads, but not from the council estates. Since then, however, for thousands of these people it has come to exclude them from the entire village.

It is interesting to compare the central parts, or cores, of villages today with photographs of them taken several decades ago, when they were still populated by agricultural communities and when motor vehicles were too few in number to disturb the tranquillity of the scene (see Plates 20 and 21). Many of the admirable black-and-white photographs that appear in the Batsford 'The British Heritage' and 'The Face of Britain' series of architectural and topographical books, published in the 1930s and early 1940s, are excellent for this purpose.[18] In most cases, including some village centres that came to be designated as village conservation areas under the terms of the Civic Amenities Act of 1967, the difference is quite striking. Along the main streets, which are now full of noisy traffic and are often cluttered with modern road signs, advertisements and traffic-calming devices, the old photographs show just the occasional parked or passing car, an unobtrusive county-council direction post, and perhaps one of Giles Gilbert Scott's familiar post-office telephone boxes. And, whilst there are many more cars and other vehicles in the landscape today, there are fewer people. Two generations ago, there had been children at play, people wandering about or riding bicycles, and a few rustics sat happily gossiping on the village green or in front of the village inn. Now, at most times of the day, the pavements and grass spaces are empty.

Even more striking, however, are the changes in the building-fabric. In village after village a row of labourers' cottages, a disused farmstead and an old wall or grassy bank have been pulled down to make way for projects such as a wider road junction, some housing redevelopment, or just a new car park for a much-altered country pub. In some villages there is a reasonable balance between preservation of old buildings and essential renovation, whilst external restorations have been carefully done and structural extensions have been hidden from view. In other villages, however, the effects of so-called cottage 'improvements' and 'upgradings' are all too evident. The new owners can easily afford one or other of the various fashionable (and often quite out of character) alterations to cottage doorways, porches and window-frames which, for properties that are not 'listed' buildings and lie outside specially protected areas, either come within the sphere of permissible development or would meet with planning refusal only in the worst cases. Inappropriate repointing and re-roofing have likewise become commonplace as also, in response to the growing 'fortress' mentality and fixation with electronic technology, has the installation of burglar alarms, security lights and satellite-receiver dishes. Moreover, no sooner have some of the incomers settled into their dream cottages than they find these too small and too cramped for all their needs; hence the popularity of extensions and conservatories, some of which may blend quite well with the original building and its surrounds, but many of them can destroy an old cottage garden, are constructed from the wrong materials, and do not have the right lines and texture. Quite often cottage enlargements, either to create extra living space or merely to provide a garage, are made simply by buying up and incorporating a property next door. Thus, what had once been two homes, formerly accommodating family after family of native villagers, have become just a single dwelling. Taking over cottages in this way, especially if the purpose is simply to double the size of what is just the weekend retreat or second home of some anonymous affluent outsider, quickly becomes a focus of resentment to any native inhabitant who is having to search against the odds for somewhere to live within his or her own village.

Destruction or insensitive modification of old buildings has not been confined to cottages and village farmhouses. Innumerable old workshops and centuries-old farm outbuildings have also been lost, some of them being bulldozed away entirely and others being turned into private garages or storage premises. Indeed, the enthusiasm for converting and modernizing old buildings has extended to just about anything that has a pretension to historical character and is not a complete ruin. Thus, former barns, granaries, water mills, oast houses, windmills and even closed-down village schools and countryside railway stations have all been treated to the process; some of them, especially in tourist areas with a large potential for new 'country-style' consumerism,[19] being extensively refurbished to house an up-market 'crafts' shop, a delicatessen, or a rustic-themed restaurant. In recent years, barn conversions have become particularly popular. For one thing, changes in farming practice and the advent of the 'new agricultural depression' (brought about largely through the phasing out of European Union Common Agricultural Policy – CAP – price-support guarantees on crops and dairy produce) are causing more and more of these buildings to become redundant and available for new uses. For another, derelict barns had, of course, formerly functioned as agricultural buildings and are, therefore, more likely to gain consent for conversion than are other types of old properties. Some barns are in fact 'listed' buildings of architectural and historical merit, and are situated within the heart of a village or the centre of a hamlet. More often than not, however, the need to find a new role for a redundant farm building is seen as a greater priority than preservation pure and simple, even if it requires major modification. Indeed, for a barn to be properly habitable, windows have to be inserted, the interiors have to be divided into rooms, and, if there is to be a fireplace, a chimney has to be built.[20] The building will be much changed and, unless the alterations are handled carefully, little, if anything, will be left of its vernacular quality.

The process of converting old agricultural buildings is now taking place outside villages as well as within them. Since the mid-1990s there has been a steep decline in the profitability of British agriculture, with many farmers giving up their struggle or going to the wall. Thus, there has been an increasing incidence of whole farmsteads being put up for sale, including some of the fine assemblages of buildings that had been constructed, standing on their own, in the golden ages of the Georgian parliamentary enclosures and Victorian high farming. The appearance of these on the property market has given the opportunity for specialist building firms to slip in some new residential development into the open countryside and to effect one more breach into the containment principles of the 1947 Town and Country Planning Act. Typically the farmsteads in question are treated to thorough refurbishment and partial rebuilding to create a luxurious 'neo-mansion' or a group of exclusive dwellings and garages. Their isolation is a drawback to most people but, for some, these developments offer the compelling attractions of social exclusiveness, detachment from other settlements, and something of an agricultural image. To allay fears of visits from motorized urban criminals, many of them are designed to have a protective, fortress-like, aspect with high surrounding walls or railings, bright security lighting, video cameras, and electronically operated iron gates all being standard features. More so than any other new feature in the English rural landscape, they signify today's eclipse of the agricultural spirit and the supremacy of the dormitory function. Together with the recent boom in constructing completely new country mansions (encouraged by further liberalization of the planning process by the Major government in 1997), the more lavish of these farmstead conversions also reflect the emergence of a new era of private wealth accumulation – on a scale not seen since Edwardian times.[21] What we are seeing, and what their mock Baroque and Palladian styles emphatically symbolize, is the ostentation of a new plutocracy; an extremely wealthy 'super rich' class of city financiers, corporate magnates, foreign tax-exiles and highly paid football and entertainment stars who, whilst choosing to live in the English countryside, are connected to the globalized world and have little real interest in the locality and the village idea. The new mansions look odd and ill-fitting in a rural landscape that is neither adorned by eighteenth-century parkland nor complemented by an estate of tenant farms and a community of servants, gardeners and gamekeepers.

Conversion of old farm buildings into exclusive new residences, however, is just one amongst several changes that are taking place in the present-day agricultural landscape. Of the farmsteads still in agricultural use, a large number have already been extensively modernized to accommodate the latest machinery, to provide greater storage space, and to give the farmer an easier working life. Agricultural buildings (with less than 465 square metres of ground-floor area) have always been exempt from the planning process and, unless they carry 'listed' status or are situated within a protected area, can be altered or replaced more or less at will. Thus, both within village England and in the open countryside, the architectural achievements of past ages of farming prosperity are being replaced by a plethora of unsightly concrete sheds, steel-fabricated roofs, and metallic silo-towers that are as much out of place in the rural landscape as they would be in place within a modern urban or suburban industrial estate. Fields too are being rearranged and enlarged to create optimum conditions for what in arable farming has now become an entirely mechanized mode of agricultural production. Since the Second

World War, hedgerows have been disappearing at an alarming rate of 5,000 miles each year.[22] Indeed, if present trends continue, in some localities little or nothing will be left of the historic field patterns – the familiar chequer-boards of the parliamentary enclosures and the irregular patchwork quilts of earlier ages. Year by year, these are being replaced by a prairie landscape in which, amidst an unending vista of monoculture, the only features to catch the eye are the combine-harvesters in late summer and the tractors and ploughs in autumn and winter. Paradoxically a change in CAP policy in the 1980s and 1990s, from one of subsidizing the cultivation of massive quantities of cereals crops to one of actually paying farmers to cease working pieces of their land, has led to some reduction of arable acreages. Thus 'set-aside' and 'wildlife' fallow, much of it in small patches along the edges and in the corners of fields, is becoming an increasingly common sight in the rural landscape. Quickly becoming filled with long grass and weeds, this soon begins to resemble some of the abandoned 'tumbledown' land of the late nineteenth- and early twentieth-century agricultural depression, though the reason for its presence is not the same.

Epilogue

> In short, there is no room for sentimentality about village life. Could its
> annals be written they would make no idyll.
>
> (George Sturt, *Change in the Village*, 1912)

The real history of village England and the English countryside has been
anything but idyllic, neither before nor since George Sturt wrote these
words. It has in reality been one of huge social disparity between the rich
and the poor, and between the powerful and the powerless; of constant
change and destruction of tradition; of the vulnerability of many villagers
to poverty and downturns in the agricultural condition; and, since the
First World War, the ruination of much of the traditional rural landscape
through suburbanization, provision of infrastructure, and agricultural
modernization. However, these are general trends and issues, and it is
important to recognize that not all villages have undergone the same
experience. At various stages in this book distinction has been made
between close and open villages, the former being landowner-dominated
and the latter being independent from such authority. There have always
been some villages in between these two polarities, but in the large
majority of cases the distinction holds true and relates to two markedly
different rural working-class lifestyles. On the one hand, inhabitants of
close villages lived a deferential life under constant paternal control, but
in a picturesque habitat and blessed by some shelter from poverty. On the
other hand, people living in open villages did have a more independent
existence, but for most this was at the expense of much poorer living conditions and always being exposed to the caprices of capitalized agriculture
and the hardships that these could create.

This book presents an inclusive social history of village England in
which all classes of people – not just the benevolent squire, the parson
and one or two interesting and well-behaved rustics – have significance.
Romanticized versions of rural history overlook or even deny the existence of poverty, which is why the impoverished 'Hodge' and the
struggling craftsman, if they feature at all, are treated only as marginal
figures. Moreover, this 'nice' rural history, and its reinforcement by

appealing media and advertising images, distorts our perceptions of the village landscape and its visual qualities. Almost invariably it focuses on the ancient church, the squire's mansion or manor house and the pictur-esque, rose-covered, cottages; but it ignores those numerous other features – the craftsmen's workshops, the Nonconformist chapels, the rows of labourers' dwellings, the parish hall, the inter-war ribbon devel-opment and the council-housing colony – that, taken together, constitute much the greater part of most English villages. Each of these, however, has important things to say about village history and is a significant piece of the historic building fabric, even if it does not have any pretensions to beauty and charm. They inform us of a very different rural world.

Whereas the romanticized, and in most cases the oldest, features of vil-lage England – the church, the manor house, the yeomen's cottages and the green – are in many cases now being protected as parts of a village conservation area or because they are in a National Park or an Area of Outstanding Natural Beauty, the less-valued 'monuments' to past rural life are everywhere being displaced. The poorest of labourers' dwellings were pulled down some decades ago, mostly in the rural slum clearances of the inter-war and early post-war years; and few of the better ones have not been substantially refurbished and modernized. Soon, if present trends continue, the living conditions of the labouring class will be observable only in old photographs and occasional museum reconstruc-tions: all traces of this under-publicized aspect of village history and heritage will have been erased from the landscape. The same will be true of the craftsmen's workshops, which for centuries had played a vital role in the village economy and social life. Traditional village craftsmen and tradesmen have become virtually extinct, but in many cases their premises are still to be seen; some standing in a sadly disused and derelict condi-tion, some being used as a storage shed, and some having been converted into a dwelling. Derelict craftsmen's workshops, often regarded as eye-sores and rarely deemed worthy of preservation, are now disappearing rapidly, either to clear the way for some infill housing development or as part of a general 'tidying up' process. Some of those that have been con-verted will live on for posterity, but more often than not the building has been so extensively altered that it is only if it is given the name of 'old smithy', 'old bakery', or 'old shop' that we are able to identify its original function. Recent decades have also seen widespread changes to long-established community institutions. Hundreds of village schools have been closed down and sold off in the property market. Nonconformist chapels, which once provided for the spiritual life of the rural working class, are likewise diminishing in numbers, either being left derelict or being put to some new use. And parish halls, proud symbols of the inter-war spirit of rural self-help and community revitalization, are now being upgraded or completely transformed. Prior to these changes the village building-fabric stood as a visual record of the way of life, past and present, of the whole community. Today, however, anyone in search of a balanced and realistic social history has to look carefully amongst all the gentrification and refurbishment. Indeed, in some villages it is a test of one's observation to find any visual reminders of the darker past. If this book helps its readers first to identify and then empathize with this deeper and more inclusive history, it will have achieved its prime purpose.

Notes

Introduction

1 Martin J. Wiener, *English Culture and the Decline of the Industrial Spirit* (Harmondsworth, Penguin Books, 1992), pp 27–40
2 David Marsh, *The Changing Social Structure of England and Wales* (London, Routledge & Kegan Paul, 1965), p 108
3 Patrick Wright, *On Living in an Old Country* (London, Verso, 1985), p 16
4 Angus Calder, *The People's War* (London, Jonathan Cape, 1991), p 196
5 Wiener, *English Culture*, p 77
6 Howard Newby, *Green and Pleasant Land: Social Change in Rural England* (London, Hutchinson, 1979), p 154
7 Peter Laslett, *The World We Have Lost* (London, Methuen, University Paperbacks, 1965)
8 Alan Armstrong, *Farmworkers: a Social and Economic History* (London, Batsford, 1985), p 244
9 Raymond Williams, *The Country and the City* (London, Hogarth Press, 1993), pp 9–12

Chapter One
Origins, Organic Quality and Geographic Context

1 Sidney R. Jones, *The Village Homes of England* (London, Bracken Books, 1912), p 3
2 Sidney R. Jones, *English Village Homes and Country Buildings* (London, Batsford, 1936), p 44
3 W. G. Hoskins, *The Making of the English Landscape* (London, Hodder & Stoughton, 1955), p 42
4 Christopher Taylor, *Village and Farmstead: a History of Rural Settlement in England* (London, George Philip, 1983), pp 116–17
5 Carenza Lewis, Patrick Mitchell-Fox and Christopher Dyer, *Village, Hamlet and Field: Changing Medieval Settlements in Central England* (Manchester, Manchester University Press, 1997), pp 1–30
6 Maurice Beresford and John G. Hurst, *Deserted Medieval Villages* (London, Lutterworth Press, 1971)
7 Brian Roberts, *Rural Settlement in Britain* (Folkestone, Dawson, 1977), p 109

8 Gordon E. Mingay, *The Rural Idyll* (London, Routledge, 1989), p 2

9 Richard Muir, *The Lost Villages of Britain* (London, Book Club Associates, 1985), p 132

10 Hoskins, *English Landscape*, p 97

11 Maurice Beresford, *The Lost Villages of England* (London, Lutterworth Press, 1954), pp 234–9

12 Hoskins, *English Landscape*, p 122

13 Frank R. Leavis and Denys Thompson, *Culture and Environment: the Training of Critical Awareness* (London, Chatto & Windus, 1964), p 87

14 Harry Batsford and Charles Fry, *The English Cottage* (London, Batsford, 1938), p 2

15 P. H. Ditchfield, *Vanishing England* (London, Methuen, 1910), p 62

16 H. J. Massingham, *The English Countryman: a Study in the English Tradition* (London, Batsford, 1942), p 57

17 Massingham, *English Countryman*, p 57

18 Massingham, *English Countryman*, p 55

19 Michael J. Wise and Basil L. C. Johnson, 'The Changing Regional Pattern in the Eighteenth Century', in R. H. Kinvig, J. G. Smith and M. J. Wise (eds), *Birmingham and its Regional Setting* (Birmingham, British Association, 1950), pp 161–72

20 Massingham, *English Countryman*, p 31

21 Tom Williamson and Elizabeth Bellamy, *Property and Landscape: a Social History of Landownership and the English Countryside* (London, George Philip, 1987), p 125

22 W. G. Hoskins and L. Dudley Stamp, *The Common Lands of England and Wales* (London, Collins, 1963), p 4

23 Colin Ward, 'The Unofficial Countryside, in A. Barton and Roger Scruton (eds), *Town and Country* (London, Jonathan Cape, 1998), pp 190–8

24 Beresford, *Lost Villages*, p 231

25 Trevor Rowley, *Villages in the Landscape* (London, Dent & Sons, 1978), p 36

26 Alan Everitt, 'Common Land', in Joan Thirsk (ed), *The English Rural Landscape* (Oxford, Oxford University Press, 2000), pp 214–18

27 Harry Thorpe, 'The Green Villages of County Durham', *Transactions of the Institute of British Geographers*, 15 (1951), pp 155–80

28 June Sheppard, 'Medieval Village Planning in Northern England: Some Evidence from Yorkshire', *Journal of Historical Geography*, 2/1 (1976), pp 3–20

29 Harry Thorpe, 'Rural Settlement', in J. W. Watson and J. B. Sissons (eds), *The British Isles* (London, Thomas Nelson, 1964), p 358

30 Angus Calder, *The Myth of the Blitz* (London, Jonathan Cape, 1991), p 182

Chapter Two
The First Transformation

1 W. G. Hoskins, *The Making of the English Landscape* (London, Hodder & Stoughton, 1955), pp 177–8

2 Michael Turner, *Enclosures in Britain 1750–1830* (London, Macmillan, Studies in Economic and Social History, 1984), p 16

3 William E. Tate, *The English Village Community and the Enclosure Movement* (London, Gollancz, 1967), p 88

4 Hoskins, *English Landscape*, p 139

5 John L. and Barbara Hammond, *The Village Labourer 1760–1832* (London, Longmans, Green & Co, 1911)

6 H. J. Massingham, 'Our Inheritance from the Past', in Clough Williams-Ellis (ed), *Britain and the Beast* (London, J. M. Dent & Sons, 1937), p 9

7 Edward P. Thompson, *The Making of the English Working Class* (London, Gollancz, 1963)

8 Eric J. Hobsbawm and George Rude, *Captain Swing* (London, Lawrence & Wishart, 1969, reissued Penguin University Books in 1973 and Penguin Peregrine Books in 1985)

9 James Yelling, *Common Field and Enclosure in England 1450–1850* (London, Macmillan, 1977), pp 20–1

10 Hammonds, *Village Labourer*, p 53

11 Thompson, *English Working Class*, pp 237–8

12 Hammonds, *Village Labourer*, p 43

13 Yelling, *Common Field*, p 9

14 Tate, *English Village Community*, p 135

15 Michael Turner, *English Parliamentary Enclosure: its Historical Geography and Economic History* (London, Dawson, 1980), p 26

16 Hoskins, *English Landscape*, p 178

17 J. D. Chambers and Gordon E. Mingay, *The Agricultural Revolution 1750–1880* (London, Batsford, 1966), p 77

18 Turner, *Parliamentary Enclosure*, pp 17–22

19 Michael B. Gleave, 'The Settlement Pattern of the Yorkshire Wolds', *Institute of British Geographers Transactions and Papers*, 30 (1962), pp 105–18

20 Howard Newby, *Country Life: a Social History of Rural England* (London, Wiedenfeld & Nicolson, 1987), p 87

21 Lord Ernle, *English Farming Past and Present* (London, Longmans, Green & Co, 1912), p 149

22 W. G. Hoskins, *Midland England* (London, Batsford, 1949), p 60

23 Newby, *Country Life*, p 57

24 Hammonds, *Village Labourer*, pp 83–97

25 Michael B. Gleave, 'The Settlement Pattern of the Yorkshire Wolds, 1750–1850' (University of Hull Department of Geography, unpublished MA thesis, 1960); also Gleave, 'Settlement Pattern', *Institute of British Geographers*, pp 105–18

26 Brian Holderness, 'Open and Close Parishes in England in the Eighteenth and Nineteenth Centuries', *Agricultural History Review*, 20 (1972), pp 126–39

27 Enid Gauldie, *Cruel Habitations: a History of Working-Class Housing 1780–1918* (London, Allen & Unwin, 1974), p 34

28 Holderness, 'Open and Close Parishes', p 135

29 Stewart Bennett, 'Landownership and Parish type c. 1830', in Stewart Bennett and Nicholas Bennett (eds), *An Historical Atlas of Lincolnshire* (Hull, University of Hull Press, 1993), pp 94–5

30 Pamela Horn, *Labouring Life in the Victorian Countryside* (Dundee, Gill & Macmillan, 1976), p 14

31 Horn, *Labouring Life*, pp 23–4

32 Tom Williamson and Elizabeth Bellamy, *Property and Landscape: a Social History of Land Ownership and the English Countryside* (London, George Philip, 1987), p 137

33 Raymond Williams, *The Country and the City* (London, Hogarth Press, 1993), p 106

Chapter Three
Villages of Poverty and Rioting

1 William Cobbett, *Rural Rides* (1830). This quotation and subsequent references are from the J. M. Dent Everyman's Library edition published in 1924, which includes the Eastern and Northern Tours.

2 Eric J. Hobsbawm and George Rude, *Captain Swing* (Harmondsworth, Penguin Peregrine Books, 1985), p 10

3 John L. and Barbara Hammond, *The Bleak Age* (Middlesex, Pelican Books, 1947)

4 Christopher M. Law, 'The Growth of the Urban Population in England and Wales', *Institute of British Geographers Transactions*, 41 (1967), p 126

5 George D. H. Cole and Raymond Postgate, *The Common People 1746–1946* (London, Methuen, 1949), p 125

6 Cobbett, *Rural Rides*, p 142

7 Cobbett, *Rural Rides*, p 207

8 John L. and Barbara Hammond, *The Village Labourer 1760–1832* (London, Longmans, Green & Co, 1911), pp 97–122

9 Hammonds, *Village Labourer*, p 191

10 Edward P. Thompson, *The Making of the English Working Class* (London, Gollancz, 1963), p 244

11 John D. Marshall, *The Old Poor Law 1795–1834* (London, Macmillan, 1968), p 20

12 Joyce Marlow, *The Tolpuddle Martyrs* (London, Andre Deutsch, 1971), p 20

13 Hobsbawm and Rude, *Captain Swing*, pp 73–4

14 Karel Williams, *From Pauperism to Poverty* (London, Routledge & Kegan Paul, 1981), p 148

15 Williams, *Pauperism to Poverty*, p 148

16 William Cobbett, *Political Register*, 70 (1830), p 711

17 Hobsbawm and Rude, *Captain Swing*, pp 89–90

18 Hobsbawm and Rude, *Captain Swing*, p 196

19 Hobsbawm and Rude, *Captain Swing*, Appendix I

20 Reproduced in John H. Clapham, *Economic History of Modern Britain*, vol. 1, 'The Early Railway Age' (Cambridge, Cambridge University Press, 1932), p 147

21 Hobsbawm and Rude, *Captain Swing*, Appendix I

22 Adrian Randall and Edwina Newman, 'Protest, Proletarians and Paternalists: Social Conflict in Rural Wiltshire', *Rural History*, 6/2 (1995), pp 205–27

23 Hobsbawm and Rude, *Captain Swing*, pp 205–14

24 Hammonds, *Village Labourer*, pp 261–2

25 Hobsbawm and Rude, *Captain Swing*, p 262

26 Howard Newby, *Country Life: a Social History of Rural England* (London, Wiedenfeld & Nicolson, 1987), p 42

27 Thompson, *English Working Class*, p 250

28 Thompson, *English Working Class*, p 266

29 Felix Driver, 'The Historical Geography of the Workhouse System in England and Wales', *Journal of Historical Geography*, 15/3 (1989), p 280

30 Williams, *Pauperism to Poverty*, p 158

31 Thompson, *English Working Class*, p 296

32 Williams, *Pauperism to Poverty*, p 108

33 Cole and Postgate, *Common People*, p 274

34 Williams, *Pauperism to Poverty*, p 77

35 Driver, 'Workhouse System', pp 280–1

36 Hammonds, *Bleak Age*, p 115

37 Dennis Mills, 'The Poor Laws and the Distribution of Population, c 1600–1860, with Special Reference to Lincolnshire', *Transactions of the Institute of British Geographers*, 26 (1959), pp 185–9

Chapter Four
High Farming and the 'Ordered' Rural Society

1 Howard Newby, *The Deferential Worker: a Study of Farm Workers in East Anglia* (London, Allen Lane, 1979), p 162

2 Hugh Prince, 'Victorian Rural Landscapes', in G. E. Mingay (ed), *The Victorian Countryside* (London, Routledge & Kegan Paul, 1981), vol. 1, pp 17–29

3 Mark Girouard, *Sweetness and Light: the 'Queen Anne' Movement, 1860–1900* (Oxford, Clarendon Press, 1977), p 5

4 H. J. Massingham, *Faith of a Fieldsman* (London, Museum Press, 1951), p 91

5 P. H. Ditchfield, *Vanishing England* (London, Methuen, 1910), p 152

6 Ditchfield, *Vanishing England*, pp 156–7

7 Flora Thompson, *Lark Rise to Candleford* (London, Penguin Books, 1973) pp 211–12

8 Francis M. L. Thompson, *English Landed Society in the Nineteenth Century* (London, Routledge & Kegan Paul, 1963), p 32

9 Anne Mitson, 'The Earls of Yarborough: Interests and Influences', in Stewart Bennett and Nicholas Bennett (eds), *An Historical Atlas of Lincolnshire* (Hull, University of Hull Press, 1993), pp 62–3

10 Thompson, *English Landed Society*, pp 112–13

11 Alan Armstrong, 'The Workfolk', in G. E. Mingay (ed), *The Victorian Countryside*, vol. 2 (London, Routledge & Kegan Paul, 1981), p 492

12 Registrar-General, *The Census of Great Britain, 1851: Ages, Civil conditions, Occupations and Birthplace of the People* (London)

13 Registrar-General, *The Census of Great Britain, 1871: Ages, Civil conditions, Occupations and Birthplace of the People* (London)

14 Victor Bonham-Carter, *The English Village* (London, Pelican, 1952), p 136

15 E. R. Kelly, *The Post Office Directory of the North and East Ridings of Yorkshire with the City and Ainsty of York* (London, Kelly's Directories, 1872)

16 Richard Olney, *Labouring Life on the Lincolnshire Wolds; a Study of Binbrook in the mid 19th Century* (Lincoln, The Society for Lincolnshire History and Archaeology, 1975), p 32

17 Pamela Horn, *Labouring Life in the Victorian Countryside* (Dundee, Gill & Macmillan, 1976), p 103

18 Registrar-General, *Census 1871*

19 Thompson, *Lark Rise*, p 389

20 A. D. Gilbert, 'The Land and the Church', in G. E. Mingay (ed), *The Victorian Countryside* (London, Routledge & Kegan Paul, 1981), vol. 1, p 52

21 Anne Mitson and Barrie Cox, 'Victorian Estate Housing on the Yarborough Estate, Lincolnshire', *Rural History*, 6 (1995), p 34

22 Michael Havinden, 'The Model Village', in G. E. Mingay (ed), *The Rural Idyll* (London, Routledge, 1989), p 24

23 Charles Rawding, 'The Iconography of Churches: a Case Study of Land Ownership and Power in Nineteenth-Century Lincolnshire', *Journal of Historical Geography*, 16 (1990), pp 157–76

24 Thompson, *Lark Rise*, p 302

25 Nigel Everett, *The Tory View of Landscape* (London and New York, Yale University Press, 1994)

26 Horn, *Labouring Life*, p 169

27 Newby, *Deferential Worker*, pp 52–3

Chapter Five
Villages in Decay

1 T. W. Fletcher, 'The Great Depression in English Agriculture', in P. J. Perry (ed), *British Agriculture 1873–1906* (London, Methuen, 1973)

2 P. J. Perry, *British Farming in the Great Depression* (Newton Abbot, David & Charles, 1974), p 139

3 Christopher M. Law, 'The Growth of the Urban Population in England and Wales, 1801–1911', *Institute of British Geographers Transactions and Papers*, 41 (1967), pp 127–44

4 Francis M. L. Thompson, 'Free Trade and the Land', in G. E. Mingay (ed), *The Victorian Countryside* (London, Routledge & Kegan Paul, 1981), vol. 1, p 103

5 Alan Armstrong, 'The Flight from the Land', in G. E. Mingay (ed), *The Victorian Countryside*, (London, Routledge & Kegan Paul, 1981), vol. 1 p 119

6 John Saville, *Rural Depopulation in England and Wales* (London, Routledge & Kegan Paul, 1957), p 56

7 Wilhelm Hasbach, *A History of the English Agricultural Labourer*, 2nd edition (London, King & Son, 1920), vol. 1, pp 253 & 354

8 Hasbach, *English Agricultural Labourer*, vol. 1, pp 400–5

9 Henry Rider Haggard, *Rural England, Being an Account of Agricultural and Social Research* (London, Longmans, Green & Co, 1902), vol. 1

10 F. E. Green, *The Tyranny of the Countryside* (London, Fisher Unwin, 1913), pp 144–9

11 H. V. Morton, *In Search of England* (London, Methuen, 1927), p 84

12 Armstrong, 'Flight from Land', p 129. His figures are based on rural Registration Districts, most of which contained at least one market town.

13 Howard Newby, *Country Life: a Social History of Rural England* (London, Wiedenfeld & Nicolson, 1987), p 10

14 Brian A. Holderness, 'Agriculture and Industrialization in the Victorian Economy', in G. E. Mingay (ed), *The Victorian Countryside* (London, Routledge & Kegan Paul, 1981), vol. 1, p 185

15 Perry, *British Farming*, p 40

16 Perry, *British Farming*, pp 51–2

17 Perry, *British Farming*

18 L. Dudley Stamp, *The Land of Britain: its Use and Misuse* (London, Longmans, Green & Co, 1948), Appendix vii

19 P. H. Ditchfield, *Vanishing England* (London, Methuen, 1910)

20 Ditchfield, *Vanishing England*, p 139

21 Thomas Sharp, *English Panorama* (London, J. M. Dent & Sons, 1936), p 90

22 H. J. Massingham, *The Wisdom of the Fields* (London, Collins, 1945), p 204

23 John T. Coppock, 'Agricultural Changes in the Chilterns', in P. J. Perry (ed), *British Agriculture 1875–1906* (London, Methuen, 1973), pp 56–76

24 L. Dudley Stamp, *The Land of Britain: Report of the Land Utilization Survey of Britain* (London, Geographical Publications, 1936–46), published as 'County Volumes'

25 Stamp, *Land: Use and Misuse*, p 303

26 Fletcher, 'Great Depression', p 54

27 Stamp, *Land: Use and Misuse*, p 139

28 Joan Thirsk, *English Peasant Farming: the Agrarian History of Lincolnshire from Tudor to Recent Times* (London, Routledge & Kegan Paul, 1957), pp 315–18

29 David Grigg, *English Agriculture: an Historical Perspective* (Oxford, Blackwell, 1989), p 192

30 Thomas Sharp, *Town and Countryside: some Aspects of Urban and Rural Development* (London, Oxford University Press, 1932), p 75

31 C. H. Gardiner, 'The Vale of Evesham Group', in H. J. Massingham (ed), *The Small Farmer* (London, Collins, 1947), p 120

32 Massingham, *Wisdom of Fields*, p 207

33 Lord Ernle, *English Farming Past and Present* (London, Longmans, Green & Co, 1912), p 418

34 Flora Thompson, *A Country Calendar and Other Writings* (London, Oxford University Press, 1979): she finished writing 'Heatherley', pp 151–307, just before her death in 1947.

35 Waldorf Astor and Seebohm Rowntree, *British Agriculture: the Principles of Future Policy* (London, Penguin Books, 1939), p 219

36 Gardiner, 'Vale of Evesham', p 128

37 H. J. Massingham, *Remembrance* (London, Batsford, 1941), p 168

38 Gordon E. Mingay, *A Social History of the Victorian Countryside* (London, Routledge, 1991), p 217

39 Pamela Horn, *Labouring Life in the Victorian Countryside* (Dundee, Gill & Macmillan, 1976), pp 101–6

40 Horn, *Labouring Life*, p 91

41 Adrian Bell, 'The Farm', in B. T. Batsford (ed), *The Legacy of England* (London, Batsford, Pilgrims' Library, 1935), p 40

42 H. J. Massingham, *The English Countryman: a Study in the English Tradition* (London, Batsford, 1942), p 66

43 H. M. Burton, *The Education of the Countryman* (London, Kegan Paul, 1943)

44 W. P. Baker, *The English Village* (London, Oxford University Press, Home University Library, 1953), p 177

Chapter Six
Village England in the Inter-War Years

1 H. V. Morton, *I Saw Two Englands* (London, Methuen, 1942), p 31

2 Ralph Dutton, *The English Country House* (Batsford, London, 1935), p 2

3 Francis M. L. Thompson, *English Landed Society in the Nineteenth Century* (London, Routledge & Kegan Paul, 1963), p 322

4 John Moore, 'The Cotswolds', in Clough Williams-Ellis (ed), *Britain and the Beast* (London, J. M. Dent & Sons, 1937), p 88

5 Patrick Wright, *The Village that Died for England: the Strange Story of Tyneham* (London, Vintage, 1996), pp 176–202

6 Flora Thompson, *A Country Calendar and Other Writings* (London, Oxford University Press, 1979), 'Heatherley', p 298

7 Alan Armstrong, *Farmworkers: a Social and Economic History 1770–1980* (London, Batsford, 1985) pp 160 & 171

8 H. V. Morton, *In Search of England* (London, Methuen, 1927), p 30

9 Nick Mansfield, 'Class Conflict and War Memorials', *Rural History*, 6/1 (1995), p 67

10 Sidney R. Jones, *English Village Homes and Country Buildings* (London, Batsford, 1936), p 36

11 John Burnett, *A Social History of Housing 1815–1970* (London, Methuen, 1978), p 251

12 Cyril E. M. Joad, *The Untutored Townsman's Invasion of the Country* (London, Faber & Faber, 1945)

13 Ministry of Works and Planning, *Report of the Committee on Land Utilization in Rural Areas* (London, HMSO, 1942), 'The Scott Report'

14 Agricultural Economics Research Institute, *Country Planning: a Study of Rural Problems* (London, Oxford University Press, 1944), pp 1–2

15 W. P. Baker, *The English Village* (London, Oxford University Press, Home University Library, 1953), p 78

16 Jones, *English Village Homes*, p 12

17 Baker, *English Village*, pp 186 & 194

18 Agricultural Economics Research Institute, *Country Planning*, p 111

19 George Sturt, *Change in the Village*, (London, Duckworth, 1912), p 3

20 M. Trevor Wild, 'Population Change 1801–1981', in Susan Neave and Stephen Ellis (eds), *An Historical Atlas of East Yorkshire* (Hull, University of Hull Press, 1996), p 52

21 Baker, *English Village*, p 186

22 Robin H. Best, 'The Extent and Growth of Urban Land', *The Planner*, 62 (1978), pp 8–11

23 Arthur M. Edwards, *The Design of Suburbia: a Critical Study in Environmental History* (London, Pembridge Press, 1981), p 118

24 Burnett, *History of Housing*, p 262

25 Thomas Sharp, *Town and Countryside: Some Aspects of Urban and Rural Development*, (London, Oxford University Press, 1932), p 44

26 Moore, 'Cotswolds', p 88

27 Clough Williams-Ellis, *England and the Octopus* (London, Geoffrey Bles, 1928), p 12; see also Clough Williams-Ellis (ed), *Britain and the Beast* (London, J. M. Dent & Sons, 1928)

28 Joad, *Untutored Townsman's Invasion*, pp 25–47

29 H. J. Massingham, *Chiltern Country* (London, Batsford, 1940) p 100

30 J. B. Priestley, 'Britain is in Danger', in J. B. Priestley (ed), *Our Nation's Heritage* (London, J. M. Dent & Sons, 1939), pp 163–9

31 A. G. Street, 'The Countryman's View', in Clough Williams-Ellis (ed), *Britain and the Beast* (London, J. M. Dent & Sons, 1937), p 123

32 Sharp, *Town and Countryside*, p 46

33 John Punter, 'A History of Aesthetic Control: Part 1, 1909–1953', *Town Planning Review*, 57/4 (1986), pp 351–81

34 Williams-Ellis, *England and Octopus*, pp 166–7

35 Moore, 'Cotswolds', p 89

36 S. P. B. Mais, *Round about England* (London, Richards Press, 1935), p 138

37 Sharp, *Town and Countryside*, p 130

38 Denis Hardy and Colin Ward, *Arcadia for All?* (London, Mansell, 1984), p 24

39 John Lowerson, 'Battles for the Countryside', in Frank Gloversmith (ed), *Class, Culture and Social Change: a New View of the 1930s* (London, Harvester, 1980), p 260

40 Hardy and Ward, *Arcadia*, p 2

41 S. P. B. Mais, 'The Plain Man looks at England', in Clough Williams-Ellis (ed), *Britain and the Beast* (London, J. M. Dent & Sons, 1937), p 213

42 Joad, *Untutored Townsman's Invasion*, p 37

43 Sharp, *Town and Countryside*, p 158

44 Howard Marshall, 'The Rake's Progress', in Clough Williams-Ellis (ed), *Britain and the Beast* (London, J. M. Dent & Sons, 1937), p 166

45 D. M. Matheson, 'The Work of the National Trust', in James Lees-Milne (ed), *The National Trust: a Record of Fifty Years Achievement* (London, Batsford, 1945), p 123

46 Reproduced in Vaughan Cornish, *The Scenery of England: a Study of Harmonious Grouping in Town and Country* (London, Council for the Preservation of Rural England, 1932), pp 97–101

47 David N. Jeans, 'Planning and the Myth of the English Countryside', *Rural History*, 1/2 (1990), pp 254–5

Chapter Seven
The Second Transformation

1 J. B. Cullingworth and V. Nadin, *Town and Country Planning in Britain* (London, Routledge, 1994), p 9

2 Patrick Wright, *The Village that Died for England: the Strange Story of Tyneham* (London, Vintage, 1996)

3 Angus Calder, *The Myth of the Blitz* (London, Jonathan Cape, 1994), p 60

4 W. P. Baker, *The English Village* (London, Oxford University Press, Home University Library, 1953), p 194

5 Arthur M. Edwards, *The Design of Suburbia: a Critical Study in Environmental History* (London, Pembridge Press, 1981), p 108

6 W. Randolph and S. Roberts, 'Population Redistribution in Great Britain, 1971–1981', *Town and Country Planning*, 50 (1981), pp 227–30

7 David Rowan, 'One-Person Households', *Guardian*, 20 January 1998

8 P. Hetherington and T. May, 'Middle England's Mad, Bad Dream in Bricks and Mortar', *Guardian*, 27 January 1998

9 Andrew W. Gilg, *An Introduction to Rural Geography* (London, Edward Arnold, 1985), p 152

10 The creation of two more National Parks – the New Forest and the South Downs – has recently been announced. This will bring the total in England to nine, and will reduce the northern and western emphasis.

11 Caroline McGhie, 'Quaint, Cosy and Loved to Death', *Sunday Times Supplement*, 13 August 1989

12 Howard Newby, *Green and Pleasant Land: Social Change in Rural England* (London, Hutchinson, 1979), pp 156–64

13 Paul Cloke, *An Introduction to Settlement Planning* (London, Methuen, 1983), p 40

14 Caroline Hitchman, 'The Reality of Rural Poverty', in Michael Sissons (ed), *A Countryside for All* (London, Vintage, 2001), p 130

15 Clive Aslet, *Countryblast: Your Countryside Needs You* (London, John Murray, 1991), p 5

16 Aslet, *Countryblast*, p 212

17 Edwards, *Design of Suburbia*, p 208
18 For example: Humphrey Pakington, *English Villages and Hamlets* (1934); H. J. Massingham, *English Downland* (1936) and *Cotswold Country* (1937); and S. P. B. Mais, *The Home Counties* (1942).
19 M. Bunce, *The Countryside Ideal: Anglo-American Images of Landscape* (London, Routledge, 1994), p 99
20 Aslet, *Countryblast*, p 7
21 Anthony Sampson, 'The New Edwardians', *Observer*, 14 July 2002
22 Countryside Commission, *Monitoring Landscape Change* (Cheltenham, Countryside Commission, 1997)

Bibliography

History and Related Subjects

Agricultural Economics Research Institute, *Country Planning: a Study of Rural Problems* (London, Oxford University Press, 1944)

Armstrong, Alan, 'The Flight from the Land', in G. E. Mingay (ed), *The Victorian Countryside* (London, Routledge & Kegan Paul, 1981), vol. 1

Armstrong, Alan, 'The Workfolk', in G. E. Mingay (ed), *The Victorian Countryside* (London, Routledge & Kegan Paul, 1981), vol. 2

Armstrong, Alan, *Farmworkers: a Social and Economic History* (London, Batsford, 1985)

Aslet, Clive, *Countryblast: Your Country Needs You* (London, John Murray, 1991)

Astor, Waldorf, and Rowntree, B. Seebohm, *British Agriculture: the Principles of Future Policy* (London, Penguin Books, 1939)

Baker, W. P., *The English Village* (London, Oxford University Press, Home University Library, 1953)

Bell, Adrian, 'The Farm', in B. T. Batsford (ed), *The Legacy of England* (London, Batsford, Pilgrims' Library, 1935)

Bennett, Stewart, 'Landownership and Parish Type c.1830' in Stewart Bennett and Nicholas Bennett (eds) *An Historical Atlas of Lincolnshire* (Hull, University of Hull Press, 1993)

Bennett, Stewart, and Bennett, Nicholas, (eds), *Historical Atlas of Lincolnshire* (Hull, University of Hull Press, 1993)

Beresford, Maurice, *The Lost Villages of England* (London, Lutterworth Press, 1954)

Beresford, Maurice, and Hurst, John G., *Deserted Medieval Villages* (London, Lutterworth Press, 1971)

Best, Robin H., 'The Extent and Growth of Urban Land', *The Planner*, 62 (1978), pp 8–11

Bonham-Carter, Victor, *The English Village* (London, Pelican, 1952)

Boyes, Georgina, *The Imagined Village: Culture, Ideology and the English Folk Revival* (Manchester, Manchester University Press, 1993)

Brett Young, Francis, *Portrait of a Village* (London, William Heinemann, 1937)

Bunce, M., *The Countryside Ideal: Anglo-American Images of Landscape* (London, Routledge, 1994)

Burnett, John, *A Social History of Housing 1815–1970* (London, Methuen, 1978)

Burton, H. M., *The Education of the Countryman* (London, Kegan Paul, 1943)

Calder, Angus, *The Myth of the Blitz* (London, Jonathan Cape, 1991), chapter 9, 'Deep England'

Cannadine, David, *The Rise and Fall of the British Aristocracy* (London, Yale University Press, 1990)

Chambers, J. D., and Mingay, George E., *The Agricultural Revolution 1750–1880* (London, Batsford, 1966)

Clapham, John H., *Economic History of Modern Britain* (Cambridge, Cambridge University Press, 1932), vol. 1 'The Early Railway Age'

Cloke, Paul, *An Introduction to Settlement Planning* (London, Methuen, 1983)

Cole, George, D. H., and Postgate, Raymond, *The Common People 1746–1946* (London, Methuen, 1949)

Coppock, John T., 'Agricultural Changes in the Chilterns', in P. J. Perry (ed), *British Agriculture 1875–1906* (London, Methuen, 1973)

Cornish, Vaughan, *The Scenery of England: a Study of Harmonious Grouping of Town and Country* (London, Council for the Preservation of Rural England, 1932)

Countryside Commission, *Monitoring Landscape Change* (Cheltenham, Countryside Commission, 1997)

Cullingworth, J. B., and Nadin, V., *Town and Country Planning in Britain* (London, Routledge, 1994)

Ditchfield, P. H., *Vanishing England* (London, Methuen, 1910)

Dutton, Ralph, *The English Country House* (London, Batsford, 1935)

Driver, Felix, 'The Historical Geography of the Workhouse System in England and Wales', *Journal of Historical Geography*, 15/3 (1989), pp 261–75

Edwards, Arthur M., *The Design of Suburbia: a Critical Study in Environmental History* (London, Pembridge Press, 1981)

Ernle, Lord, *English Farming Past and Present* (London, Longmans, Green & Co, 1912)

Everett, Nigel, *The Tory View of Landscape* (London, Yale University Press, 1994)

Everitt, Alan, 'Common Land', in Joan Thirsk (ed), *The English Rural Landscape* (Oxford, Oxford University Press, 2000)

Fletcher, T. W., 'The Great Depression in English Agriculture', in P. J. Perry (ed), *British Agriculture 1875–1906* (London, Methuen, 1973)

Gardiner, C. H., 'The Vale of Evesham Group', in H. J. Massingham (ed), *The Small Farmer* (London, Collins, 1947)

Gauldie, Enid, *Cruel Habitations: a History of Working-Class Housing 1780–1918* (London, Allen & Unwin, 1974)

Gilbert, A. D., 'The Land and the Church', in G. E. Mingay (ed), *The Victorian Countryside* (London, Routledge & Kegan Paul, 1981)

Gilg, Andrew W., *An Introduction to Rural Geography* (London, Edward Arnold, 1985)

Girouard, Mark, *The English Country House* (New Haven, Yale University Press, 1971)

Girouard, Mark, *Sweetness and Light: the 'Queen Anne' Movement, 1860–1900* (Oxford, Clarendon Press, 1977)

Gleave, Michael B., 'Dispersed and Nucleated Settlement in the Yorkshire Wolds', *Institute of British Geographers, Transactions and Papers*, 30 (1962), pp 105–18

Gloversmith, Frank, (ed), *Class, Culture and Social Change: a New View of the 1930s* (London, Harvester, 1980)

Gonner, E. C. K., *Common Land and Enclosure* (London, Macmillan, 1912)

Green, F. E., *The Tyranny of the Countryside* (London, Fisher Unwin, 1913)

Grigg, David, *English Agriculture: an Historical Perspective* (Oxford, Blackwell, 1989)

Haggard, Henry Rider, *Rural England, Being an Account of Agricultural and Social Research* (London, Longmans, Green & Co), vol. 1

Hammond, John L., and Hammond, Barbara, *The Village Labourer 1760–1832* (London, Longmans, Green & Co, 1911)

Hammond, John, L., and Hammond, Barbara, *The Bleak Age* (Middlesex, Pelican Books, 1947)

Hardy, Denis, and Ward, Colin, *Arcadia for All?* (London, Mansell, 1984)

Hasbach, Wilhelm, *A History of the English Agricultural Labourer*, 2nd edn (London, King & Son, 1920)

Havinden, Michael, 'The Model Village', in G. E. Mingay (ed), *The Rural Idyll* (London, Routledge, 1989)

Hitchman, Caroline, 'The Reality of Rural Poverty', in Michael Sissons (ed), *A Countryside for All* (London, Vintage, 2001)

Hobsbawm, Eric J., and Rude, George, *Captain Swing* (London, Penguin Peregrine Books, 1985)

Holderness, Brian A., 'Open and Close Parishes in England in the Eighteenth and Nineteenth Centuries', *Agricultural History Review*, 20 (1972)

Holderness, Brian A., 'Agriculture and Industrialization in the Victorian Economy', in G. E. Mingay (ed), *The Victorian Countryside* (London, Routledge & Kegan Paul, 1981), vol. 1

Horn, Pamela, *Labouring Life in the Victorian Countryside* (Dundee, Gill & Macmillan, 1976)

Horn, Pamela, *Rural Life in England in the First World War* (London, Gill & Macmillan, 1984)

Hoskins, W. G., *Midland England* (London, Batsford, 1949)

Hoskins, W. G., *The Making of the English Landscape* (London, Hodder & Stoughton, 1955)

Howard, Ebenezer, *Garden Cities of Tomorrow* (London, Faber & Faber, 1946)

Howkins, Alun, 'Labour History and the Rural Poor, 1850–1980', *Rural History*, 1/1 (1990), pp 113–22

Jeans, David N., 'Planning and the Myth of the English Countryside', *Rural History*, 1/2 (1990), pp 249–64

Joad, Cyril E. M., *The Untutored Townsman's Invasion of the Country* (London, Faber & Faber, 1945)

Jones, Sidney R., *The Village Homes of England* (London, 'The Studio', 1912)

Jones, Sidney R., *English Village Homes and Country Buildings* (London, Batsford, 1936)

Laslett, Peter, *The World We Have Lost* (London, Methuen, University Paperbacks, 1965)

Law, Christopher M., 'The Growth of the Urban Population in England and Wales', *Institute of British Geographers Transactions*, 45 (1967), pp 125–41

Leavis, Francis R., and Thompson, Denys, *Culture and Environment: the Training of Critical Awareness* (London, Chatto & Windus, 1964)

Lewis, Carenza, Mitchell-Fox, Patrick, and Dyer, Christopher, *Village, Hamlet and Field: Changing Medieval Settlements in Central England* (Manchester, Manchester University Press, 1997)

Lowerson, John, 'Battles for the Countryside', in Frank Gloversmith (ed), *Class, Culture and Social Change: a New View of the 1930s* (London, Harvester, 1980)

McGhie, Caroline, 'Quaint, Cosy and Loved to Death', *Sunday Times Supplement*, 13 August 1989

Mais, S. P. B., *Round about England* (London, Richards Press, 1935)

Mais, S. P. B., 'The Plain Man looks at England', in Clough Williams-Ellis (ed), *Britain and the Beast* (London, J. M. Dent & Sons, 1937)

Mais, S. P. B., *The Home Counties* (London, Batsford, 1942)

Mansfield, Nick, 'Class Conflict and War Memorials', *Rural History*, 6/1 (1995), pp 67–87

Marlow, Joyce, *The Tolpuddle Martyrs* (London, Andre Deutsch, 1971)

Marsh, David, *The Changing Social Structure of England and Wales* (London, Routledge & Kegan Paul, 1965)

Marshall, Howard, 'The Rake's Progress', in Clough Williams-Ellis (ed), *Britain and the Beast* (London, J. M. Dent & Sons, 1937)

Marshall, John D., *The Old Poor Law 1795–1834* (London, Macmillan, 1968)

Massingham, H. J., *English Downland* (London, Batsford, 1936)

Massingham, H. J., *Cotswold Country* (London, Batsford, 1937)

Massingham, H. J., 'Our Inheritance from the Past', in Clough Williams-Ellis (ed) *Britain and the Beast* (London, J. M. Dent & Sons, 1937)

Massingham, H. J., *Chiltern Country* (London, Batsford, 1940)

Massingham, H. J., *Remembrance* (London, Batsford, 1941)

Massingham, H. J., *The English Countryman: a Study in the English Tradition* (London, Batsford, 1942)

Massingham, H. J., *The Wisdom of the Fields* (London, Collins, 1945)

Massingham, H. J., (ed), *The Small Farmer* (London, Collins, 1947)

Massingham, H. J., *Faith of a Fieldsman* (London, Museum Press, 1951)

Matheson, D. M., 'The Work of the National Trust', in J. Lees-Milne (ed), *The National Trust: a Record of Fifty Years Achievement* (London, Batsford, 1945)

Matless, David, *Landscape and Englishness* (London, Reaktion Books, 1998)

Mills, Dennis, 'The Poor Laws and the Distribution of Population, c 1600–1860, with Special Reference to Lincolnshire', *Transactions of the Institute of British Geographers*, 26 (1959), pp 185–9

Mingay, George E., (ed), *The Victorian Countryside* (London, Routledge & Kegan Paul, 1981), vols 1 & 2

Mingay, George E., (ed), *The Rural Idyll* (London, Routledge, 1989)

Mingay, George E., *A Social History of the English Countryside* (London, Routledge, 1990)

Mingay, George E., *A Social History of the Victorian Countryside* (London, Routledge, 1991)

Ministry of Works and Planning, *Report of the Committee on Land Utilization in Rural Areas* (London, HMSO, 1942), 'The Scott Report'

Mitson, Anne, 'The Earls of Yarborough: Interests and Influences', in Stewart Bennett and Nicholas Bennett (eds), *An Historical Atlas of Lincolnshire* (Hull, University of Hull Press, 1993)

Mitson, Anne, and Cox, Barrie, 'Victorian Estate Housing on the Yarborough Estate, Lincolnshire', *Rural History*, 6 (1995), pp 29–45

Moore, John, 'The Cotswolds', in Clough Williams-Ellis (ed), *Britain and the Beast* (London, J. M. Dent & Sons, 1937)

Morton, H. V., *In Search of England* (London, Methuen, 1927)

Morton, H. V., *I Saw Two Englands* (London, Methuen, 1942)

Muir, Richard, *The Lost Villages of Britain* (London, Book Club Associates, 1985)

Neave, Susan and Ellis, Stephen, (eds), *An Historical Atlas of East Yorkshire* (Hull, University of Hull Press, 1996)

Newby, Howard, *The Deferential Worker: a Study of Farm Workers in East Anglia* (London, Allen Lane, 1977)

Newby, Howard, *Green and Pleasant Land: Social Change in Rural England* (London, Hutchinson, 1979)

Newby, Howard, *Country Life: a Social History of Rural England* (London, Wiedenfeld & Nicolson, 1987)

Olney, Richard, *Labouring Life on the Lincolnshire Wolds; a Study of Binbrook in the mid 19th Century* (Lincoln, Society for Lincolnshire History and Archaeology, 1975)

Pakington, Humphrey, *English Villages and Hamlets* (London, Batsford, 1934)

Perry, P. J., (ed), *British Agriculture 1873–1906* (London, Methuen, 1973)

Perry, P. J., *British Farming in the Great Depression* (Newton Abbot, David & Charles, 1974)

Priestley, J. B., 'Britain is in Danger', in J. B. Priestley (ed), *Our Nation's Heritage* (London, J. M. Dent & Sons, 1939)

Prince, Hugh, 'Victorian Rural Landscapes', in G. E. Mingay (ed), *The Victorian Countryside* (London, Routledge & Kegan Paul, 1981)

Punter, John, 'A History of Aesthetic Control: Part 1, 1909–1953', *Town Planning Review*, 57/4 (1986), pp 351–81

Randall, Adrian, and Newman, Edwina, 'Protest, Proletarians and Paternalists: Social Conflict in Rural Wiltshire', *Rural History*, 6/2 (1995), pp 205–27

Randolph, W., and Roberts, S., 'Population Redistribution in Great Britain, 1971–1981', *Town and Country Planning*, 50 (1981), pp 227–30

Rawding, Charles, 'The Iconography of Churches: a Case Study of Land Ownership and Power in Nineteenth-Century Lincolnshire', *Journal of Historical Geography*, 16 (1990), pp 157–76

Roberts, Brian, *Rural Settlement in Britain* (Folkestone, Dawson, 1977)

Rowley, Trevor, *Villages in the Landscape* (London, Dent & Sons, 1978)

Saville, John, *Rural Depopulation in England and Wales* (London, Routledge & Kegan Paul, 1957)

Sharp, Thomas, *Town and Countryside: Some Aspects of Urban and Rural Development* (London, Oxford University Press, 1932)

Sharp, Thomas, *English Panorama* (London, J. M. Dent & Sons, 1936)

Sheppard, June, 'Medieval Village Planning: Some Evidence from Yorkshire', *Journal of Historical Geography*, 2/1 (1976)

Stamp, L. Dudley, *The Land of Britain: the Report of the Land Utilization Survey of Britain* (London, Geographical Publications, 1936–46), published as 'County Volumes'

Stamp, L. Dudley, *The Land of Britain: its Use and Misuse* (London, Longmans, Green & Co, 1948)

Stamp, L. Dudley and Hoskins, W. G., *The Common Lands of England and Wales* (London, Collins, 1963)

Strong, Roy, *Country Life 1897–1997: the English Arcadia* (London, Boxtree, 1996)

Tate, William E., *The English Village Community and the Enclosure Movement* (London, Gollancz, 1967)

Taylor, Christopher, *Village and Farmstead: a History of Rural Settlement in England* (London, George Philip, 1983)

Thirsk, Joan, *English Peasant Farming: the Agrarian History of Lincolnshire from Tudor to Recent Times* (London, Routledge & Kegan Paul, 1957)

Thirsk, Joan, (ed), *The English Rural Landscape* (Oxford, Oxford University Press, 2000)

Thompson, Edward P., *The Making of the English Working Class* (London, Gollancz, 1963), chapter 7, 'The Field Labourers'

Thompson, Francis M. L., *English Landed Society in the Nineteenth Century* (London, Routledge & Kegan Paul, 1963)

Thompson, Francis M. L., 'Free Trade and the Land', in G. E. Mingay (ed), *The Victorian Countryside* (London, Routledge & Kegan Paul, 1981)

Thorpe, Harry, 'The Green Villages of County Durham', *Transactions of the Institute of British Geographers*, 15 (1951), pp 155–80

Thorpe, Harry, 'Rural Settlement', in J. W. Watson and J. B. Sissons (eds), *The British Isles* (London, Thomas Nelson, 1964)

Turner, Michael, *English Parliamentary Enclosure: its Historical Geography and Economic History* (London, Dawson, 1980)

Turner, Michael, *Enclosures in Britain 1750–1830* (London, Macmillan, 1984)

Ward, Colin, 'The Unofficial Countyside', in A. Barton and R. Scruton (eds), *Town and Country* (London, Jonathan Cape, 1998)

Wild, M. Trevor, 'Population Change 1801–1981', in Susan Neave and Stephen Ellis (eds), *An Historical Atlas of East Yorkshire* (Hull, University of Hull Press, 1996)

Williams, Karel, *From Pauperism to Poverty* (London, Routledge & Kegan Paul, 1981)

Williams, Raymond, *The Country and the City* (London, Hogarth Press, 1993)

Williams-Ellis, Clough, *England and the Octopus* (London, Geoffrey Bles, 1928)

Williams-Ellis, Clough, (ed), *Britain and the Beast* (London, J. M. Dent & Sons, 1937)

Williamson, Tom, and Bellamy, Elizabeth, *Property and Landscape: a Social History of Land Ownership and the English Countryside* (London, George Philip, 1987)

Wise, Michael J. and Johnson, Basil L. C., 'The Changing Regional Pattern in the Eighteenth Century', in M. J. Wise, J. G. Smith and B. L. C. Johnson (eds), *Birmingham and its Regional Setting* (Birmingham, British Association, 1950)

Wright, Patrick, *On Living in an Old Country* (London, Verso, 1985)

Wright, Patrick, *The Village that Died for England: the Strange Story of Tyneham* (London, Vintage, 1996)
Yelling, James A., *Common Field and Enclosure in England 1450–1850* (London, Macmillan, 1977)

Literary Works

Brett Young, Francis, *Portrait of a Village*, 1937
Clare, John, *The Village Minstrel*, 1821
Clare, John, 'To a Fallen Elm', (c. 1820s)
Cobbett, William, *Rural Rides*, 1830
Disraeli, Benjamin, *Sybil, or The Two Nations*, 1845
Eliot, George, *Silas Marner*, 1859
Eliot, George, *Adam Bede*, 1861
Engels, Frederick, *Condition of the Working Class in England in 1844*, 1845, chapter 10, 'The Agricultural Proletariat'
Forster, E. M., *Howard's End*, 1910
Hardy, Thomas, *Under the Greenwood Tree*, 1872
Hardy, Thomas, *Far from the Madding Crowd*, 1874
Hardy, Thomas, *The Mayor of Casterbridge*, 1881
Hardy, Thomas, *Tess of the d'Urbervilles*,1891
Jefferies, Richard, *Hodge and his Masters*, 1880
Lee, Laurie, *Cider with Rosie*, 1959
Sturt (Bourne), George, *Change in the Village*, 1912
Thompson, Flora, *Lark Rise to Candleford*, 1945
Thompson, Flora, *A Country Calendar and Other Writings*, first published posthumously in 1979
Trollope, Anthony, *Doctor Thorne*, 1858

Index

Abercrombie, Patrick, 132, 145, 149, 155

agriculture, capitalization of, 3, 9, 22, 24–5, 28, 34, 36, 48–9, 70–1, 75, 95, 102–3, 176; cereals farming, 36, 48, 50, 54–7, 59, 70–1, 75, 78, 89, 95–7, 132; dairy farming, 56, 59, 97, 99, 101; regional specializations, 57, 97, 99–102; traditional open-field culture, 2–3, 8–10, 22–4, 28–31, 33, 35

agricultural buildings, conversion of, 173–4

agricultural depression, *see* Great Agricultural Depression

agricultural labourers, 34–5, 40, 42–3, 46, 49, 51, 70–1, 77–9, 81, 86, 88–90, 103, 107–8, 124, 126, 176–7; decline in numbers, 77, 89; casual workers, 38, 51–2, 77–8, 81; gang workers, 78, 81;

agricultural labourers' dwellings, *see* cottages

agricultural mechanization, xviii, 68, 70–2, 77, 89, 93, 96, 132, 151, 174–5; threshing machines, 53–4, 56, 59–60, 70, 90; use of steam power, 90

Agricultural Revolution, xviii, 23, 37, 75, 103; 'new husbandry', 22, 25, 28, 43; scientific cattle and sheep breeding, 22, 25, 28

agricultural wages, 45, 47–8, 50–4, 56, 59, 89, 96; regional differences, 47–8

Aldbourne (Wilts), 13, 147–8

allotments, 34, 83, 128

Anglican church, *see* church

Areas of Outstanding Natural Beauty (AONBs), 156–8, 169, 177

aristocracy, *see* landed aristocracy

Arts and Crafts movement, 121, 134

Ashbury (Berks), 119

Ashdown Forest (Sussex), 143

Ashridge House (Bucks), 72

Avon valley (Warks), 6, 11, 56

Aylesbury (Bucks), Vale of, 57, 155

Batsford 'The British Heritage' and 'The Face of Britain' books, 147, 171

Bayons Manor (Lincs), xi

Beckford, William, 60, 72

Bell, Adrian, 108

Bentham, Jeremy, 51

Beresford, Maurice, 3

Berkhamsted Common (Herts), 143

Bibury (Glos), 5

Binbrook (Lincs), xi–xii, 79, 122

Black Death, 2–3

Blackmore Vale (Dorset), 90

blacksmiths, *see* craft industries

'Bleak Age', xviii, 45–69

Blockley (Glos), 13

Boyton (Wilts), 60

Bradfield (Berks), 66

Brett Young, Francis, 91–2

Brocklesby (Lincs), xi, 75

Brown, Lancelot 'Capability', 44

bungalows, xvii, 101, 134–5, 137, 141, 150, 163

bus services, 114, 120, 162–3

Caird, James, his 'cereal line' and 'wage line', 55–7

Canvey Island (Essex), 139

Captain Swing, *see* Swing riots

Castle Combe (Wilts), 5

Cavendish (Suffolk), xx

census, *see* population census

Cerne Abbas (Dorset), 66

chapels, xii, 43, 60, 73, 82–3, 118, 124, 17

Chedzoy (Somerset), 21

Chesterton (Warks), 3, 7